THE NEW TESTAMENT: AN INTRODUCTION
Volume 1
Paul and Mark

THE NEW TESTAMENT: AN INTRODUCTION

Volume 1
Paul and Mark

Paul Nadim Tarazi

ST VLADIMIR'S SEMINARY PRESS
CRESTWOOD, NEW YORK 10707
1999

The publication of this book has been made possible through the generosity and support of Elsie Skvir Nierle, in honor of her brother, Joseph Skvir, a devoted member of the Orthodox Church.

Library of Congress Cataloging-in-Publication Data
Tarazi, Paul Nadim, 1943-
    The New Testament: an introduction / Paul Nadim Tarazi.
        p.   cm.
    Includes bibliographical references and index.
    Contents: v. 1. Paul and Mark.
    ISBN 0-88141-188-4
    1. Bible.   N.T.—Commentaries.   I. Title.
BS2341.2.T37   1999
225.6'1—dc21   98-40713
                                                                CIP

THE NEW TESTAMENT: AN INTRODUCTION

Copyright © 1999 by
Paul Nadim Tarazi

Vol. 1: Paul & Mark
Vol. 2: Luke & Acts
Vol. 3: John & Revelation
Vol. 4: Matthew & The Canon

ISBN 0-88141-188-4

PRINTED IN THE UNITED STATES OF AMERICA

Contents

vi

Abbreviations

Books of the Old Testament[1]

Gen	Genesis	Job	Job	Hab	Habakkuk
Ex	Exodus	Ps	Psalms	Zeph	Zephaniah
Lev	Leviticus	Prov	Proverbs	Hag	Haggai
Num	Numbers	Eccl	Ecclesiastes	Zech	Zechariah
Deut	Deuteronomy	Song	Song of Solomon	Mal	Malachi
Josh	Joshua	Is	Isaiah	Tob	Tobit
Judg	Judges	Jer	Jeremiah	Jdt	Judith
Ruth	Ruth	Lam	Lamentations	Wis	Wisdom
1 Sam	1 Samuel	Ezek	Ezekiel	Sir	Sirach (Ecclesiasticus)
2 Sam	2 Samuel	Dan	Daniel	Bar	Baruch
1 Kg	1 Kings	Hos	Hosea	1 Esd	1 Esdras
2 Kg	2 Kings	Joel	Joel	2 Esd	1 Esdras
1 Chr	1 Chronicles	Am	Amos	1 Macc	1 Maccabees
2 Chr	2 Chronicles	Ob	Obadiah	2 Macc	2 Maccabees
Ezra	Ezra	Jon	Jonah	3 Macc	3 Maccabees
Neh	Nehemiah	Mic	Micah	4 Macc	4 Maccabees
Esth	Esther	Nah	Nahum		

Books of the New Testament

Mt	Matthew	Eph	Ephesians	Heb	Hebrews
Mk	Mark	Phil	Philippians	Jas	James
Lk	Luke	Col	Colossians	1 Pet	1 Peter
Jn	John	1 Thess	1 Thessalonians	2 Pet	2 Peter
Acts	Acts of the Apostles	2 Thess	2 Thessalonians	1 Jn	1 John
Rom	Romans	1 Tim	1 Timothy	2 Jn	2 John
1 Cor	1 Corinthians	2 Tim	2 Timothy	3 Jn	3 John
2 Cor	2 Corinthians	Tit	Titus	Jude	Jude
Gal	Galatians	Philem	Philemon	Rev	Revelation

Books by the author

OTI1   *The Old Testament: An Introduction, vol.1, Historical Traditions*, St Vladimir's Seminary Press, Crestwood, 1991.

OTI2   *The Old Testament: An Introduction, vol.2, Prophetic Traditons*, St Vladimir's Seminary Press, Crestwood, 1994.

OTI3   *The Old Testament: An Introduction, vol.3, Psalms & Wisdom*, St Vladimir's Seminary Press, Crestwood, 1996.

I Thess   *I Thessalonians: A Commentary*, St Vladimir's Seminary Press, Crestwood, 1982.

Gal   *Galatians: A Commentary*, St Vladimir's Seminary Press, Crestwood, 1994

---

1   Following the larger canon known as the Septuagint.

To Imkje

Foreword

This is the first of four volumes in a projected New Testament Introduction series. It deals with the earliest NT writings: Paul's epistles and the gospel of Mark. The second volume will discuss Luke and Acts, the third—John and Revelation, and the fourth—Matthew, the other writings, and the formation of the New Testament canon. The reason for this arrangement is first and foremost chronological: to introduce writings roughly in the sequence they were themselves produced, building a familiarity with the earlier ones first so that their use as sources for later ones can more readily be understood when the later ones are discussed. The rationale undergirding my interpretation of the textual relationships is based in part on the determination of their dates of authorship by the field of biblical scholarship in general, and in part on a firm conviction—arising out of years of study and research—that with few exceptions the New Testament is a unitary production in the sense that it does not present us with discordant voices or "differing points of view" as is often claimed. In this sense it is similar to the Old Testament: just as Ezekiel and his school were behind virtually the entire Old Testament, so also it is Paul and his disciples who authored the writings that came to be known as the New Testament. Therefore it is with Paul that I begin, and as I cover the remaining New Testament books I will be showing their links to the "Pauline school."

Like its predecessor, the three-volume *Old Testament Introduction*, this series is not a "typical" introduction to scripture. It does not survey or even cite existing scholarly opinions about the texts, nor does it try to touch upon every significant issue of interpretation within each scriptural book. What it does do is focus on explaining each book's central purpose or theme—the primary message the author set about to convey—and the literary techniques employed to get that idea across to the intended audience. My own main goal in these introductory volumes is thus to provide my reader with the *key* to understanding any given text *as a whole*, and in order to accomplish this more effectively within the limited space available to me, I will at times skip over matters that readers may be interested in. That more detailed level of coverage must be reserved for commentaries, publication of which, by St Vladimir's Seminary Press, will continue when this New Testament Introduction series is complete.

My sincere gratitude goes to Tom Dykstra, my editor, who, more than ever before, has earned the title of "co-worker" by undertaking the thankless task of making my difficult manuscript on Mark more manageable for the general reader. It remains a difficult text. A bare minimum of preparation necessary for understanding this book adequately would be to read at least the third volume of my Introduction to the Old Testament series (preferably all three), and, even more importantly, to become thoroughly familiar with the New Testament books covered here. Beyond that, the greatest possible benefit from the book will be realized when it is used in study groups led by someone with a greater knowledge of scriptural scholarship than the average layperson.

A word of explanation is in order here for the reason behind my dedication of this book in particular to my wife, Imkje. The thought of this dedication was not postponed, let alone forgotten; it was saved. I had for years planned to put in writing what has all along been a reality in daily life: Imkje and the apostle Paul were and are, for me, intertwined. She genuinely, almost effortlessly, lived what Paul taught as being the quintessence of God's will, and thus his love, for us: unconditional love for the neighbor, any neighbor, simply for being the neighbor. This entailed care, true care, for the other: finding out the other's true need—which is not always equivalent to felt need—and acting accordingly. I witnessed this in her on two exacting levels: motherhood and nursing (as an RN she must handle the "unknown" other). Both "levels" require, besides warmth and genuine interest in a person, a keen discernment between the real and fake needs of that person, and then—which is the most difficult—acting, whatever the cost, upon that conviction. Whenever Paul's teaching irritatingly challenged my egotism and my sloth, I watched her; she smoothed out the gospel for me and for that I am eternally grateful to her, more than she will ever be capable of imagining. I have always wished that she and the Apostle would meet but, since it is impossible for me to introduce him to her, I am settling for the possible: introducing her to Paul's written legacy. May she and my readers find solace as well as wisdom and power in the gospel of Paul, my only father in Jesus, the Christ, who was crucified for our sake and rose unto the glory of his Father, our God. My sincere prayer is that she and they realize, at the least, that the hard work the present volume reflects could not have been a product of mere egotism, and at best, that it is an expression of the love God commanded me through Paul to have for them.

Paul Nadim Tarazi

I

Paul

1

Paul and His Letters

Paul was a latecomer to the movement within first-century-A.D. Judaism that espoused a belief in Jesus as the long awaited Messiah of God, and this fact was destined to hang over his head as a sword of Damocles throughout his life. It is for this reason that a great deal of his writings are devoted to defending the stature of his apostleship as being equal to that of the other apostles. Understandably, both his apostleship and his teaching about Jesus were questioned; he constantly had to defend the truth of his "gospel," which he referred to as "*the* gospel."

But how could a latecomer, who by his own confession had persecuted the church with the intention of destroying it (Gal 1:13), openly stand opposed to Peter and James—who had known Jesus personally and were preeminent among the church leadership? He must have had an objective basis for doing so, or else these "pillars" James, Cephas (Peter), and John would not have given him their "right hand" of friendship, which they did at their first official encounter (2:9). Had Paul's position not been defensible based on principles universally acknowledged among the church leadership, he would not have gotten far in Jerusalem where he was challenging the "pillars" on their own turf and in the midst of their supporters.

The issue at that time was whether circumcision was necessary for believing Gentiles, and Paul was even successful in backing up the theoretical talk with a "test case" to prove his point: he brought along the Gentile Titus in order to secure proof that an uncircumcised believer had truly been accepted by the Jerusalemite leadership without having circumcision forced upon him

(2:1-3). He simultaneously established official recognition of the equality of his apostleship with that of Peter, his field being the uncircumcised "sinners," while Peter's was the Jews, the primary addressees of God's promises. All of this was based on a recognition that the same God who was at work in Peter's mission was also at work in Paul's gospel to the Gentiles (2:8), and this fact, that all understood themselves to be serving the same God witnessed to in the same (what we now call Old Testament) scriptures, is what ultimately put Paul on an equal footing with the other apostles.

For the first-century Jews, who were not only strict monotheists but also prohibited any pictorial or statuary representation of their deity, God was reflected in their Holy Writ, the books of the Torah, the Prophets, and the Writings. Since there was no iconic representation of him, any reference to him was de facto a reference to those scriptures; in other words, to speak of him amounted to or required quoting those scriptures.[1] It is only when we take seriously this premise that we can fathom the possibility of such a meeting as the one referred to above between Paul and the Jewish Christian leadership: if Jesus is the Messiah of God, then he can only be the "scriptural" Messiah of the "scriptural" God; that is to say, Jesus is whatever scripture says he is, and what God has done through him is whatever scripture says that God will do in the last days in order to bring to fulfillment the divine plan revealed in scripture.

Paul, the Pharisee, was well reared and drilled in the scriptures, and well able to debate with anyone about their content and meaning. But what was the point he made that convinced the "pillars" of the plausibility of his "gospel," even if it did not make them enthusiastic in adopting it? In all probability—and in historical research this is the most one can hope for—it must have

---

1   Were it not so, the Jews, or at least a number of them, would not have been able to resist the heavily syncretistic world in which they were living.

been what had triggered the turning point in his life: the experience of conversion that turned him into defender, builder and servant of the church he had at first set out to bring to extinction. What could have triggered such a conversion? Before attempting an answer, let me say once again that for Paul, the Jew-Israelite and Pharisee, the only valid reference for God's will, intentions, plans and workings in our world, is scripture. Scripture told him that the Messiah, the chosen representative of the scriptural God, would have to be victorious in order to ensure God's *yeŝuʿah* (victory/salvation), but Jesus had been crucified, which was the most abject and shameful kind of death in the Roman Empire. It seemed impossible then that he would have been the scriptural God's Messiah, and the new movement among Jews that considered him so was to be declared "anathema," i.e., cursed by God and thus to be cast out, eliminated from the congregation of Israel. So Paul was on a "sacred" mission to subdue the emerging community of people who believed in the Messiahship of Jesus. While pursuing his goal at Damascus he was aghast at the stubbornness of at least some of them. Either they were "blind" to the content of scripture, or they were "seeing" something in it that justified their position. This would have prompted Paul to take a second look at the book of Isaiah, that mini-scripture telling the story of God with his city Jerusalem, the story ending with the establishment of the heavenly Jerusalem.[2] This is the Messianic book par excellence, replete with Messianic prophecies, and Paul must have been struck by the repeated descriptions of the *'ebed yahweh* (the servant of the Lord) in the "Book of the Consolation of Israel" (Is 40-55) that announces the "good news" of the rebuilding of God's city, Jerusalem. Reflections on these passages would then have led him to "see" clearly that the shameful "defeat" of Jesus on the cross was actually an integral part of God's plan of salvation which God would implement in his city.

2 See *OTI2* 197.

But the Isaianic "Book of Consolation" spoke of this divine *mišpat* (just judgment) bringing about salvation as being something so stunning that it would attract all nations to come to Jerusalem to witness the glory of its God and present him with offerings, as was the habit in the ancient Near East, to honor him and to acknowledge his mighty deeds. It is in this sense that God's glory lighting up Jerusalem will be a "light to the Gentiles." Thus, the other facet of Yahweh's victory enacted through his "servant" is God's universalism, his acknowledgment as God by all nations. Put otherwise, unless the nations flock into Jerusalem to see the glory of Yahweh and walk in its light, Isaiah's prophecy concerning the new Jerusalem will not have been realized, and consequently the death of his "servant" will have been in vain, which would contradict what is stated in the "servant of the Lord" poems. If the crucified Jesus is God's Messiah, then the nations are to be informed and invited. Even more, strictly speaking, their acceptance of the crucified Jesus as their *kyrios* (lord) is the corroboration of the fact that he is indeed the Messiah. Paul read correctly that the Isaianic message was not an "intra-Jewish" matter, but rather the universal God's matter, more specifically that, through his "servant," God has shown himself to be the God of Jews and Gentiles alike. This entailed his acceptance by both as such. However, if God was indeed the God of all through the crucified Jesus—and he was according to Peter and James as well as Paul—he had to be equally so, i.e., his acknowledgment as such by the Gentiles may not be considered contingent upon his endorsement as such by the Jews. The Isaianic message was offered to both and was to be received unconditionally by both. The "hardening" of the Jews may not be used to block the access of the Gentiles to God, as Paul will put it in his letter to the Romans. Any one could become, through faith that God had indeed realized his plan in the crucified Jesus, part of the "olive" tree that is God's, and only God's, and that blossoms out of *his* promise to the *forefathers* of Israel (Rom 11: 16; 28), and not to the Jews. Indeed, "not all who are from Israel, are Israel." (9:6b)

That understanding was at the heart of the agreement reached at the meeting in Jerusalem between Paul and the "pillars," and it led to the acknowledgment that Paul's mission to the Gentiles was equivalent to Peter's mission to the Jews. That Paul's understanding of the agreement was not one-sided can be gathered from the fact that Peter comprehended it as Paul did. Paul summarizes his view in Romans: "...there is no distinction between Jew and Greek; the same Lord is Lord of all and bestows his riches upon all who call upon him. For, 'every one who calls upon the name of the Lord will be saved'." (10:12-13) Peter initially acted in accordance with this view. At Antioch, *after* the Jerusalem encounter, both Barnabas, Paul's companion at the meeting, and Peter, one of the "pillars" and the apostle to the circumcision, were sharing meals with the Gentiles on an ongoing basis. It was only the later intervention of James' men that put pressure on all of them to cease this practice, thus reinstating the "distinction" between Jews and Gentiles. Paul saw this as a breach of the prior "official," and thus binding, agreement, and he decided to abide by that agreement on his own.[3] Whatever was agreed upon in Jerusalem, God's city, was for him the most authoritative expression of *vox Dei* (the voice [will] of God). The dilemma was clear-cut and so was his choice: "Am I now seeking the favor of men, or of God? Or am I trying to please men? If I were still pleasing men, I should not be a servant of Christ." (Gal 1:10) It is as the slave/servant of Christ that he viewed himself all along, and he makes that clear repeatedly throughout his correspondence. A slave/servant abides by the will of his master whom he seeks to please. In Paul's case, that master was ultimately God *who spoke out at the Jerusalem meeting* where Paul was given the "right hand" of the "pillars," i.e., the representatives of God's will within the community of all Jewish believers in Jesus the Messiah. Reneging on that decision meant for him reneging on a pledge to God himself!

3 Gal 2:11-14.

Excursus on the Greek term doulos

The strict translation of the Greek *doulos* is "slave," although quite often one finds it rendered as "servant." The reason for my opting for the former is that it fits better the context of the 1st century Roman empire. *doulos* referred to someone who was owned by, the property of, a *kyrios* (master). This meant that the *doulos* had to do whatever his master willed regardless of his own personal feelings; the *doulos* had no will of his own *de jure* or *de facto*:

> Will any one of you, who has a servant plowing or keeping sheep, say to him when he has come in from the field, "Come at once and sit down at table"? Will he not rather say to him, "Prepare supper for me, and gird yourself and serve me, till I eat and drink; and afterward you shall eat and drink"? Does he thank the servant because he did what was commanded? So you also, *when you have done all that is commanded you, say, "We are unworthy servants; we have only done what was our duty."* (Lk 17:7-10)

A *doulos* is literally *bound by*, enslaved to, his master's will. In the case of Paul, this meant *forfeiting his own will*:

> For if I preach the gospel, that gives me no ground for boasting. *For necessity*[4] *is laid upon me.* Woe to me if I do not preach the gospel! For if I do this of my own will, I have a reward; *but if not of my own will, I am entrusted with a commission.* What then is *my reward?* Just this: that in my preaching I may make the gospel free of charge, *not making full use of my right* in the gospel. (1 Cor 9:16-18)

After the infamous episode at Antioch Paul had no choice but to proceed on his own, carrying out his part of the agreement sealed at Jerusalem, that is, acting as the plenipotentiary apostle to the Gentiles according to the gospel sanctioned by God himself. How Peter would carry out his part was not a concern of Paul's according to the following two principles:

1) Paul would answer to God, not to Peter or to any other leaders, for only God himself will pronounce judgment on the Lord's day:

4   The Greek *anagke* means something imposed, forced upon.

"This is how one should regard us, as servants of Christ and stewards of the mysteries of God. Moreover it is required of stewards that they be found trustworthy. But with me it is a very small thing that I should be judged by you or by any human court. I do not even judge myself. I am not aware of anything against myself, but I am not thereby acquitted. It is the Lord who judges me. Therefore do not pronounce judgment before the time, before the Lord comes, who will bring to light the things now hidden in darkness and will disclose the purposes of the heart. Then every man will receive his commendation from God." (1 Cor 4:1-5)

2) Every apostle is responsible only for the turf assigned to him, not for territory assigned to others:

"We do not boast beyond limit, in other men's labors; but our hope is that as your faith increases, our field among you may be greatly enlarged, so that we may preach the gospel in lands beyond you, without boasting of work already done in another's field." (2 Cor 10:15-16) "...thus making it my ambition to preach the gospel, not where Christ has already been named, lest I build on another man's foundation." (Rom 15:20)

Paul could not simply forget about Jerusalem, however. His gospel required that the Gentiles bring their offerings to the God who had wrought his salvation in his city, Jerusalem. And who else save James and those around him could represent the face of God for the Gentiles flocking into that city in order to present their offerings to God? Yet James and the Jerusalemite leadership did not want these offerings, and Paul would spend years trying to convince them to do so in order that the truth of the gospel, as the fulfillment of God's promises made "through his prophets in the holy scriptures" (Rom 1:1-2), would be corroborated in the eyes of Jews and Gentiles alike. Only then would Jerusalem truly be God's city in which his glory would shine and in whose light all Jews and Gentiles throughout the world would be summoned to walk. James chose to hold stubbornly onto his Jewishness rather than accept the will of the scriptural God revealed in his word of promise realized in the gospel. This stubbornness created an impediment to Peter's mission to the Jews as well as to Paul's gospel to the Gentiles. Both Jews and Gentiles who had not accepted Jesus as the Messiah could use the stand of James, the "pillar" par excellence, as an excuse to shy away from the gospel's portrayal of "Christ crucified, a stumbling block to Jews and folly to Gentiles" (1 Cor 1:23-24). And there was great incentive to reject "Christ crucified" due to the connotation of shame[5] the crucifixion entailed in the Roman empire in the eyes of all, Jews as well as Gentiles.

In order to express symbolically the basic tenet of his stand, that there is only one community of God comprising Jews and Gentiles on the same footing,[6] Paul, now alone after his break with Barnabas, recruited Timothy the Jew alongside Titus the uncircumcised Greek, making them his main official companions in the carrying out of his mission.[7] Thus, he definitely had no intention of compromising. However, what is striking in Paul's decisions is that they reflect a steady and unchanging understanding of the gospel coupled with a keen sense as to the consequences of accepting or rejecting it at a particular time. When he went up to Jerusalem to defend the truth of God's gospel in the presence of the Jewish "pillars" he took along the uncircumcised Gentile Titus. When he embarked on his journey into the heart of the Gentile world he chose as his top aide the Jew Timothy, whom he made sure to circumcise, underscoring before the Jerusalem "pillars" as well as the Gentiles that neither circumcision nor uncircumcision matters as far as the gospel is concerned; whoever decides to accept the gospel must do so on its own terms:

> ...it [the gospel] is the power of God for salvation to every one who has faith, to the Jew first and also to the Greek. For in it the righteousness of God is revealed through faith for faith; as it is written, "He who through faith is righteous shall live." (Rom 1:16-17)

> ...there is no distinction between Jew and Greek; the same Lord is Lord of all and bestows his riches upon all who call upon him. For, 'every one who calls upon the name of the Lord will be saved.' (Rom 10:12-13)

5   See Gal 6:14 and *Gal* 14 and 324.
6   See *Gal* 38-39 and 140-143.
7   1 Cor 4:15-17; 16:10; 2 Cor 2:13; 7:5-16; 8:6, 16-24; Phil 2:19-24; 1 Thess 3:1-6.

But why did I refer to Macedonia and, more specifically, Philippi, Paul's first stop outside Asia Minor, as the heart of the Gentile world? As I have just said in regards to Titus and Timothy, Paul expresses his commitment to the truth of the one gospel in a highly symbolic manner depending on the aspect of the gospel he is intending to stress or test. Until his dispute with his colleague, Barnabas, in Antioch, Paul had evangelized with him areas that used to be part of the Seleucid kingdom[8] that extended over Syria, Babylonia and Asia Minor, i.e., the "home" of the Judaism of apostolic times as well as of nascent Judaism. Upon his break with Barnabas Paul left his Jewish "home" and ventured alone outside its safe boundaries into Macedonia (the land of Alexander, the father of Hellenism) and later into Achaia (the land of the "Greeks", i.e., Gentiles par excellence). There, his gospel—and by the same token, his apostleship—was about to be put to the test since he was "the apostle to the Gentiles." Besides being a Macedonian city, Philippi in Paul's time was also a Roman colony, i.e., a city whose main inhabitants were Roman veteran soldiers and their families. It was a small settlement until 42 B.C. when Octavian and Antony defeated Cassius and Brutus, Julius Caesar's assassins, in its vicinity. By order of Antony, some of the Roman soldiers settled there and it was declared a "Roman colony" and given the name Colonia Vitrix Philippensis in honor of the victory just won. After Antony's defeat by Octavian at Actium in 30 B.C., the latter dispossessed many members of the Praetorian Guard who had sided with Antony of their lands in Italy and granted them allotments in Philippi, which was then refounded with the title Colonia Julia Philippensis in honor of Octavian's daughter, and later Colonia Julia Augusta Philippensis when Octavian received the designation "Augustus" from the Senate in 27 B.C. Moreover, its importance is mirrored in the fact that it lay on

---

8 Pamphylia, Pisidia and Lycaonia. Even if Cyprus is considered to have been more under Ptolemaic hegemony, the same general reasoning would apply.

the Via Egnatia, the famous Roman road that crossed the Balkan peninsula and linked Italy to the East. So, in a manner of speaking, Philippi was in Paul's eyes a "little Rome" and, for him, anchoring the gospel there was tantamount to planting it at the heart of the Roman empire itself, which was the *oikoumene*, the entire "inhabited world" for a Jew and Roman citizen like him. Should one Philippian accept the gospel, then Paul would have proven "that in Christ Jesus the blessing of Abraham" has indeed "come to the Gentiles" (Gal 3:14) and, by extension, so had the "truth of the gospel" he fought so hard to "preserve" (2:5) at the Jerusalem summit. The close connection with the latter can also be clearly seen in that, already at that time, Paul gave his word that he "would remember the poor" of Jerusalem (2:10), i.e., he would make sure the Gentiles always acknowledge that they are "a wild olive shoot...grafted...to share *through the [holy] root [viz. the fathers]* in the olive tree" (Rom 11:17). Indeed, Paul followed through and did his utmost to make out of the monetary collection for the Jerusalem church among his Gentile churches a necessary matter (2 Cor 8-9). As I indicated earlier, for Paul this "offering" by his churches to the Lord of Jerusalem was an integral component of the Isaianic word of salvation.

Only this understanding can explain the following strange passage in Philippians: "And you Philippians yourselves know that in the beginning (at the outset—*en arkhe*) of the gospel, when I left (went out of—*exelthon apo*) Macedonia..." (3:15) Strange indeed, for why would Paul link the "beginning" (*arkhe*) of the gospel with his departure from Macedonia rather than his arrival there? The only answer is that this "beginning" reflected the time that in Paul's own mind the truth of the gospel he was preaching was corroborated, the time when it became *the gospel* in the eyes of *all*, Jews and Gentiles, because the "nations"—represented by the Philippians—as well as the Jews accepted it. Only then did Isaiah's "good news" become a reality; only then could Paul write boldly and assertively "to the church of God which is in

Corinth," the capital of the Roman province of Achaia, the land of the "Greeks/Gentiles" par excellence:

> For Jews demand signs and Greeks seek wisdom, but we preach Christ crucified, *a stumbling block to Jews and folly to Gentiles,* but *to those who are called, both Jews and Greeks,* Christ the power of God and the wisdom of God...He [viz. God] is the source of *your* [the Gentiles'] life in Christ Jesus, whom God made our wisdom, *our righteousness and sanctification and redemption.* (1 Cor 1:22-23, 30)[9]

From the immediately following "For *I decided* to know nothing among you except Jesus Christ and him crucified" (2:2) it seems even that starting in Philippi he drew for himself a fixed path he would abide by until the end—and later when he penned his letter to the Philippians he referred back to that determination as the "beginning of the gospel."

Upon leaving Philippi Paul visited Thessalonica, capital of the Roman province Macedonia, where he founded his second Gentile church. While in Athens, on his way to Corinth, he sent Timothy back to Thessalonica to check on the status of his flock there (1 Thess 3:1-2). Timothy reached him in Corinth and reported to him his findings, and those findings sparked Paul's first letter ever to a Gentile church, 1 Thessalonians. Corinth being the capital of the Roman province Achaia, the apostle decided to spend enough time there to plant the seed of God's word in the heart of Greece proper and as close to Athens as possible; here again he intended to add a major symbolic conquest to the roster of his gospel. This required a lengthy stay, at least eighteen months according to Acts 18:11, 18.

The same Book of Acts describes Paul's sojourn in Corinth in a manner that seems to reflect the significance he attributed to that city as an opportunity to prove how his gospel could indeed unite Jew and Gentile in one church. Thus, we find mention of both

---

9 In v.30 Paul is applying the scriptural terminology of righteousness, sanctification, and redemption to Gentiles as well as Jews, with no differentiation.

Jews and Gentiles in Acts: there is a *Jewish* couple Aquila and Priscilla who had just arrived from Italy (18:2-4); there is a debate *in
the synagogue* where Paul successfully persuaded both *Jews and
Greeks* (v.4); his temporary residence was a house *adjacent* (*syno-
morousa*) to the synagogue (v.7); and the ruler of the synagogue is
said to have *believed in the Lord, together with his household* (v.8).
Only then are we told that, upon the Lord's command, Paul
"stayed a year and six months, teaching the word of God among
them" (v.11) and prolonged his stay (v.18) even after the subsequent ruler of the synagogue was beaten by his fellow Jews (v.17),
presumably for having also endorsed the Pauline gospel.[10] All the
aforementioned seems to reflect Paul's intention to implant at the
symbolic heart of the Gentile world the *one* church of the *one* gospel, the *one* community (of Jews and Gentiles) of the *one* God (of
the scripture of the synagogue) gathered around the *one* crucified
Lord (the essential content of the Pauline gospel). This one community of Jews and Gentiles stands *outside* the synagogue since
"not all who are (descended) from Israel, are Israel" (Rom 9:6b),
but the Jews are in a sense "closest" to the gospel, or "first" according to the terminology of Romans. Nevertheless, they too must
accept or reject Paul's gospel, and unless they accept it there can
be no salvation for them (Rom 1:16-17). All this means that in
his letter to the Romans, Paul was calling upon his addressees re-
siding in the capital of the empire to follow the example he had
set for the entire world (*oikoumene*)[11] in Corinth, capital of
Greece and therefore representative of the *oikoumene*. This in turn
explains the extent of the correspondence he dedicated to the *pres-
ervation* of the Corinthian church: it serves as a "prototype" of the
Pauline church, meeting and overcoming all kinds of adversity,
from within as well as without.

---

10 He bears the same name as Paul's co-sender of 1 Corinthians (1:1). Given that these
    are the only two instances of the name Sosthenes in the New Testament, it is rea-
    sonably certain that the person intended in both cases is the same.
11 See below my comments on Romans.

In spite of all his efforts a major failure was awaiting Paul in Jerusalem: James and his party refused the collection Paul raised among the Gentiles. This outcome can be gathered from the change in tone between the letter to the Romans and that to the Philippians.[12] It may also be detected in Acts 18:22 where Paul's Jerusalemite visit is glossed over: "When he had landed at Caesarea, he went up and greeted the church, and then went down to Antioch." The visit to Antioch, where the original break between Paul and the other apostles took place, is treated in a similar manner: "After spending some time there he departed..." (v.23a) Paul was hurrying to check on and strengthen the Galatian churches he had founded earlier (v.23b) before settling in Ephesus and making his headquarters there (1 Cor 15:8-9; see also Acts 19; 20:17-38).[13]

The choice of that city may well have been dictated by its status as capital of the Roman province of Asia (which facilitated travel and communication) as well as its geographical situation at the center of a circle encompassing the realm of Paul's Gentile churches, Galatia, Philippi, Thessalonica, and Corinth. On the other hand, it had a symbolic significance in that it lay at the westernmost end of what used to be the Seleucid kingdom and across the sea from Greece, i.e., at the border between Judaism and Gentility. It is from these headquarters that Paul wrote his letters to the Galatians and the Corinthians. The Letter to the Romans was written either from Ephesus or from Corinth during his last visit to his Macedonian and Achaian churches (Acts 20:1-6), at any rate before his last visit to Jerusalem and before the final break with the church leaders there when they again rejected the Gentile monetary collection for the "poor." An "intra-Jewish"

12 See further on Romans and Philippians.
13 He left in Ephesus Priscilla and Aquila (18:18-21), two of his top co-workers (see 18:24-26 where they play a major role in introducing Apollos to Paul's teaching; Rom 16:3 where they head the greeting list; 1 Cor 16:9 where they are singled out among the brethren; 2 Tim 4:9-19 which shows that they remained until the end among Paul's few followers).

conflict ensued that ended with Paul's imprisonment by the Roman authorities in Caesarea of Palestine. His appeal to Caesar brought him to Rome, and from there he wrote his letters to the Philippians and Philemon before his execution. Another possibility is that Paul was imprisoned by the Roman authorities at Ephesus where he will have written the latter two letters and most probably met his death as well.

2

The First Letter to the Thessalonians

When Timothy returned to Corinth from his mission trip to Thessalonica he informed Paul of the difficulties facing the believers there. First and foremost was the stunning fact that the Jerusalemite leadership was determined to place impediments in the way of the gospel Paul was preaching to the Gentiles; his proclamation of freedom from the necessity of circumcision and obedience to the Mosaic Law was deemed unacceptable. Paul responded to this situation by writing a letter in which no less than three out of the five chapters address this matter.

Upon reading this letter, one will immediately notice that, together with commenting on his gospel, Paul devotes as much time and energy to an apologia of his apostleship. The reason is obvious. Paul's opponents realized that proving him wrong materially was a difficult matter; being a Pharisee and thus very well trained in scripture, he was able to counter-argue each and every one of their points. Moreover, already at the Jerusalem meeting he was able to force the "pillars" themselves to acknowledge his equality ("give him the right hand"). So Paul's opponents resorted to attacking his person by suggesting that Paul was a late comer, not an original disciple of Jesus, and thus not an authority per se; that anything he might say is by the same token always questionable. In other words, they were telling his followers to question Paul's authority specifically when he explained to them what was and was not the content of the gospel. This could have been a powerful argument, for it was largely on Paul's personal authority that his churches had been established. Were that undermined, those flocks would then seek the next "higher authority," which presumably would be the Jerusalem Jewish-Christian leadership. And there authorities were clearly in opposition to Paul on key points of scriptural interpretation. Not only did they reject his interpretation of the Jerusalem agreement, but they even induced Peter and Barnabas, apostles themselves, to side with them against him. And if Paul could be "proven" wrong once, he could be wrong again at any time; to make sure that he was not erring, his followers would continually have to check the tenets of his teaching against that of the "pillars" and the "other apostles"—and in any disagreement it would be the latter who would be deemed correct.

Paul was thus forced to defend his gospel and his apostleship *in the same breath*. This is precisely what he does here in 1 Thessalonians and will continue to do throughout his subsequent correspondence.

Salutation (1:1)

The letter was addressed to the church (*ekklesia*) of the Thessalonians, i.e., to the entire gathered congregation; thus, it was meant to be authoritative. However, preferring a more paternal tone or perhaps even fearing an initial negative reaction on the part of his hearers that could undermine his message by putting them in the "wrong mood," Paul opted to name himself without his title of apostle and alongside his helpers, Silvanus and Timothy. After all, his apostleship was under fire.

Introduction (1:2-9)

Given that virtually all Thessalonians were from Gentile stock (v.9b), Paul begins by reminding them of the two basic assets of their new life: faith in the sense of commitment to their new God, and love which is the epitome of what he requires of them. He also reminds them that ultimately they must answer not to human authorities but to God himself at the Lord's coming (v.3), thus exhorting them to realize the seriousness of the fact that they are God's "chosen" people, through the gospel he brought them (v.4-5).

The gospel, however, required that they share with him afflictions as well as the joy granted by God's spirit (v.6). They did just that, and now the example they set is inspiring others; the gospel that originated in Macedonia[1] is on its way not only to Achaia, where Paul already is, but also throughout the known world, i.e., the Roman empire to which even now Paul intends to bring it (vv.7-8). The essential content of this gospel lies in turning toward the scriptural God and awaiting from heaven his resurrected Son who will deliver us from the coming wrath of divine judgment (vv.9-10).

Recalling Paul's Apostolic Ministry (2:1-16)

Paul then proceeds to remind them that they themselves were privy to the afflictions he had to endure for the gospel's sake; indeed, he brought them the gospel in the midst of the sufferings he had to undergo in Philippi (vv.1-2). Those sufferings actually served as a sign that he was on the right track and thus emboldened him to continue, for they showed that he had been found trustworthy of the gospel and of apostleship (vv.4-5). And once he received approval from God himself, there was no need to seek it from men (v.6). That is the reason why he didn't make use of his apostolic authority (v.7a) but rather acted toward them as a nursing mother or a father would (vv.7b-8, 11). He didn't even require them to honor him as an apostle by taking care of his material needs while among them (v.9). And yet, they received his words as God's word, thus confirming his apostleship (v.13), and their acceptance extended even to their own sharing in sufferings connected with the gospel (v.14). It is also in this sense that they proved to be on a par with Jewish Christians in Judea, who underwent the same rough treatment by their fellow Jews (v.14). As for the latter, their attempts to hinder the Gentiles' salvation through the preaching of the gospel makes them enemies of God and thus deserving of his

---

1 See previous chapter.

wrath, just as the biblical Israel did by refusing God's prophets and killing them (vv.15-16).[2] This statement may well have been also intended as a caveat to James and his party who were trying to hinder Paul's preaching of the gospel among Gentiles.

Paul's Concern for the Thessalonians (2:17-3:13)

Paul's worries about the steadfastness of the Thessalonian believers is connected with his view of himself as an apostle accountable to the Lord when the Lord's Day of judgment comes. It is only then that the winner's crown will be bestowed upon him, and it will only happen *if* the Thessalonians by then have still kept the faith. That will then be proof that they did receive God's word from Paul. Given this perspective, he sees the hindrance to his visiting them as the work of Satan, the enemy whose job will be to show that Paul did not actually take good care of the flock assigned to him (2:17-20; 3:5). Not having been able to visit them himself, he sent the second best, Timothy, "God's co-worker in the gospel of Christ," to strengthen them in their faith by reminding them that the gospel entails their sharing in afflictions for its sake (3:1-4). As I explained in the previous chapter in conjunction with Paul's preaching at Philippi, for him there will have been no gospel—God's promises given through Isaiah's words will not have been realized—unless some Gentiles have accepted (and kept) it. Only such an understanding can explain the otherwise strange use of *evangelizomai* (preach the gospel) to speak of the good news Timothy was *bringing to Paul*; the "gospel" here is the news that the Thessalonians have kept the faith and love Paul had preached to them (v.6). Whereas he had sent Timothy to comfort/exhort (*parakalesai*) them (v.2), it is he who was comforted (*paraklethemen*) by their endurance in the faith despite all affliction and distress (v.7). Indeed he asserts his own dependence on them ("now

---

2　By paralleling Jesus and the prophets and equating God's word with the gospel (to the Gentiles), Paul is already expressing what he will later magisterially state in Rom 1:1-6.

we live, if you stand fast in the Lord," v.8) and is so overwhelmed that he cannot find the adequate thanksgiving he could render to God (v.9). Still, until the Lord comes (v.13) he cannot afford to relax: he continues his supplication for the opportunity to see them again in order to strengthen their faith (v.10), and he hopes that he will be granted his wish (v.11), but until then he supplicates the Lord himself to take care of the matter (v.12).

Other Pressing Concerns (4:1-12)

Paul's contemporary Jews were molded and challenged by scripture, in the teachings of the prophets and in the Torah, the biblical God's official instruction for the biblical Israel. They were privy to God's will. The Gentiles, however, were the biblical "nations" whose ways were consistently condemned in scripture and considered to be deserving of God's wrath. Since persistent behavior is essentially a habit, any slight change in it, let alone a thoroughgoing one, requires a continuous effort and incessant reminders. Paul's Gentiles had to get away from the ways of the "nations," which were their own ways. This is what they already learned from him (vv.1-2) and this is what he begins by reminding them of. That Paul was trying to "mold" his Gentiles according to the will of the scriptural God can be easily detected in the biblical terminology he uses: the will of God; holiness (*hagiasmos*)[3] versus harlotry (*porneia*);[4] heathen who do not know God;[5] the Lord as an avenger; uncleanness (*akatharsia*)[6] versus holiness (vv.3-7). These all refer to old, now proscribed forms of behavior vs. the new encouraged ones.

Paul concludes this section dedicated to the relationship between the Thessalonians and God with a sudden reference to God as the

---

3   Which is the basic quality of God and, consequently, the members of his community.
4   Which is the epitome of sin. In the prophetic books it refers to abandoning the Lord in order to follow other deities.
5   Compare with Ps 79:6; Jer 10:25. See also 1 Cor 8:1-6; Gal 4:8-9.
6   Which is a reference to being an outsider to God's community.

grantor of the Holy Spirit: "Therefore whoever disregards this, disregards not man but God, who gives his Holy Spirit to you." (v.8) The previous mention of the Holy Spirit occurs in 1:5-6:

> For we know, brethren beloved by God, that he has chosen you; for our gospel came to you not only in word, but also in power and in the Holy Spirit and with full conviction. You know what kind of men we proved to be among you for your sake. And you became imitators of us and of the Lord, for you received the word in much affliction, with joy inspired by the Holy Spirit.

The Thessalonian Gentiles were chosen and became God's people just as the "chosen" biblical Israel was, through the gospel that was both preached and accepted *in the Holy Spirit.* The next reference to the Spirit is found in 5:19-20 in conjunction with prophecy: "Do not quench the Spirit, do not despise prophesying." What can be made of all this?

My conviction is that Paul himself raised to prominence the biblical element "Holy Spirit" among his Gentile churches in order to minimize any chance that the Jerusalemite church would be able to gain and keep hegemony over them. He took the lead mainly from his predecessor Ezekiel, the Jerusalemite priest who made out of the Babylonian, and thus Gentile, locality Chebar not only a place where the God of Jerusalem could also speak, but actually *the* location from which he would authoritatively address Jerusalem itself. To do so, God and his prophet Ezekiel, or their spoken word, had to be eminently mobile and it was God's spirit that supplied the agency for that mobility of the divine/prophetic word and allowed it to travel from the Gentile Babylonia to Jerusalem. Paul followed Ezekiel's pattern and made it clear to his churches that they were, through the Pauline gospel, in direct contact with God's word through his spirit, and not via Jerusalem and its leaders. Those Jerusalem leaders were actually bound by God's word in the gospel, and not vice-versa. Thus, Paul was actually laying the foundation for his churches' dependence on the gospel and, at the same time, their independence from Jerusalem.

He was prompted to do so by the continual awareness that his own inevitable death would leave his churches truly "orphaned" since he was the sole apostle on their side. Hence, his letters were consciously intended to become their "written gospel," i.e., God's written last word about how to correctly interpret his word consigned in scripture. Paul's letters themselves were thus intended to serve as scripture from the moment they were written![7]

If the Gentiles are the "chosen" ones of God, they are his people and consequently they are to abide by his will expressed in his Law. No wonder then that the other side of Paul's basic concern regarding his Gentile churches entailed the "practical" aspect of his gospel: God's people must follow God's rules and regulations. And, as he will expressly declare to the Judeo-Gentile community of Rome (Rom 13:8-10) as well as to his Gentile churches in Galatia (Gal 5:14), the fullness of the Law lies in love of one's neighbor. Already in this early epistle one can detect the centrality of this matter for Paul. Regarding it he says to the Thessalonians that they are "taught by God" (*theodidaktoi*), which is a reference to the Jeremianic "new covenant" (Jer 31:31-34)[8] where we read that God's Law would be written on people's hearts, and there would be no need for teaching it since everyone would be abiding by it.

The Resurrection of the Dead and the Lord's Coming (4:13-5:11)

Having reminded his addressees of the two principles of his gospel to the Gentiles, their having been chosen by the scriptural God and thus their responsibility to do his will, Paul deals with the specific issue that was bothering them: the death of some of them. They had heard him teaching that those who accepted the gospel would be freed from the domain of the idols and brought

7   See also the chapter on the letter to the Galatians.
8   See *I Thess* 142-143.

under that of the scriptural God, from whose wrath they will be delivered at his son's coming in glory (1:9-10). Their conclusion was that they would be still living to join the Lord's glorious procession as victor over all his enemies. But some, or at least one, of the Thessalonian believers died since Paul left them, and this was a cause for grief within the church there. Paul meets this concern by saying that grief pertains to those who have no hope, the Gentiles, whereas his Thessalonians were no longer part of the "nations," for they now believe that the one coming in glory is the *dead and risen* Christ, and his companions will include some like him, who died, or rather "fell asleep," since God will raise them as he did his Christ (4:13-14). Actually, the deceased have it better in that they will *precede* those still living in the victorious procession of God's Son (v.15). To explain the matter Paul refers to the setting of the *parousia* (coming), a word he used to speak of Christ's coming in glory. *Parousia* meant the coming of a king, emperor, or governor to visit one of his cities, or the coming of a general, victorious in a major battle, to the (capital) city where the king, emperor, or governor at the head of the entire populace would be awaiting the general to crown him with the wreath of victory. The latter imagery fit perfectly the case of Jesus whose victory was, for the believers, a reality since they accepted the news of it in the gospel offered them as a word of proclamation.[9] Still, just as citizens who have *heard the news* that their general won the battle *yet cannot see* him victorious and so must await his return to their city, the believers await their victorious Christ coming in glorious apparel; only then will they be able to join in his procession.

It is against this background of *parousia* that Paul consoles the Thessalonians. The deceased among them are actually in a better position. Just as Jesus arose (v.14) they also will arise at his coming (v.15) and will be part of the victorious Christ's entourage, coming

9   See 1 Cor 15:12 and Rom 10:8-10, 14-17.

along with him (v.14). The rest will be like those awaiting him at the gates of their city and will join him upon his arrival; they will be part of the welcoming party. At that time, all, the deceased and the living, will be together with the Lord for ever (v.17). The main message here is that not only will the dead not be left behind (v.15) but they will actually be first (v.16), ahead of the living. Consequently, the Thessalonians have no reason to bemoan "those who fell asleep" (v.14), "the dead in Christ" (v.16). "Therefore comfort one another with these words," says the apostle (v.18).

Immediately, however, he cautions them against any speculations concerning the timetable of the Lord's coming. His "day will come like a thief in the night" (5:2), unexpectedly even as to its results, for it will cause destruction instead of escape (v.3). So instead of trying to predict when the Lord will come, which is not necessary for people who are assured that it will be to their own benefit and they cannot miss it (v.3), they had better make sure to be on that day indeed ready to meet it, as "sons of the light, awake and sober" (vv.6-7), i.e., *persevering* in the path of faith, love, and hope (v.8) that Paul's gospel set them on (1:2-5). It is only on this condition that both the deceased and living can secure eternal life with Christ (5:10). "Therefore encourage one another and build one another up, just as you are doing" says again the apostle (v.11) at the end of the entire section. He wants to make sure that the words of comfort concerning the dead (4:13-18) *not* cause the Thessalonians to worry about the coming's timetable, out of eagerness to be reunited with them soon. Since those who fell asleep died in Christ (v.16) they will be brought with him by God (v.14); the Thessalonians ought not worry about them. Rather, if they really want to be reunited with them, they should worry about themselves being found awake and ready at the sound of the herald's trumpet announcing the nearing of the Lord. If they are found dead asleep of drunkenness, incapable of either hearing the trumpet's sound or, should they be able to hear it, unable to join the welcoming party, they will wind up being left altogether out of the festivity and God's kingdom. And there will be no excuse since the apostle did exhort, encourage, and charge them "to *lead a life worthy of God,* who calls you into his own kingdom and glory" (2:11-12).

Miscellaneous Exhortations (5:12-25)

Having taken care of the most important matter causing concern among the Thessalonians, Paul proceeds to give recommendations pertaining to the general well-being of their church. First on the list, as always, is the issue of order (*taxis*) at their gatherings. This is important because the church is the community of the scriptural God, and the God of scripture is portrayed as a king seated on his throne, preserving peaceful and life-giving order throughout his realm. Any disorder within such a king's realm would reflect an inability on his part to control the chaotic powers threatening the very existence of his kingdom and those within it, and ultimately would put under question his kingship itself along with his ability to rule.[10] Hence, the lion's share of Paul's exhortations are intended to encourage respect and obedience for the community elders who "stand at the head [as leaders] (*proistamenous*) [of the church] in the Lord" and as such are required to care for it (vv.12-14). The other side of the same coin is the brotherly love which must be expressed mainly in mutual tolerance of one another (v.15). Without this combination of conditions the community's very existence is at risk.[11]

Paul then enjoins his hearers to always express their joy (v.16) in the Holy Spirit, God's gift granted through the word of the gospel despite all adversities (1:5-6). In so doing they will emulate Christ himself who also was a victor though apparently vanquished on the cross. Consequently, an essential feature of prayer is thanksgiving (5:17-18a) to God who granted the Thessalonians

---

10 *OTI3* 17-32.
11 See Gal 5:15 and my comments thereon in *Gal* 289-90.

in Christ victory together with his glory and kingdom. Actually, that was his *will* for them in the Christ Jesus (v.18b). And if God's spirit, the guarantor of their joy, was granted to them, they are not to quench that spirit's presence by despising its work manifested through prophetic teachings (vv.19-20) within their church. There would be concrete negative consequences of despising prophecy, for it could lead to their being enslaved to the earthly Jerusalem and its leaders. Rather, they are to serve the divine Spirit, and in his light they are to test everything and stand by what is genuinely from him and is therefore good (v.21-22).

Having covered all the conditions for the maintenance of God's life-giving peace, Paul lifts his prayer to that God of peace to keep the Thessalonians on the right path all the way until the Lord Jesus Christ's *parousia* (v.23). Furthermore, he is convinced that his prayer will indeed be heard since God, who "called" them through the gospel, will also carry through on his promise (v.24). Paul then requests that he be included in their prayers (of thanksgiving) at their gatherings (v.25) since all that God did and will do for them was through the gospel Paul brought to them (2:13).

Final Words (5:25-27)

Paul intended his letter to be read at an official gathering, i.e., as a scriptural reading would; this would be the simplest way to have the letter read to *all* the brethren. Moreover, his "adjuring them by the Lord" (making them take an oath) to do so can only mean that, by accepting this exhortation, "all" would become bound *under oath* to consider what they read from him to be truly the gospel as they received it from him: not a human word, but as the genuine "word of God" (2:13).

In Paul's Gentile churches his letter was to be read alongside the Old Testament scriptural readings and so will have acted as their authoritative (scriptural) interpretation. Since, on the other hand, *all* brethren present are to receive it as such and treat *all* those present as equally holy through the "holy" kiss, his rule applied to any Jews who were part of that gathering. In other words, his *one* gospel was equally binding to the entire *one* church of God, "the Jew first and the Gentile."

Paul concludes his letter by asking that *all* the Thessalonian brethren remain faithful to God's grace revealed through the Jesus Christ preached in that *one* gospel.[12]

12 See Gal 1:6

3

The Letter to the Galatians: Background

Paul wrote Galatians from his headquarters in Ephesus soon after a trip to Galatia, to which he had traveled in order to strengthen those churches in the faith he had originally taught them when he founded them.[1] He wrote this letter so soon after being there personally because news had reached him that members of James' party had followed in his footsteps and were trying to lure the Galatian believers away from his gospel. But why would he have cause for concern that the Galatian Christians would desert him so quickly, in spite of his repeated efforts and the official stamp of approval of the Jerusalem agreement? What made his opponents' argument appeal to the Galatians to the extent that a number among them, if not their majority, were already reneging on their commitment to his gospel? Those opponents must have had an extremely convincing argument to offer.

The Background for the Opponents' Argument

The first and basic scripture of Judaism is the Torah or Pentateuch. As with any set of scriptures, even those containing apparently independent "rules" within them, this one was never intended to be used as it were "magically," by a reader who would pick and choose passages that seem at face value to apply to any given situation. But for those who read it both then and now, the temptation to do that is too strong to resist. Consider, for example, the typical section in a present-day Bible where the reader is given a list of biblical passages to read and refer to for each and every situation in life: birth or bereavement, sorrow or joy, success

1 See *Gal* 5-9.

or failure, and so forth. It is as though the biblical God were the sum total of a collection of pagan deities, each in charge of a different area or aspect of our lives![2] But as I have shown throughout my Old Testament Introduction series and am now showing again with regard to the New Testament, the scriptural books are individually and collectively written *as a story* with a beginning and an end, a story whose meaning cannot be gathered except when taken in its entirety.[3]

Nevertheless, people are people, and they constantly fall into the trap of singling out for special emphasis those parts of the story that seem to them more pertinent to their particular situation. One such mishandling of scripture, with particularly severe consequences, has afflicted both Jews and Christians over the centuries down to our own day and can be termed "the Maccabean complex." The biblical story of Israel's deliverance from Egypt has a place of honor in the Torah or Pentateuch, the first scripture of Judaism, and it has undoubtedly promoted among Jews an abhorrence for the state of slavery and a trend toward financial independence through the learning of a trade; this explains the high percentage of free or freedmen among the Jews of the Roman empire in Paul's time, when compared to others. However, the exodus is not an end in itself but a preamble to the giving of the Law—and the Law defines sin, not slavery, as God's nemesis. Moreover, the Law was given to be the rule of life in Canaan, a criterion by which Israel would be judged, as is stated explicitly and repeatedly in Deuteronomy, the Torah's last book. Later, in the Prophets, the second scripture, the same emphasis on sin over

---

2 This is at best a slothful attitude: while the poor pagans had to remember the name and the function of each deity in order to make the proper request and insure prompt answer, we circumvent this nuisance and ask from the same god whatever behooves us and according to our need or pleasure. At its worst, this attitude makes out of the living biblical God who does "what no eye has seen, nor ear heard, nor the heart of man conceived" (1 Cor 2:9), a web-site masterminded by humans to satisfy *their* whims of the moment.

3 *OT2* 197-99; *OT3* 99-104.

slavery is maintained, for here we learn that Israel faltered and sinned and was *exiled by God because it sinned,* not vanquished by an adversary because it was weak.

In the first half of the second century B.C. a family of rural priests, the Maccabees, led an armed revolt against the Seleucids that ended with the recapture of Jerusalem and Maccabean rule there. These people were not hailed by all Jews as deliverers, since they used the revolt to declare themselves exarchs and later kings. They were harshly criticized by the *hasidim,* who opted for strict allegiance to the Torah in its totality[4] and started a trend that stressed the study and explication of the Torah, the Prophets, and the Writings as God's ultimate voice for good and forever. The Pharisees, one of whom was Paul, were an offshoot of this trend.

But the Maccabean "success" remained appealing to many Jews who tried unsuccessful revolts under Pompei (63 B.C.), between 66 and 70 A.D., at which time Jerusalem was vanquished and the temple burned down, and between 132 and 135. In 134 Jerusalem fell again to the Romans, and in 135 it was renamed Aelia Capitolina by Emperor Hadrian in honor of Jupiter, Juno, and Minerva, the main deities of the Capitoline Hill in Rome. Despite defeat after defeat, the appeal of the Maccabean success complex never died; it can never die since it strikes a sensitive chord, the Promethean[5] chord latent in every human being and which John D. Rockefeller once identified as especially characteristic of the American spirit. I shall limit myself to a recent example in the contemporary life of the USA. In their legitimate effort to introduce Hannukah as an "American" holiday alongside Christmas, some Jewish organizations have advertised it as being in commemoration of "the first

4 For example, by not fighting on the sabbath.
5 In Greek mythology Prometheus was one of the Titans, the original Greek deities. It is said that he stole fire from the gods and gave it to man. So he was considered the giver of arts and sciences to man and became the prototype of human beings who would fight their way to attain knowledge, and thus power, that was reserved only to the gods.

(successful) fight for religious freedom." This phraseology was aptly chosen to ensure it would strike a responsive chord in the minds of Americans, who could be counted on to support all who sought "freedom." The plan worked because although this kind of "freedom" is not endorsed by scripture as a whole, and Americans in general are familiar with scripture, they also in general adopt the "Maccabean complex." Remember the American adage: Nothing succeeds like success.

The Opponents' Argument

Paul's opponents can be considered as having the Maccabean attitude linking the gospel with the notion of "success." In the Roman empire the greatest honor, and thus the greatest sign of success, was to be designated a free Roman citizen or at least a freedman, i.e., a slave who had been released from the status of slavery. Indeed, it was natural that this would be commonly perceived as a high goal because the overwhelming majority of people within the Roman realm were slaves. The argument Paul's opponents made to the members of the Pauline churches in Galatia built upon these values may be paraphrased as follows:[6]

> Paul says that you are Abraham's children through your faith in Jesus as God's Christ. This cannot be true since you are still slaves in your overwhelming majority, while the Jews, Abraham's true children, are by and large free; and this ought to be so since Abraham's true progeny was saved by God from (the) slavery (of Egypt). It is thus contradictory to still be a slave and consider oneself Abraham's child; and God's promise was made to Abraham *and his progeny which is Isaac and, after him, Jacob/Israel* to whom was granted the Torah to honor and implement. Thus, unless you are circumcised and follow the commandments of the Torah you are not a member of Israel, and God's promise to Abraham does not apply to you. So Paul is actually fooling you into believing that

6   This paraphrase and the one below for Paul's response are based on a fuller discussion of these issues in my *Galatians: A Commentary.*

you are part of those who will join the victorious procession of Jesus at his parousia, while in reality you will be thrown out as part of the "nations," God's and his Christ's enemies.

Why is it that Paul is not telling you the entire saving truth? It is because circumcision is both a hardship on an adult and a sign of shame in the Hellenistic mentality[7] that pervades the Roman empire. He realized that it would put off virtually all Gentiles who would then refuse the gospel and thus prove "the apostle to the Gentiles" unsuccessful in his mission. Being the boastful person he is to the extent that he came to Jerusalem with Titus to show him off, he cannot afford to be proven wrong in his thesis that the Gentiles will flock in numbers to accept his gospel. So he decided to allow his Gentile converts to forego circumcision to make the gospel easy on the Gentiles who would not have to bear the "shame" of circumcision for the sake of Christ who is the fulfillment of God's promise to Abraham, fulfillment offered in the gospel to all those who would accept to become his children. There is one way to do that: have one's foreskin circumcised as scripture mandates. In other words, Paul betrayed the true gospel for his own glory: Paul is actually ashamed of what God himself considered a sign of his (promise of) salvation, and is thus doing nothing less than perverting the one gospel.

Galatians, beware of Paul! By luring you away from the shame and hardship of cutting off your foreskins, he is actually cutting you off from entering the kingdom of God which the gospel is supposed to bring to you. Ultimately it is God's glory he is betraying for his own; and this is the consummate sin according to scripture.

Paul's Counter-Argument

Since the opponents' forceful and, at face value, highly convincing argument revolved around the notion of hardship and shame, Paul rebuts it by using it *ad hominem*, i.e., by turning it around *as it stands* against them. Thus he tells the Galatians:

---

7 The Hellenistic mentality was rooted in the Greek view that the human body is perfect as is; any mutilation to it is an abhorrence to the gods that created the human beings. So, at the common baths for instance, a circumcised would be ridiculed.

"O foolish Galatians! Who has bewitched you, before whose eyes Jesus Christ was publicly portrayed as crucified?" (Gal 3:1) This was my unflinching preaching since the beginning to all Gentiles in the Roman empire, for whom the cross is the foremost sign of hardship, shame, and ultimate humiliation in defeat.[8] So you can imagine what it means if you would have to say before the Roman authorities that your lord, i.e., owner and master of your life, to whom you owe full allegiance, is someone who was crucified under their orders. This sounds as though you were reviving the revolt of slaves headed by Spartacus less than a hundred years ago which ended with a large number of them being crucified along a road leading to Rome, as a warning to other slaves. It is tantamount to signing one's death sentence, even for a Roman citizen like me, Paul. The "danger" of circumcision fades in comparison: the latter can be hidden by clothes or by refraining from going to public baths. No, I will not myself, nor will I let you, get off the hook by opting for circumcision, a fake shame compared to that of the cross.

Thus, as you can see, if you have eyes to see, it is my opponents who are actually luring you away from the gospel by offering you an easy way out through a "cheap" sacrifice. Actually, it is they "who want to make a good showing in the flesh that would compel you to be circumcised, and only in order that they may not be persecuted for the cross of Christ. For even those who receive circumcision do not themselves keep the law, but they desire to have you circumcised that they may glory in your flesh. But far be it from me to glory except in the cross of our Lord Jesus Christ" (Gal 6:12-14a). If there is anyone whose intention is to show off, it is definitely they, not I!

Galatians, an Apologia

As always, Paul's opponents attacked his apostleship as well as his teaching.[9] Hence, just as he did in 1 Thessalonians, Paul here also starts his letter with a defense of his apostleship as well as his gospel. But this time he devotes so much space to these two interconnected topics that the letter takes on the tone of an apologia, a

8 See p. 5.
9 See p. 17.

written formal defense:[10] Gal 1:1-2:14 deals with Paul's apostle-ship while 2:15-4:7 anchors his gospel in (the Old Testament) scripture, God's word. Moreover, the official nature of Paul's defense is reflected in two striking features right at the start of this writing: (a) Paul stresses his apostleship and its nature already in the salutation (1:1), and (b) he omits the traditional "thanksgiving" formula in order to delve immediately into the matter at hand by strongly reproving his addressees and issuing an ultimatum to them.

Galatians, a Scripture

However, it is clear that Paul intended something much more than a mere apologia in writing this letter. The reason for the attack on his apostleship along with his gospel is obvious: it was his status as an apostle that lent authority to his teaching, so the opponents needed to undermine that authority. They directed their efforts toward doing just that, and since their questioning of Paul's authority was taken seriously, they succeeded in weakening the absolute nature of Paul's gospel in the Galatians' mind. Again and again Paul's opponents returned to the same theme because it proved so effective, and each time Paul had to defend both himself and his teaching.

To put an end to this sly maneuvering, he presented his letter *as scripture* after the pattern of Deutcronomy, the last book of the Torah, where Moses, God's emissary, reiterates[11]—just as Paul does in Galatians (1:9)—his message of salvation together with the conditions that will allow the hearers to abide safe and sound under his aegis while going about their daily life. Deuteronomy is God's *last* word to an Israel which, after accepting salvation from

10 H. D. Betz in his momentous commentary, *Galatians: A Commentary on Paul's Letter to the Churches in Galatia* (Hermeneia, Philadelphia 1979) takes the position that the structure of the letter follows that of a Greco-Roman apologia (pp.14-25).

11 See Deut 5:22; 29:1.

him, betrayed him time and again in the wilderness. It is a final word delivered before Israel's embarkation on a journey among the nations. So is Paul's letter: it is his *last* word to the Galatians who, after having received from him the gospel of the justification and blessing promised to Abraham and his progeny, betrayed him time and again under his opponents' pressure; henceforth they have only this word in their remaining journey within the Roman empire. Just as Deuteronomy ended with the promise of God's blessings on those who would follow the book's injunctions and with the threat of his curses on those who would not abide by them, so does Paul's letter put under a curse *anyone,* even himself or an angel from heaven, who would desert the God offered in the Pauline teaching (Gal 1:6-9). Conversely, it promises God's peace and mercy upon all those who follow the "rule" (*kanon*) of this gospel as delineated in the letter (6:16). Finally, just as God's word in the Torah was given "at the *hand* of Moses,"[12] God's only and authoritative representative in Deuteronomy, so this letter is God's word written by *Paul's own hand* (6:11),[13] by God's only authoritative representative to the Galatians (1:1-2,[14] 6-9, 11-18, 21; 2:5; 6:17). The Galatians must now beware: the Prophets, the second scripture, tell us that the curses of Deuteronomy did strike Israel, sentencing it to death by exile. So they cannot afford to take Paul's warning lightly:

> Now I, Paul, say to you that if you receive circumcision, Christ will be of no advantage to you. I testify again to every man who receives circumcision that he is bound to keep the whole law. You are severed from Christ, you who would be justified by the law; you have fallen away from grace. (Gal 5:2-4)

---

12 See e.g. Num 4:37, 45, 49; 9:23; 10:13; 15:23; 36:13.

13 Though he wished to be present with them in order to utter it (4:20).

14 Notice how, unlike the salutations in his other letters, Paul separates himself as apostle from his collaborators (see my comments in *Gal* 19-23).

4

The Letter to the Galatians: Content

Salutation (1:1-5)

In this long salutation Paul underscores that his apostleship comes from God and from Christ, not from any human agency. He then offers a brief synopsis of the apostolic message he originally preached to the Galatian churches and continues to preach now: we have all been rescued, liberated from our subjection to the present evil age through Christ's redemption of us all, Jews as well as Gentiles,[1] freed from our sins (vv.3-4). Now that we have been redeemed, purchased back, we are bound only to our new master, the Lord Jesus Christ; we are his.[2] Consequently, we are no longer under the authority of whatever human agency used to govern us, be it the Roman emperor or Jerusalem; both are of this present age. And the impetus behind this liberation is nothing less than the will of the biblical God who, through this redemption, became the Father of us all (v.4). "Us" in this case means both Jews and Gentiles; the Jews who had been bound to the earthly (present) Jerusalem, whose sin was the reason for the exilic punishment of Israel in scripture; and the "nations" (Gentiles) who were by definition sinners.[3]

There Is Only One Gospel (1:6-10)

Given the nature and clarity of the message Paul brought to Galatia, he is astonished at the Galatians' desertion from it (v.6). The notion of desertion applies to both a slave who escapes his master's

---

1 See 3:29a.
2 See 4:25.
3 See 2:15 and *Gal* 83-84.

house and, more importantly, to a soldier who turns his back on his general to join the enemy's army. The imagery came immediately to Paul's mind because in his view, being Christ's entails membership in his army under the leadership of the Spirit as its chief commander.[4] In this case "desertion" is utter foolishness[5] since the other side to which one might desert does not even exist: there is one and only one gospel. Any "other" gospel (v.7) can only be a perversion of the real one, a phantasm. The same "curse" will be borne by anyone who preaches the phantasm of a false gospel (vv.8-9) and, by the same token, all those who might follow such a leader. As for Paul, he intends to remain the slave/servant of the true Christ (v.10) proclaimed in the one true gospel.[6]

Paul Is the Apostle of this One Gospel (1:11-24)

There follows an argument in defense of Paul's claim to be an apostle: that he is such can be clearly seen from his life story. From a persecutor and destroyer of God's church (v.13) he became a preacher of the gospel before having met any of the apostles and thus without consultation with, or approval from, Jerusalem (vv.16-19), and he continued to act as an apostle before any formal discussion of the matter with any (other) apostle or Jerusalem (vv.21-24). To use scriptural terminology, he must have been chosen by God himself just as the other apostles were (v.15), and consequently the gospel he was preaching was clearly from God and not his own human fabrication (vv.11-12).

The Jerusalem Meeting and the Incident at Antioch (2:1-14)

This same gospel he was already preaching for years was vindicated at a summit in Jerusalem itself and in the presence of the

---

4 See 5:25 and my comments thereon in *Gal* 304.
5 See 3:1.
6 See 2:5, 14.

"pillars" themselves (vv.1-2), a summit made necessary due to the constant harassment by "false brethren" who are actually "spying"—as only an enemy would—on the Pauline churches (vv.4-5). As for himself, Paul was so open about the matter that he brought along his uncircumcised helper Titus (v.3). That meeting endorsed Paul's teaching, and all agreed that the gospel and apostleship were as much *one* as their originator, God himself (vv.6-9).[7] To ensure that this agreement would be as binding on Jerusalem itself as it was on the Gentiles, Paul accepted the task of raising an "offering" for the church of Jerusalem from his own churches (v.10). His subsequent bone of contention with the "pillars" was that such an agreement made under God's auspices[8] could not be reneged on by either party;[9] the "pillars" were not above God!

And yet, they did renege later at Antioch when a party from James put pressure on Jews to abandon full table fellowship between them and Gentiles, which until then even Cephas himself had been practicing (vv.11-12). Even Barnabas fell to this pressure (v.13), betraying his fellow-soldier Paul and thus "deserting" God. An open confrontation ensued (v.14).

When It Comes to Christ, Jews and Gentiles Are on a Par (2:15-21)

Both parties, Paul and the "pillars," are in agreement that Jews can only attain righteousness through faith in Jesus as God's Christ (vv.15-16), and thus that just doing things specified by the Law is insufficient. However, their conclusions regarding such "works of the Law" are different: Paul believes it is *not necessary*

---

7 See my comments on vv. 7-8 in *Gal* 69-70.
8 Notice the "I went up by revelation" in v.2a, the same divine revelation that sanctioned his apostleship and gospel (1:12).
9 Notice the exchange of the right hand of fellowship between the "pillars" on the one hand, and Paul and Barnabas on the other (v.9).

anymore, whereas the others maintain that it is. Paul considers his opponents' stand to be contradictory: if one concedes that God's righteousness is granted freely, as a gift (v.21a), then it is not given either to the Jew Paul or the "pillars'" as a reward for abiding by the Law. If it were, and if believing Gentiles likewise had to fulfill the Law to receive righteousness, that would mean Christ died in vain (v.21b). In that case there would have been no gospel and, by the same token, no apostleship either to Gentiles or to Jews, because the gospel is about righteousness freely granted through Christ. Yet this was the effect of Cephas' sudden about-face in Antioch: by making it look as though Gentiles still remained a kind of "second-class citizen" he effectively forced them to "judaize" (*ioudaizein*; v.14), i.e., to become Jews and acknowledge that their faith in Christ was insufficient!

Paul and the "pillars" are Jews and thus are themselves in this position of having been granted the "life" from God which the Torah promises in Deuteronomy, yet as believers in Christ Jesus they received it without having fulfilled all the requirements of the Torah. If any of them attempts now to try to make out of Torah observance a *necessary* condition for that life, that person will be rejecting the will of God, who has already freely granted it through his Christ. If they do that, they will have proven themselves as "transgressors" against God's will (vv.18-19).

Faith Versus Works of the Law (3:1-14)

Paul challenges the "foolish Galatians" by asking whether they can possibly have forgotten the crucifixion of Christ that was so clearly depicted to them in Paul's preaching (v.1). He then reminds them that God's spirit, the grantor of the life promised within the Law itself,[10] was bestowed upon them at that time when they accepted this apostolic teaching in faith (vv.2, 5). So

10 See Ezek 37:1-14.

why would they want to go back to the realm of the flesh,[11] especially after all they have endured (vv.3-4)? Besides, not only their own experience, but also scripture itself shows that faith is what counts, because Abraham himself, the one to whom the promise was made, was granted righteousness on the basis of his faith (v.6). How could his real children expect things to be different for them (v.7)? Furthermore, scripture foretold the "gospel" to Abraham, namely that the Gentiles would receive God's blessing through him (vv.8-9). The Torah, on the other hand, is a two-sided sword: while it does make promises to those who obey it fully, it also and emphatically puts under a curse all who would not fully abide by everything written in it (v.10). And again, scripture itself, in Habakkuk, declares that life will be granted to the one who is righteous on the basis of faith (v.11), whereas the Torah stresses the necessity of abiding by its requirements, and thus does not speak the language of faith (v.12). God's Christ himself was actually hit by the curse spoken of in Deuteronomy (v.13), i.e., in the Torah, so that the blessing of Abraham spoken of in Genesis, i.e., in the Torah, would be preached unto the Gentiles as having reached them through that "cursed" Christ—and this happened *in order that* everyone, Jews as well as Gentiles, would receive the promised Spirit through faith, not works of the Law (v.14).

The Promise to Abraham and the Subsequent Giving of the Law (3:15-25)

To make things easier on his readers Paul then appeals to a human example (v.15a): the legal testament or will. Once someone's will has been ratified, no one else can annul it or add to it (v.15b). And since God's word is incontrovertible, his promise stands particularly firm, unchanged from when it was first spoken (v.17). Proof of this is in Genesis, where it is reiterated verbatim—hence

11 Further discussion of this matter will take place at 5:16-26.

the plural "promises"—to Abraham's progeny, Isaac and Jacob (v.16a). What are we to make of Paul's insistence on the fact that Genesis speaks of "progeny" (singular) rather than "progenies" (plural; v.16b)? Paul could not have been oblivious of the fact that both the Hebrew *zera'* and the Greek *sperma* are as generic singulars as the English "progeny" is, each applying to the totality of someone's descendants. So why would he make a case of that?

Beginning with Jeremiah the message of restoration to the kingdom of Judah included also the previously fallen kingdom of Israel (Ephraim),[12] so much so that as Ezekiel repeatedly relates the story of God and his recalcitrant people, God's people are represented as two sisters.[13] But ultimately, when forgiveness and reconciliation are announced, stress is put on the two becoming one, in a text[14] immediately following the promise of the life-regenerating spirit.[15] Likewise, Paul's intention is to say that, in God's purview, at the time of the realization of his promise of salvation and blessing there cannot be two communities, but one. Consequently, his opponents are ignoring scripture when they keep a wall between the Gentiles and the Jews in the eschatological community of the Messiah.[16]

But if the Law was eventually proven as unnecessary for God's realization of his promise to Abraham, why did he bother promulgating it in the first place (v.19a)? The reader of scripture will notice that only in the return from Babylonian exile could Abraham's progeny emulate his journey. The biblical Abraham's beginnings are in Ur of the Chaldeans: "And he said to him, 'I am the Lord who brought you from Ur of the Chaldeans, to give you this land to possess.'"[17]

---

12 See Jer 2:6-13, 18; 7:15; 23:13-14; 31:27, 31-34.
13 Chs. 16 and 23.
14 Ezek 37:15-28
15 Ezek 37:1-14.
16 See for more details *Gal* 138-143
17 Gen 15:7; notice that this verse follows immediately the first biblical quotation by Paul in his discussion of the Abarahamic promise: "And he believed the Lord; and he reckoned it to him as righteousness." (v.6) See also 11:28, 31; 12:2.

We are also told that there, in Ur of the Chaldeans, "Sarai [Sarah] was barren; she had no child."[18] Now, in the entire Old Testament, the only mention of Sarah outside the book of Genesis occurs at Is 51:2 in the following text directed at Israelites living in the Babylonian captivity:

> Hearken to me, you who pursue deliverance, you who seek the Lord; look to the rock from which you were hewn, and to the quarry from which you were digged. Look to Abraham your father and to Sarah who bore you; for when he was but one I called him, and I blessed him and made him many. For the Lord will comfort Zion; he will comfort all her waste places, and will make her wilderness like Eden, her desert like the garden of the Lord; joy and gladness will be found in her, thanksgiving and the voice of song. (Is 51:1-3)

Shortly thereafter, although Sarah is not mentioned, Jerusalem (which is compared to her in the above text) is addressed in "nomadic" terms reminiscent of the times of Abraham and Sarah:

> Sing, O barren one, who did not bear; break forth into singing and cry aloud, you who have not been in travail! For the children of the desolate one will be more than the children of her that is married, says the Lord. Enlarge the place of your tent, and let the curtains of your habitations be stretched out; hold not back, lengthen your cords and strengthen your stakes. (Is 54:1-2)[19]

These texts illustrate how it was only when Abraham's progeny was in the Babylonian exile that his story could be meaningful for them. As for the exiles themselves, they did not happen to have taken a leisurely trip to Babylon; they were exiled by God himself because they had sinned against him. And God was implementing his righteousness when he exiled them, precisely because he had told them in Deuteronomy—the last book of the Torah whose first book, Genesis, speaks of Abraham—that he would do so if they didn't follow his precepts. After the people lived in exile for a time,

---

18 Gen 11:30.
19 One cannot help but notice that this is precisely the text quoted in Gal 4:27 in conjunction with the discussion of Abraham's progeny.

however, God implemented his righteousness again, this time after the Abrahamic mode. Abraham's progeny found themselves in the same position as he had been when he was fully at the mercy of God who was calling him. While Abraham had no future because he was childless, the exiles were hopeless because their exile was the punishment of God himself, their only possible hope.

The function of the Law was precisely to put Abraham's progeny in this same predicament as their forefather. It did that by "producing" the transgressions that resulted in their exile (v.19a). And it "produced" them in the sense that a "transgression" can only exist when there is a specific prescription to transgress against. The Law was thus the beginning of the story that ended in exile to the land where Abraham came from. It was the only possible way to make the Jews realize that they could not have access to the Abrahamic promise unless they approached it from the perspective of the "nations," i.e., as sinners like the Gentiles (vv.21-22). Only thus could the foremost promise to Abraham be fully realized, namely that he would become a great nation[20] *and* that all nations would encounter God's blessing in him.[21] This finally took place at the advent of God's Christ, who is Abraham's progeny (v.19b) and who now leads his people out of exile as well as out of the rule of the Law that caused their exile. In order to make clear in the mind of the Galatians the full equation between the Jews and the Gentiles when it comes to the Abrahamic promise, Paul likens the Law to a "pedagogue" (vv.23-25), using a Roman household term that refers to a slave appointed by the house master to be in charge of his children until they come of age. Though a slave himself, he temporarily *ruled* over the freeborn children.[22]

---

20 Gen 12:2.
21 Gen 12:3, quoted in Gal 3:8.
22 This imagery applied perfectly to the Law and its function in scripture, in view of what he is about to say later (4:1-7) concerning the under-age child.

All, Gentiles as Well as Jews, Are Equally God's Children (3:26-4:7)

In regard to the Abrahamic promise and blessing, there is no longer any differentiation between Jews and Gentiles. *All* can become God's children, but they can only do it by joining the one Messianic community founded on the one faith preached in the one gospel (3:26). Indeed, one joins this community by being baptized "into Christ" as he is presented in the gospel,[23] and through baptism one belongs to this same Christ (v.27). Thus it is not only Jew and Gentile who are fully equal within this community but also slave or free (v.28a);[24] there is only one rank or kind of member in the Messianic community (v.28b).[25] And it is through becoming Christ's that all can become Abraham's progeny and, as such, children according to the promise, i.e., true heirs (v.29) according to scripture, following its teaching that only Isaac, Abraham's son by divine promise, was Abraham's heir.

Just as earlier he compared the biblical Law with a Roman pedagogue in order to bring home his point to his Galatian addressees, so too here and for the same purpose Paul draws a parallel between the biblical notion of heir/inheritance and its counterpart in Roman terminology. There he spoke of the slave pedagogue, here he moves to the under-age child who is under the authority of slaves appointed by the head of the family as caretakers of his house (4:1-2). Just as the Jews were under the authority of a pedagogue—the Law—that ruled over them without being able to grant them freedom when they would come of age, so also the Gentiles were subjected to guardians and trustees, the "ele-

---

23 See my comments on Gal 3:27 in *Gal* 172-173.
24 The expression "there is no male and female" is intended to forestall any possible understanding of baptism in terms of mystery religion rites; see my comments in *Gal* 173-176.
25 See my comments on Gal 3:28b in *Gal* 185-186.

ments of the world" (v.3), i.e., their own (false) deities[26] that could not grant the freedom they now have in Christ. But at the assigned time for the realization of the promise made to Abraham, God sent his son as a Jew, i.e., subject to the Law (v.4) in order to redeem his fellows from this Law (v.5a) by voiding its sting since he accepted its curse and rendered it null and void.[27] The result was that the apostles, Jews "freed" from the curse of the Law through the crucified Christ, embarked on the path proclaimed in Isaiah: they brought forth this good news, the "gospel," to all the "nations" and offered them true sonship through this Christ (v.5b), as to children having come of age. And the sign that the Gentiles did become "sons" can be seen in the fact that they received the Spirit without works of the Law.[28] This Spirit gave them access to address God as *'abba*, as God's Son himself did and as only a true child would (v.6). If all this is true, then you Gentile Galatians, affirms Paul, are no longer slaves but sons; and if sons, then full heirs (v.7).

Paul's Appeal that the Galatians Not Allow Themselves to Be Misled (4:8-20)

Since the Mosaic Law is as much a slave overlord as the pagan deities are, the Galatians would be reverting to square one, just exchanging one overlord for another, if they were to accept circumcision and start following the Law's prescriptions (vv.8-10). And, if so, then Paul's preaching to them the gospel, through which he "begat" them,[29] would have been in vain (v.11).

This thought allows him to digress and appeal to their hearts. Since he and they are a "family" then it is love that reigns and whatever they do as children they could not possibly "wrong" him, for he loves them as a father (v.12). He reminds them of the

26 See 4:8-9.
27 See 3:13 and my comments thereon in *Gal* 129-133.
28 3:2, 5.
29 See 1 Cor 4:14-15.

first time they met, when they treated him as only children would treat their father, accepting him fully in spite of his appearance which was in some way offensive or repulsive (vv.13-14a, 15); and by accepting him in this way they also accepted the crucified Christ of the gospel in spite of his repulsive appearance on the cross (v.14b). So how did he suddenly become their enemy (v.16)? The reason can only be that others are trying to seduce them away from him (vv.17-18). As a father writing to his children, this thought leaves him at a loss for words (vv.19-20).

The Scriptural Story of Abraham and His Two Sons from His Two Wives (4:21-31)

Paul needed the previous "psychological" preparation to lay down his counter-argument to his opponents' main contention that his gospel did not deliver the Galatians from their status as slaves.[30] As usual, his argument is based on scripture, and more specifically the Torah (v.21). There one reads that Abraham had two sons, the first from Hagar, the slave woman, and the second through God's promise from Sarah, the free woman (vv.22-23). Now, the first covenant, the one contained in the Torah, was broken by the inhabitants of Jerusalem and as a consequence they experienced the curse of exile and slavery (vv.24-25), as is witnessed in the Prophets, the second scripture. The same second scripture also tells us that only while in Babylonia, among the "nations," was Israel offered the chance to be like Isaac rather than Hagar's son. As the children of the promise they could experience salvation from slavery (v.27), in a new Jerusalem that would be entirely God's handiwork and thus "heavenly" (v.26). Likewise, the Galatians have now been offered through Paul's gospel a chance to be children of the promise the way Isaac was (v.28). And the present opposition to their attaining the salvation and freedom promised

30 See p. 32.

them is also foretold in scripture, for according to it the free woman's progeny (Isaac) suffers persecution at the hand of the slave woman's progeny (Ishmael; v.29). Finally, scripture prescribes the solution to this problem: it advises that the slave woman and her progeny be "cast out" (v.30). The Galatians are thus advised to follow this advice by refusing to deal with Paul's opponents who are the "fleshly" Abrahamic progeny. Paul backs up this interpretation by asserting that "we," i.e., his Gentile addressees *together* with himself the Jew, are all and *in the same way* children of the free woman and not of the slave (v.31).

The Only True Freedom Is that Offered in the Gospel (5:1-15)

Here we begin with another exhortation: It was to bring us to this full freedom, as God's children through the promise, that Christ was crucified; the Galatians ought to stick by their freedom and not fall back into "another" state of slavery (v.1). But then the text takes on a new tone; whereas in 4:8-11 Paul begged them not to succumb, here, after having presented them with God's word through scripture itself, which the opponents thought to be their bulwark, he warns the Galatians of dire consequences if they do let themselves be circumcised (vv.2-4). In Christ, whether a person is circumcised or not no longer makes any difference; the only hope for attaining God's righteousness is to abide in the faith taught by Paul, which requires love to all as to full brethren (vv.5-6).

After the Galatians had started on the right track (v.6) they were lured away from God, who had called them through Paul's gospel (v.7). Those who lured them away shall answer to God (vv.8-9); they are deceivers who stoop even to impugning Paul's own motives (v.10).[31] Paul closes with an ironic remark: if his opponents put so much weight on the cutting off of a piece of flesh,

31 See *Gal* 13-14 and 281.

then they themselves ought to go all the way and make themselves eunuchs! (v.11).

After this aside meant to shake up the Galatians for the last time, Paul picks up where he left off, returning to love of one's neighbor. The Galatians were not freed from their previous masters so that they could follow their own whims; rather, they are to subject themselves to their new lord's will (vv.13-14). And his will, that they love one another, is for them a matter of life and death. If they don't take it seriously, they may risk not being among those whom Christ will come to invite into his Father's kingdom (v.15).

The Spirit Versus the Flesh (vv.16-26)

Christ is their new master and as such he has a "law" or "rule" for them to walk by: they are not to follow the desires of their "flesh," i.e., their humanity, but rather the will of the "spirit" of God (v.16), even when it contradicts theirs (v.17). The fact that they are not under the Mosaic Law does not mean they are "free" even from God (v.18). Following their own desires will end in their disinheritance from the kingdom of God that was promised them (vv.18-21). It is only those who let themselves be guided by the Spirit who will inherit that kingdom, for it is the Spirit who produces the fruit of love in those who are the slaves of the crucified Christ (vv.22-26).[32]

Love in Practice (6:1-10)

In order to put into practice the required love, leaders are to deal with gentleness toward those in their charge, remembering that they are appointed house masters who will have to answer to their master at his coming (vv.1-5).[33] Conversely, the brethren are to honor those who toil for their upbuilding through the word (v.6). Everybody must always remember that the Lord is coming to judge

32 For more details on this extremely rich passage see my comments in *Gal* 297-305.
33 For more details see my comments in *Gal* 309-314.

all and each will reap whatever he has sowed (vv.7-9); so as long as there is still time, everyone is to practice love toward all (v.10).

Paul's Final Word (6:11-18)

Finally Paul puts his personal signature on the letter in order to give the word it contains official status (v.11), and he appends yet another warning. Paul's opponents' use of circumcision voids the cross of Christ of its meaning for the Galatians (v.12), and those opponents seek converts for no purpose other than their own glory (v.13). As for Paul himself, he refuses to glory except in the ultimate sign of shame, the cross, because for him it is the cross of Jesus Christ, his new Lord (v.14) who has brought about a "new creation" in which one's status as circumcised or not is of no account (v.15). This is the new rule for the "Israel of God" (by which he means himself and any Jews who share his faith) and for the Gentiles who are with them; only upon them will God's peace and mercy be bestowed (v.16). This is Paul's *final* word to the Galatians (v.17) on which basis he asks that the grace of Christ, which is in this his gospel,[34] encompass them (v.18).

---

34 1:6.

5

The First Letter to the Corinthians: Miscellaneous Issues

The Corinthian Correspondence

At Ephesus, after having sent out his letter to the churches of Galatia, Paul began to receive troubling news about the church he had founded in Corinth: beliefs and practices contradicting or betraying the Pauline gospel abounded, to the extent of jeopardizing its very existence in that city. Furthermore, as might have been expected, Paul's opponents had begun to spread their alternative teaching in Corinth too. The disintegration of the main Gentile church Paul had planted at the heart of the world of the "nations"[1] would greatly weaken, if not devastate, any real hope for proving the validity of his gospel. Paul understood that a turning point in his struggle with Jerusalem would take place in the battle over Corinth, and so he gave it the kind of careful attention we see evidenced in the volume of Corinthian correspondence (29 chapters) and the number and variety of issues discussed in it.

It is difficult to decide as to the form the original correspondence took. As they exist today, the two canonical letters, 1 and 2 Corinthians, seem to have been pieced together by a later editor who combined a number of smaller epistles. They are much longer than is typical of letters, longer even than Galatians, which is itself a very long one.[2] At the same time, they are not unified thematically, in contrast to the long theological argumentation in

---

1 See chapter 1.
2 The case of the subsequent letter to the Romans will be discussed later.

Romans, for example. Here we find a number of different topics,[3] and the break between any of them could have been a break between originally separate letters. In fact, it is highly unlikely that all these issues would have arisen at the same time. It is also difficult to imagine that Paul would have refrained from taking care of each one immediately rather than let the first ones continue unaddressed while he waited until sufficient problems accumulated so he could write a single long letter dealing with them all. Finally, one should not ignore the remarks in 1 and 2 Corinthians where Paul refers to letters he wrote to the Corinthians;[4] these may refer not to lost letters but to letters incorporated within the 1 and 2 Corinthians corpus.

If, then, 1 and 2 Corinthians are composites, can we determine an editorial purpose behind making two letters out of many? Or could the process have been more or less haphazard, its only goal being to make all of the letters fit into two roughly equal parts corresponding to the size of a parchment? The first alternative is more likely: 1 Corinthians deals with various issues related to the Corinthians' thoughts and behavior, while the second revolves around Paul's apostleship (and gospel). Though impossible to prove, it is not at all beyond reason to imagine that the editing took place under Paul's guidance or during his lifetime. If so, it was probably done while he was in prison[5] before his death. The reason for such an endeavor will be discussed at the end of the Introduction to Mark.

1 and 2 Corinthians as Scripture

For the time being, it is important to point out that whether taken as a whole or in parts, the contents of each of the two ca-

---

3 See 1 Cor 1:11;5:1; 6:1, 12; 7:1; 8:1; 9:1-3; 10:1-5; 10:23-25; 11:2-5; 11:17; 12:1; 15:1-5; 16:1; 2 Cor 1:13-16 (compare with 1 Cor 16:5); 2 Cor 3:1-3; 8:1 and 9:1; 10:1-3.
4 1 Cor 5:9; 16:3; 2 Cor 2:3-4; 7:8; 10:9-11
5 In Rome or more probably Ephesus.

nonical letters are addressed, like their predecessors 1 Thessalonians and Galatians, to the entire community of the Corinthians without singling out its leaders. This indicates that they were intended to be read *officially at the communal gatherings,* i.e., as scripture would be. Thus they were meant to be binding as a *kanon* (rule), as the scriptural canon was. Paul's interpretation of scripture—and his two letters to the Corinthians abound in both scriptural references and interpretations thereof[6]—was *intended* to be binding upon *all* the Corinthians; Paul brought them "the gospel of God which he promised beforehand through his prophets in the holy scriptures"[7] and consequently it is *Paul's* word alone that defines *their* relationship to the scriptural God—even if it does not carry that authority for others:

> Am I not free? Am I not an apostle? Have I not seen Jesus our Lord? Are not you my workmanship in the Lord? If to others I am not an apostle, at least I am to you; for you are the seal of my apostleship in the Lord. (1 Cor 9:1-2)

> Are we beginning to commend ourselves again? Or do we need, as some do, letters of recommendation to you, or from you? You yourselves are our letter of recommendation, written on your hearts, to be known and read by all men; and you show that you are a letter from Christ delivered by us, written not with ink but with the Spirit of the living God, not on tablets of stone but on tablets of human hearts. (2 Cor 3:1-3)

After the Galatian experience, and as is clear from the salutations at the beginning of 1 and 2 Corinthians, Paul explicitly titled himself as an *apostle* to those he was writing to.

The Corinthian Heresy

The basic thread that holds together the entire discussion of apparently unrelated issues in 1 Corinthians is what nowadays is

6 See below.
7 Rom 1:1-2.

commonly called "realized eschatology." The Corinthians misunderstood the gift of God's spirit of which Paul spoke. He taught that since the Gentiles had received God's ultimate gift, his Holy Spirit, they were not bound to follow any so-called authorities headquartered in the earthly Jerusalem, or for that matter any other "human" authority. They were free to be led by God's spirit on the path that would ultimately lead to their participation in the welcoming procession of Christ at his advent in glory, and after that their inheritance of the kingdom of God.[8] The Corinthians imagined that their "exciting"[9] experience of the Spirit was the sure sign that God's kingdom had already come. They misconstrued their "spiritual" experience as an end in itself, as if God's spirit had been brought to them by Paul solely for producing various spiritual "gifts." As a result they created their own fantasies about the character of God's spirit and perceived themselves as "spiritual" (3:1), "mature/perfected" (2:6), free of everything (6:12; 10:23) and free from *any* authority, even Paul's (9:1-3). Consequently, they also considered themselves not subject to God's final judgment (11:27-34)[10] and, in so doing, *de facto* denied Christ's coming (15:20-28) and, by the same token, even his resurrection (15:12-19).

The Apostolic Word Brought to Corinth Has All Along Been "The Messiah Crucified" (1-3)

After the salutation (1:1-3) Paul reminds the Corinthians that the gospel word he brought them was not that the coming of Jesus Christ *as Lord* took place at his resurrection. Christ will be revealed as Lord at his coming in glory—and not before then. At that time the God who called the Corinthians and is always faithful to his promise *will ensure* that they have a part in the Lord Jesus

8   See Gal 5:21b-6:10.
9   See 1 Cor 12 and 14.
10 This phenomenon is pervasive nowadays, not the least among Orthodox Christians.

Christ's welcoming procession (vv.4-9). Until then the only *real* Christ we can know is not the glorious Lord but the crucified Christ, the only way to God's wisdom and power for his "called" ones (vv.18-25), despite his rejection by Jews as well as Gentiles due to his apparent "foolishness" and "weakness." So why, Paul asks, is everyone trying to side with one or another leader considered to be particularly knowledgeable in God's matters (vv.10-17)? All the Corinthians have to do is consider who and what all of them were when the gospel reached them, for they all lacked wisdom, power, and nobility. It is upon such that God decided to bestow the wisdom sought by the Greeks and the righteousness sought by the Jews (vv.26-30).

The faith accepted by the Corinthians is *God's* wisdom expressed in *his* Christ crucified, through whom he bestows *his* spirit (2:1-13). If they are incapable of comprehending God's work, it is because they are not as "spiritual" and "mature/perfected" as they think they are (vv.14), and they had better listen again to Paul the truly "spiritual" one who has the mind of (the crucified) Christ and is now judging them (vv.15-16).

His teaching is that there is only one point of reference, God himself; any and all teachers are mere men working in God's field or building (3:1-9). *However,* Paul having been the first sent to them, *his* teaching is *de facto* the authoritative reference for them (vv.10-15). Moreover, it is God who made them his holy temple (v.16), and no one is *above* God's temple (v.17). Quite the contrary: every being, whatever its nature, with the exception of God and his Christ, is the *servant* of God's temple (vv.18-23).

The Apostles Have All Along Been Ministers of "The Messiah Crucified" (ch.4)

If God has been revealed as "foolish" and "weak," then how much more so must his ministers present the same face toward the world (vv.6-13)? It is to his, and only his, *coming* judgment that they will have to answer; until then, any other judgment, even their own about themselves, is invalid (vv.1-5). How then could the Corinthians' appraisal of themselves be of any value? Paul is sending to them, as his children through the gospel, the only valid exemplar by which they could judge themselves: his child in the Lord, Timothy. Timothy will reprove them as needed through Paul's teaching (vv.14-17). In this teaching Paul will be with them in a spirit of gentleness; but they should heed Timothy's instructions and comply with his judgments lest Paul himself be forced to come and condemn them (vv.18-21) by "delivering them to Satan."[11]

By "delivering unto Satan" Paul means "put under the aegis of Satan" or "put in the domain of Satan," in the same sense one might speak of the Roman emperor's aegis or domain. Anyone living within the boundaries of the Roman empire would be under the emperor's aegis, within his realm of authority and protection. Should a person decide to move out of the empire's boundaries, he would move to the domain of another authority. The same principle applies today in that when a person moves from one state or country to another he will find himself bound by, and protected by, a different authority. Paul viewed the baptized Gentiles as being under the authority and thus protection of their new lord (king, emperor), Jesus Christ; but then they must abide by his rules. Should they contravene those laws, they would be exiled out of his realm and back to the realm of their previous masters, their (false) deities, who were perceived by the monotheistic Jew, Paul, as demons.[12]

Examples of "Immaturity/Imperfection" (5-6:11)

In order to show that he is serious, Paul "excommunicates" a sinner, indirectly condemning them all, the "perfect" ones of God, who were tolerating such a sin within the "holy" temple of God

11 5:5.
12 See 10:19-21.

that they are (4:1-5). They are to be cleansed before joining the paschal table (vv.6-9).[13] As for outsiders, it is not the business of the Corinthians to judge them; God himself will take care of the matter (vv.9-13).[14]

Another "imperfection" of the Corinthians (6:1-11) is the way they bring their disputes before Roman courts. How, asks Paul, could God's "holy ones," who will be seated around Christ on his throne when he judges the "nations," subject themselves to the judgment of these same "nations"? This is tantamount to declaring the victory of these nations over Christ and his God. Furthermore, if the Corinthians were indeed "spiritual," they would not have been committing actions answerable to Roman justice.

Harlotry (6:12-20)

The last "imperfection" is the deadliest because it completely misunderstands the "spiritual" freedom granted by God through Jesus Christ. It involves a belief that the baptized has become fully "free" in some absolute, all-encompassing sense, though this could not have been put into practice by the Corinthians since even the most free person in their society, a Roman citizen, was bound by the state's rules and regulations.[15] The Corinthians in their "spiritual" excitement must have interpreted Paul's teaching according to their Gentile mentality that viewed deities as (super-) humans; so, for them, to have become God's holy ones must have meant that they became like the Greco-Roman deities that did as they pleased, especially when it came to food and sex.[16] For

---

13 See also 11:17-34.
14 This is a far cry from what Christians, virtually across the board, nowadays do: they uphold Christianity and point the finger at the non-Christians.
15 This misunderstanding seems to have been rampant among the Pauline churches due to their comprising mainly slaves; see Gal 5:13-26 and my comments thereon in *Gal* 283-305 as well as the previous chapter.
16 Cultic banquets were commonly associated with orgies, e.g. the Dyonisia or Bacchanalia, feasts in honor of the god Dionysus/Bacchus.

the scriptural Paul and his scriptural gospel, licentious banquets with other deities, mainly Baal, was *the* epitome of sin against God in Deuteronomy and the Prophets:[17] scripturally, the very definition of sin *is* to commit adultery against the Lord God.

The basis for Paul's correcting instructions is that the Corinthians were set free from their previous masters, the Greco-Roman deities,[18] through having been purchased from them for a price (v.20a). They now belong not to themselves (v.19b) but to a new master, the scriptural God (v.19a), and their business, as the temple of his Holy Spirit, is to glorify him (v.20b). God and they are for one another; they do not have the right to go "harloting" with someone else (v.13). He purchased them to make them members of his household, i.e., similar to his Son;[19] and, as he raised his Son from the dead, he will raise them also (v.14). They belong to Christ, the manager of God's household, and they are to obey the orders he gives through the Spirit;[20] indeed, they are of the same "spirit" as he (v.17). Leaving their new Lord to dally with their previous masters is harlotry (vv.15-16); it is the consummate insult to the head of God's household, *the* sin (v.18) whose punishment is death by exile. And, this time, the exile will be for good since they have already been redeemed from among the "nations" and marked for the resurrection through God's spirit[21] (vv.14, 16, 19).

Difficulties Related to Married Life: A Test Case for the Pauline Gospel's Validity

Since endorsement of the gospel was a personal decision, difficulties arose in case one was married or engaged. What would the believer's

---

17 That is, the Deuteronomistic History and the prophetic books.
18 See Gal 4:8-9.
19 See Gal 4:6-7.
20 See Gal 5:24-25.
21 See Ezek 37:1-14.

options be in such a situation? The question may sound moot at the end of the 20th century, but in Paul's time, given the hardships, even possibility of execution, that faith in Christ entailed, the matter was both relevant and difficult. Here Paul was faced with a real test for his gospel since he had to fight against not just the Corinthians or his opponents but the two of them together. Paul's opponents offered the Corinthians the example of Ezra, and they were all too ready to follow it:

> While Ezra prayed and made confession, weeping and casting himself down before the house of God, a very great assembly of men, women, and children, gathered to him out of Israel; for the people wept bitterly. And Shecaniah the son of Jehiel, of the sons of Elam, addressed Ezra: "We have broken faith with our God and have married foreign women from the peoples of the land, but even now there is hope for Israel in spite of this. Therefore let us make a covenant with our God to put away all these wives and their children, according to the counsel of my lord and of those who tremble at the commandment of our God; and let it be done according to the law. Arise, for it is your task, and we are with you; be strong and do it." Then Ezra arose and made the leading priests and Levites and all Israel take oath that they would do as had been said. So they took the oath...All these had married foreign women, and they put them away with their children. (Ezra 10:1-5, 44)

Paul could not go along with this for at least two main reasons:

1) It was a requirement of Judaism, and prescribing it for Gentile Christians would have been another form of judaizing, no less than forcing upon them dietary restrictions. This was a cunning trap set by Paul's judaizing opponents.[22]

2) It would create havoc in Paul's churches because they would begin to fill up with Gentiles disgruntled with their spouses, people who would thus use their partnership in God's "holy temple" to provide a convenient excuse to commit harlotry, which is *the* sin against God's holiness!

22 See Gal 2:11-14.

No way, said Paul: the scriptural God is not going to be "used"; he is our master and we are at his service. Given the delicacy of the matter, Paul painstakingly (40 verses) lays out other solutions he has to offer.

What is particularly impressive in this section is the way he repeats his advice or command addressing the woman as well as the man, which is quite striking when one considers that given the number of messages he was writing to the Corinthian community it would be natural to try to be as concise as possible. His determination to invest extra effort here even where it involves some repetition reflects his stand that, in the community of the baptized—unlike the situation within Judaism and to some extent in the Roman empire at large—woman was on a full par with man: they were each personally "holy,"[23] each members of God's "holy" temple.[24]

Directions to the Married and Advice to the Unmarried (ch. 7)

One must remain in the state one was in when called by God; this is the rule in all the Pauline churches (vv.17-24). Consequently, if one was married at the time of God's calling, then so be it (vv.10-13); the holiness of God, to whom the believer belongs, overcomes the uncleanness of the pagan deities, to whom the unbelieving spouse is attached (v.14). On the other hand, since it is actually the believing partner who broke the original agreement with the other,[25] it is the latter who is at liberty to break up the marriage, not the believer (vv.15-16).

The "slavery" to Christ through whom we were purchased (vv.22b-23) is binding even when both spouses accepted faith in

---

23 7:14. See further my comments on 11:2-16.
24 3:17.
25 When they decided to marry one another, they were both Gentile. Now, the believing partner is creating havoc by subjecting one-sidedly the family life to a new, life-threatening stress.

him. Just as in a Roman household a slave couple are not free, here also a believing husband and wife are not free to do as they please even in "spiritual" matters; their marriage becomes the property of the Lord who dictates what it takes to keep it healthy (vv.1-7).

The unmarried believers are advised to follow Paul's lead and remain so in order to dedicate themselves fully to the Lord's business (vv.25-35; 39-40). Celibacy has no value per se (vv.27-28a); rather it is in function of the Lord's coming (vv.29-31). This is confirmed by the way Paul handles betrothal (vv.36-38).

The Issue Related to the Food Offered to Idols (ch.8)

As was the case throughout the ancient Near East, social life in the Roman empire was essentially religious, and especially so in this case due to the cult of the emperor. Any official social gathering entailed offerings to the deities or emperor under whose auspices the event was taking place. There were those believers who did not care and attended such gatherings anyway since "there is but one God" and thus "an idol has no real existence" (v.4). But others took some of Paul's words[26] literally and concluded that any involvement in pagan festivities would mean betraying the Lord for Baal.

For Paul, the solution to this dilemma cannot be reached through a philosophical discussion as to whether idols exist or not; this would be sophistry since no one can prove or disprove the "existence" of such intangibles.[27] The matter at hand was rather how to solve the Corinthian dilemma. To do so, he appeals to the scriptural God himself, whom we did not know first but rather were known and loved first by him (vv.1-3) when he called us through the gospel. When we accepted his call he *became* our

---

26 In 6:12-20.

27 In a sense, idols existed more realistically than the biblical God since he did not have any tangible form while they could be represented with statues and thus "pointed out" to any one asking about them.

only God and his Christ *became* our sole lord (vv.4-6). But this God's household is made out of people whom he purchased from slavery through the death of his Christ, and he does not want to lose any of them due to someone else's arrogance. And therefore he issued his rule to all: love each other.[28] It does not take much to figure out that true love requires gentleness (*prautes*)[29] from the stronger and more knowledgeable toward the weaker and less knowledgeable[30] even if such love meant a hardship nearly impossible to bear, i.e., to refrain from eating meat, thereby curtailing one's "social" life outside the church, which required some form of involvement in offerings to idols (vv.7-13).

Paul's Apostleship (ch.9)

At this point comes a passage that presents Paul himself as a model for such a great sacrifice. He points out again to the Corinthians that nothing is yet secure for him, let alone for them, until the Lord comes and all will be judged on whether they will have abided by the will of their new master:

> Do you not know that in a race all the runners compete, but only one receives the prize? So run that you may obtain it. Every athlete exercises self-control in all things. They do it to receive a perishable wreath, but we an imperishable. Well, I do not run aimlessly, I do not box as one beating the air; but I pommel my body and subdue it, *lest after preaching to others I myself should be disqualified.* (vv.24-27)

Scriptural Precedent (10:1-22)

It is not only Paul's word but scripture itself that sets a paradigm (v.11) for what is asked of the self-confident Corinthians who have such confidence in their baptism[31] and their fellowship at

28 See Gal 5:13-15 and further 1 Cor 13.
29 See Gal 5:23.
30 See Gal 6:1; also 1 Cor 4:21.
31 See 1:10-17.

the Lord's table.[32] The Israelites, the Corinthians' scriptural fore-bears, were also established through "baptism" and were fed "spiritual food," but nevertheless were not safe from God's judgment (vv.1-10). Yet, not all died, which means that the divine test is not intended to destroy us but to encourage us to abide willingly by his will in spite of any apparent impossibility of the matter (vv.11-13). After all, what he did at the exodus, the apparently impossible salvation of the fathers from slavery, he can now do again by completing the apparently impossible task of making his own children out of the Corinthians, without subjecting them to the prerequisites of circumcision and the Law.

When it comes to sacrificial meals, one is to be aware that, as guests, we are bound by the house rules set by the host master. If this is the case with the Lord's supper, so it is with the meals at the Roman official gatherings. Here again scripture tells us that God did not tolerate Israel's sharing in Baal's sacrificial meals (vv.14-22).

How to Behave at Private Meals (10:23-11:1)

Just as in the case of sacrificial meals it is God who is to be taken into consideration, it is the neighbor, and not oneself, who is the point of reference for correct behavior in the case of private meals. The Corinthians are to eat whatever is put before them out of deference for their host; and they ought not worry since, for them, there is only one God and "the earth and everything in it are his" (vv.23-27). But if a fellow believer is present and might be scandalized, then for his sake they are to refrain from eating meat (vv.28-30). In all they do (v.31) they should follow Paul's lead (v.33)[33] and "give no offense to Jews or to Greeks or to the church of God" (v.32).

32 See 11:17-34.
33 See also 10:19-23.

Church Gatherings

By far the greatest challenge for Paul in the defense of his gospel was to make out of the assemblies of his Gentile converts orderly "church" gatherings ruled by the scriptural God the same way as their counterparts, the synagogue gatherings, were. This was easier said than done: the synagogue and its services were molded over centuries beginning with Ezekiel in the 6th century B.C. On the other hand, Paul's Corinthian converts were by and large Gentile slaves whose most impressive experiences in matters of religious gatherings were either the unruly and orgiastic festivities of Bacchus or the gladiator fights in the Roman theaters. How then could he convince the Jerusalem "pillars" that his churches were genuinely "one" with those of Judea if a Judean believer would feel as though he were at the theaters or Bacchanalia when sharing in the Pauline church gatherings? Since the "face" of a deity is reflected in the gatherings held in the honor of that deity, a Judean "brother" of a Gentile believer would hardly be convinced that it was his own scriptural God being honored at such unruly gatherings. Due to their "spiritual" excitement, the Corinthians were effectively proving the Jerusalemite leadership's case that the Gentiles could not yet be considered full and equal members of their Messianic community. Accordingly, here, even more than in ch.7, Paul had to battle the Corinthians' behavior on two fronts.

Woman's Attire at Church Gatherings (11:2-16)

For Paul, when it came to God's Holy Spirit—the actual leader of the Pauline churches—there was no differentiation between man and woman. Witness thereof is the quite large number of women among his co-workers: "Phoebe, a deacon[34] of the church at Cenchrae...Aquila, fellow worker in Christ Jesus...Mary who has toiled[35] among you...those who have toiled[36] much in the Lord,

---

34 The Greek has one word *diakonos* that applies to both sexes.
35 The same verb *kopio* that Paul uses to speak of his apostolic endeavors.
36 Again the same verb *kopio*.

Tryphaena and Tryphosa." (Rom 16:1, 3, 6, 12)[37] It is no wonder then that at Corinth there were women among the prayer leaders and prophets at the church gatherings (1 Cor 11:5). It seems that Paul was able to do that without running into too much pressure to stop it from Jerusalem. One reason may have been the scriptural precedents he could appeal to: Miriam (Ex 15:20), Deborah (Judg 4:4-16), Huldah (2 Kg 22:14-20), and Noadiah (Neh 6:14). Also, since the Jerusalem church viewed itself as God's eschatological community, Paul could have leveled against it and its "pillars" an even more directly relevant selection from scripture:

> And it shall come to pass afterward, that I will pour out my spirit on all flesh; your sons and your *daughters* shall prophesy, your old men shall dream dreams, and your young men shall see visions. Even upon the menservants and *maidservants* in those days, I will pour out my spirit. (Joel 2:28-29)

At any rate, it is clear from Paul's discussion in 1 Cor 11:2-16 that such an issue was not at stake. What was at stake is the head attire of those women and, as usual for Paul, the main reason for his response is to preempt any criticism by Jerusalem that would undermine his effort to preserve his churches' "freedom."

But what was the actual "danger" of having unveiled women leading prayers or prophesying? It was common practice in those times that women, especially the married ones, would use a veil over their heads when in public, and the church gatherings were eminently public.[38] Due to their understanding of "realized eschatology," Corinthians misunderstood Paul's allowing women to proclaim in a church gathering the prophetic "word of God" to the community, as *de facto* equating women as women to men as men, which equation in its turn would function as a proof that the "end" had already come. A "sign" thereof was the unveiling of

---

37 Later the tradition speaks of a woman, Thecla, as Paul's co-worker and who is known in Orthodox Christianity as *eisapostolos* (equal-to-the-apostles).

38 The Greek noun *ekklesia*, translated as "church," was the technical term for "the public gathering of the body politic."

women: woman *appears*, and thus *is*, the same as man. For Paul this attitude was reminiscent of mystery religion beliefs, in which there was no differentiation between the sexes when it came to "mystical" intercourse with the deity. This idea of direct access to the deity would *de facto* eliminate the need for Christ as mediator between God and human beings and thus as *sole head* of the church "until he subjects himself to God."[39] Until then, between God and us stands Christ as our Lord. Paul must respond that, no, the end has not yet come and *nothing* has changed in the surrounding human society with its rules, or in God's natural order in creation. The only "change" is that God revealed himself as "foolish" in his crucified Christ. This is the sole valid *skandalon* (stumbling block) for both Jews and Gentiles, and Paul was not about to allow a bunch of excited Corinthians to "act scandalously" and "offend Jews and Greeks and the church of God"[40] in order to "express" their *feeling* of freedom! Consequently, if the "change" brought about by Christ's death and resurrection is to be celebrated and expressed, it must be through the same medium that brought such celebration to Corinth, i.e., through the "word" (of the gospel), which now comes also through the (prophetic) "word" of the church prophet, but not through that prophet's person, and not dependent in any way on the prophet's gender.

Paul's solution is to remind everyone that the "change" brought about by the granting of God's spirit through baptism does not entail equality between man and woman (before God), i.e., "raising" woman to the level of man; rather it means that man is dislodged from his place of preeminence (as God's representative), for that position is now taken by the crucified Christ who is Lord over man. In other words, the change entails the "demoting" of man to being subdued to someone who died shamefully on the

39 15:28.
40 10:30.

cross. That this is Paul's point can clearly be seen in the way the "hierarchy" in v.3 does not follow either an ascending (woman-man-Christ-God) or descending (God-Christ-man-woman) scheme: "But I want you to understand that the head of every man is Christ, the head of a woman is her husband, and the head of Christ is God." Thus, what Paul wants the Corinthians to know is that "the head of every man is Christ," not God himself. And since Christ, not man, is the lord, then whatever *he* wills is binding. And if he wills that a woman speak the "word of the Lord," i.e., *his* word, then so shall it be. But, by the same token, this does not mean that woman per se has been "allowed" to speak in the church gatherings, not at all. It is always Christ, and only he, who speaks *his* "prophetic" word through *a prophet*, not through man or woman. And the word of the Lord has no "appearance" to be "changed." It is *within* the given order of things that the prophetic word is to be uttered. If the change is exterior, then one runs the risk of imagining that an actual tangible change took place. But if that were the case, then the word would be the word of the "changed" person himself and not of the Lord, which would be a far cry from Isaiah's reaction: "Woe is me! For I am lost; for I am a man of unclean lips, and I dwell in the midst of a people of unclean lips; for my eyes have seen the King, the Lord of hosts!"[41] In order to make out of this sinner a prophet, it was neither his person nor his gender that was "changed" but rather his *lips* that were cleansed so that he might speak God's words.[42]

As usual, for Paul, beyond the "social" (vv.4-6) and "natural" (vv.13-15) reasons to keep outward things as they are (vv.4-6), given that the end has not yet come, his main argument harks back to his divine reference, scripture, which states that woman was made for man[43] and thus she functions toward him as he

41 Is 6:5.
42 Is 6:7.
43 See Gen 2:18-23.

functions toward God (vv.7-9). However, scripture also states that "the woman is (made) from the man"[44] and "the man is (born) through the woman" (v.12a)[45] and ultimately "both[46] are from God" (v.12b).[47] It is precisely this reality that is given as the reason[48] why *in the Lord*, i.e., in the community of God's Messiah, things cannot be otherwise than the way the scriptural God himself ordered them: "woman is not independent of man, nor man of woman" (v.11) while both are dependent on him (v.12b). And this same God, in all his Messianic communities (v.16), rules through the prophetic "word of the Lord."

Disrespect toward the Lord at His Table (11:17-34)

Even more serious is the misconduct during the Lord's supper, an occasion for which the Corinthians gather to become one Messianic community in practice as well as in belief. Notice Paul's use of the expressions "come together as a church" (*synerkhomai en ekklesia*; v.18) and "come together in one place" (or "for the same purpose"; *synerkhomai epi to avto*; v.20) as well as the repeated occurrence of "come together" (*synerkhomai*; vv.17, 33, 34). The believers are not themselves ipso facto "the church" but are called to gather as one. And it is always the Lord who defines that gathering: the calling (*kerysso*) is through *his* word and the matter at hand is *his* supper (vv.20), which is not a potluck dinner (vv.21-22)! Sharing in the Lord's dinner has to be understood against the background of the ancient Near Eastern tradition that a guest must eat what the host offers; bringing something along to help out is no less than an insult to the host. In the case of the Lord's supper the insult would be especially sharp because the *entire* meal consists of *his* own "body and blood" (vv.23-25), i.e., Christ

---

44 See Gen 2:22.
45 See Gen 3:20.
46 See *Gal* 158 on my understanding *ta panta* (all) as meaning "both" in v.12.
47 It is he who both formed (*yasar*) the man (Gen 2:7) and built (*banah*) the woman (v.22).
48 Notice the conjunction *gar* (for) linking v.12 to v.11.

himself sacrificed for us. "Chipping in a dessert" or any other food would make of the gathering and the meal something fundamentally different from one focused solely on the Lord's sacrifice. And *until he comes,* the gathering cannot even be refocused upon his resurrection rather than his death without similarly disastrous consequences (v.26). But when he does come, we shall be gathered around him resurrected, as Paul will explain in ch.15.[49]

Therefore (v.27), let us watch our conduct at the Lord's suppers. These gatherings are a test (vv.28-29) as to whether we realize that the Lord seated at the head of the table is none other than the one *coming to judge* us. They are opportunities for us (v.31) to be judged by him and chastened (v.30) for the purpose of instruction (*paidevometha,* v.32a), lest at his coming we be judged worthy of condemnation (v.32b). *Therefore,* let us behave at these suppers in accordance with the host's will, that we love our neighbor (v.33); if we fail to do that we shall indeed be condemned (v.34)!

Paul thus envisions the Lord's supper rather differently from the understanding of it one frequently hears today, i.e., that it is basically a gathering of God's people to enjoy his life-giving gift. Instead, we find it described in 1 Corinthians as a gathering of God's people around him as Lord, i.e., *seated on his glorious throne*

---

49 The Liturgies of St John Chrysostom and St Basil the Great mention "the second and glorious coming (of Christ)" but do not dwell on it. It is *remembered as having come to pass* in one breath together with the events of his Passion, *before* the call to God the Father to send down his Holy Spirit and the consecration of the elements: "Having in remembrance, therefore, this saving commandment and all those things which have come to pass for us: the Cross, the Grave, the Resurrection on the third day, the Ascension into heaven, the Session at the right hand, and the second and glorious coming..." (Chrysostom); "Wherefore, O Master, we also, having in remembrance his saving Passion and life-giving Cross, his three-day burial, and Resurrection from the dead, his Ascension into heaven and Session at the right hand, his God and Father, and his glorious and terrible second coming ..." (Basil). Also, in the prayer of thanksgiving *after* communion the priest says: "Do thou, the same Lord of all, grant that the communion of the holy Body and Blood of thy Christ may be for us unto... the fulfillment of thy commandments, unto *an acceptable defense at the dread Judgment Seat of thy Christ.*" (Basil)

to judge and condemn the wicked, *within* his Messianic community as well as without it.[50] His stern face is actually turned more toward those within rather than those without[51] precisely because his lordship is hidden in his cross and thus cannot be "seen" except by the believers. Only at his coming, and not before, will his stern face be directed toward *all*. At that time those who will have learned to practice judging themselves in the light of his command to love their needy neighbor,[52] will avoid his condemnation and enjoy the life he promised through the death he died *for all*.

The Lack of Order during the Gatherings Due to the "Spiritual Ones" (ch.12-14)

Another major problem plaguing the Corinthian community was a feud between bearers of one of two spiritual gifts that were expressed publicly during the church gatherings: speaking in tongues and prophecy. Both sides, but especially the speakers in tongues, acted as though the Spirit who imparts all gifts was "free to do as he pleases," leaving them with no restraints. Paul reminds them that the Spirit is God's and as such is bound to God's will that everything should work toward the common good (*pros to sympheron*; 12:8), and the common good is that of the church, particularly its gathering together, which Paul likens pointedly to a body (vv.12-13). The body consists of a totality of members working together for the good of the whole, not each for itself; but on the other hand it is the good of the body which in turn proves to be the good of each member (vv.14-26). However, just as in the body some members (e.g. the brain, the heart, the liver) are essential whereas others are helpful (the hands and arms, the feet and legs, the eyes), so also it is in Christ's body. Priority is given to the bearers of gifts related to the "word" that both pro-

---

50 See *OT13* 39-41.
51 See 5:12-13.
52 Whether knowingly or unknowingly (Rom 2:12-16; see also Mt 25:31-46).

duces and sustains the church: apostles, prophets, and teachers (vv.27-31). Without these there is no church. On the other hand, the church can live without miracles, healings, tongues, and interpretation of tongues. Yet, before embarking on his advice for a practical solution in ch.14, Paul digresses to remind *all* that, just as the human body is maintained by the concord among its members, so is the church sustained by love of its members for one another (ch.13).

After his digression, Paul starts by asserting that prophecy is in general more valuable than speaking in tongues (14:1) for the simple reason that it builds up and sustains the church (vv.3, 4b) whereas tongues build up only the speaker (vv.2, 4a). The gift of tongues becomes useful in the church only by means of another spiritual gift, that of interpretation. It is the interpreter whose intelligible words edify the church (vv.5-12) and without whose presence the speaker in tongues should not even be allowed to function in the gathering (vv.13-19). There is, however, one positive function of tongues not dependent on interpretation, and that is to impress outsiders who would be drawn to listen to the intelligible "word" that is also preached at the same gathering (vv.20-25).

In this feud Paul is not taking sides. His main interest is the upbuilding of Christ's church through the intelligible word. So the speaker in tongues may speak as long as there is an interpreter, and the prophet may speak also. Yet, in neither case is anyone allowed to "show off" his gift at the expense of edification: both speakers in tongues and prophets are to be limited to two or three and one at a time (vv.26-31). And prophecy is not itself per se edifying just because it is intelligible: the content of the prophetic words uttered must be subject to the judgment of the other prophets (v.32). A sense of order and decorum is required in the gatherings because they are intended to be a reflection of the eschatological peace of God that will come when everything and everyone is subject to his rule (vv.33a and 37-40).

The Resurrection

The discussion in 1 Corinthians ends with the subject of the resurrection, whose complete misunderstanding by the Corinthians was at the root of all their other "mistakes." By imagining that Christ's resurrection was a tangible event lying "behind" them in time, they relegated it to something whose value lay solely in their everyday life. They viewed their "spiritual" situation as the product, if not the ultimate aim, of that resurrection; they found its fulfillment and meaning in their "experience" of the Spirit. At best, they were unintentionally making of Jesus Christ their own *doulos* (slave/servant) whereas in reality he was their *kyrios* (lord/master) and they his slaves/servants. At worst, they were consciously doing so.

The Gospel of the Resurrection of Christ (15:1-11)

No, said Paul, the Corinthians were not masters of the situation at all. They had *never* "experienced" Christ's resurrection, let alone its outcome. They had not *"seen"* the Lord. Seeing the resurrected Jesus as Lord was a sign of apostleship.[53] Had they indeed seen him, they would have been apostles; had they been apostles, they would not have needed Paul to bring them the gospel. In fact, they were just "sinners"—*unholy*—Gentiles, devoid of God's *Holy* Spirit when Paul arrived at Corinth. It was Paul who brought them the word of the gospel which they accepted and were then granted the Spirit. This same Spirit remains the Spirit of Paul's scriptural God, and Paul keeps telling them what that Spirit is all about because they continue to misunderstand. They can *never* become more knowledgeable about that Spirit than he is for a very simple reason: the Spirit came to them embedded in Paul's apostolic word as he preached it to them. Their "line" to that Spirit will *always* be Paul's word as *he* conveyed it to them. And the faith that resulted from that word will always remain de-

---

53 See 9:1.

pendent on the content of that word. Therefore the apostle Paul judges the Corinthians' faith in the light of his gospel, not they his gospel in the light of their understanding of it: "Now I would remind you, brethren, in what terms I preached to you the gospel, which you received, in which you stand, by which you are saved, *if you hold it fast—unless you believed in vain.*" (vv.1-2) Furthermore, this gospel delivered by Paul to the Corinthians was not only from Paul but was through and through apostolic: "Whether then it was I or they, so we preach and so you believed." (v.11)

As to the content of the gospel, it is defined by four main clauses of a single sentence: "(1) that Christ died for our sins in accordance with the scriptures, (2) that he was buried, (3) that he was raised on the third day in accordance with the scriptures, and (4) that he appeared to Cephas." (vv.3-5a) It is imperative here to notice that the appearance to Cephas (and the other apostles) is part and parcel of the gospel message regarding the resurrection of Christ, not separate or optional. In other words, there was *not* a resurrection *followed by* an appearance to the apostles as though one can sneak in behind the apostle's back and independently contemplate Christ's resurrection. Such imagination is, by the way, strictly ruled out, and thus forbidden, by the "resurrection" accounts extant in the four canonical books we call gospels: at no point do we have a "report" as to how Christ's resurrection took place; rather, what we always have is either the "appearance" of the resurrected Christ to his apostles or the confirmation of earlier appearances to others through later appearances to the apostles. Put otherwise, one cannot speak of Christ's resurrection except in the way it was taught by the apostles in their apostolic word(s).

Christians' Resurrection from the Dead Versus Christ's (vv.12-28)

That is why, at the start of his discussion of the Corinthian problem, Paul does not say "Now if Christ is raised from the dead, how can some of you say that there is no resurrection of the dead?" but "Now if Christ is *preached as* (*keryssetai hoti*) raised from the dead, how can some of you say that there is no resurrection of the dead?" (v.12) The point is that those who preach that Christ was raised from the dead, on whose witness our belief in that resurrection depends, do say that there is a resurrection from the dead. Even more: they actually present their understanding of Christ's resurrection *on the basis of* their understanding of *our* resurrection from the dead. That this is the direction of their reasoning is evident no less than three times in 7 verses (vv.12-19): "But if there is no resurrection of the dead, then Christ has not been raised" (v.13); "We are even found to be misrepresenting God, because we testified of God that he raised Christ, whom he did not raise if it is true that the dead are not raised" (v.15); and "For if the dead are not raised, then Christ has not been raised." (v.16) In other words, whereas in the Corinthians' thinking the talk about the resurrection from the dead *follows* that about the resurrection of Christ, in the apostles' mindset our resurrection comes first. Since there is a resurrection from the dead as scripture teaches us,[54] then "how can some of you say that there is no resurrection of the dead?" And since there is a resurrection from the dead, then Christ *may* well have been raised, and the apostles are *preaching* that indeed he was raised (vv.12, 14). But if belief in either resurrection is baseless, then that preaching is in vain and, consequently, the Corinthians' faith is futile (vv.14, 17) and, much more importantly, they are still in their sins, i.e., unholy sinners (v.17). Why? Because it is the gospel that brought them the Holy Spirit who transformed them from "sinners" into God's holy ones.[55]

So the Corinthians had better wake up and realize that their resurrection from the dead is *ahead* of, and not behind, them. And so is the resurrected Jesus Christ *ahead* of them, coming again in the

54 Dan 12:2.
55 1:2; 3:16; 5:19; 7:14.

future so that they may be raised also. As I explained when discussing 1 Thess 4:13-18,[56] the resurrected Jesus appeared to the apostles requesting them to proclaim his victory so that the celebration at his coming would be joined by all who have accepted the good news of his victory. His resurrection is thus to be viewed as a sure sign that his followers will partake of the same victory in the same way that the first fruits are a sure sign that the ripening of all fruits is at the doorstep (v.20). The Corinthians cannot have experienced Jesus' resurrection as theirs since they are still destined to die, whereas "Christ being raised from the dead will never die again; death has no longer dominion over him."[57] Death is the last enemy he will destroy (v.26), and when he does so he will complete the resurrection of all from the dead, which is the final sign of the coming of God's kingdom (vv.27-28). Until then the Corinthians are as mortal as their Gentile neighbors out of whose ranks they came;[58] that is, they are as mortal as they used to be before accepting the gospel. The only resurrected one is the Christ of the gospel, and the only valid image of him for them—until he comes again—is the image of him *dead* on the cross.[59]

The Baptism on Behalf of the Dead (vv.29-34)

Next Paul buttresses his argument by showing the Corinthians how inconsistent one of their own practices is with their view of the resurrection: some of them were practicing vicarious baptism for the sake of the deceased (v.29a). Why would they do such a thing, asks Paul, if the believers are already "spiritually" raised and there is no upcoming resurrection of the dead (v.29b)? This practice itself stems from their original correct comprehension of Paul's message: the Lord is *coming* and there *will be* resurrection

---

56 See chapter 2 and *I Thess* 145-153.
57 Rom 6:9.
58 1 Cor 6:11a.
59 1 Cor 1:23; 2:2; 11:26. See also Gal 3:1.

from the dead to be followed by judgment (vv.32b-34). Given this premise, some Corinthians were afraid that their unbaptized deceased friends and relatives would not be part of the Lord's welcoming procession.[60]

Scriptural Terminology

Having established again in his readers' mind the assuredness of the resurrection from the dead Paul moves to explicate it. In order for us today to follow his exposition we must escape from the Platonic prison in which our religious thinking has been trapped for centuries, namely the idea that the human being is *composed* of *a* soul and *a* body, the former being "divine" and thus immortal while the latter is bound to corruption and thus incapable of life after death. This is precisely how the Corinthians viewed matters and explains why they so quickly distorted Paul's original teaching to them. "Soul" and "body" are two linguistic expressions of one and the same reality, the human being. Take the English "soul" one of whose meanings is "human being" in phrases like "not a soul in sight"; the same applies to the English "body" in phrases like "what is the body count?" In scripture a soul, exactly like a body, can be cut off from the people[61] and die.[62] The Hebrew word for soul is *nephes̆*, meaning "breath"; it attests to the fact that the most immediate sign of life in a human being is breathing.

Scripturally speaking, compared to the human being, whether one uses the word "soul" or "body," God is altogether different: He is *ruah* (wind or spirit) whereas the human being is *basar* (flesh).[63] Since *ruah* refers to the wind, moving air, it was very early used in religious thought to refer to a deity who could produce an effect,

---

60 Compare with 1 Thess 4:13-18.
61 Ex 31:14.
62 Ezek 18:4, 20.
63 In scripture the expressions *kol nephes̆* (every soul) and *kol basar* (all flesh) are fully equivalent.

like destroying a hut, uprooting a tree, or even raising waves, without being seen. What is interesting about the scriptural *ruah* used to speak of God is that, although it could annihilate any and all *basar*, being air it is also "breath" and thus could also give "breath" to, "breathe life" into, the same *basar*.[64] It is only when that happens, when through the gift of the Spirit (*ruah-pneuma*) or in conjunction with the Spirit's work a human being is granted life, that in Paul's view a human being can also be called "spirit" (*pneuma*)[65] or a "spiritual" being. However, even as such, the human being never becomes a life-giving spirit as the risen Lord is (v.45b); he always remains a life-receiving spirit, the only exception being the apostle who is, *not in his person* but in his apostolic "word," the risen Christ's face toward the believers and thus brings the Spirit to them.

The "Mode" of the Resurrection from the Dead (vv.35-58)

To explicate the resurrection to the Corinthians Paul draws parallels from an area familiar to everyone at that time, agriculture. The natural phenomena of plants dying and growing in the ground provided him with readily applicable images since the human body at death is laid and "perishes" (v.42) in the ground. As he explains, even a plant's seed "does not come to life unless it dies" (v.36), which is precisely Paul's point: the resurrection from the dead takes place after, not before, our death. His image of a seed dying and sprouting also illustrates his point of "sameness despite the difference in form": a given seed produces its corresponding fruit; yet the fruit does not look like the seed (vv.36-38), it has a more "glorious" appearance (vv.39-41). Such is the difference between our body now and its resurrected form

---

64 See Ezek 37:1-14.
65 Rom 1:9; 2:29; 7:6; 8:16; 1 Cor 2:11; 5:3-4, 5; 6:17; 7:34; 14:14; 16:18; 2 Cor 2:13; 7:13; Gal 6:18; Phil 4:23; 1 Thess 5:23; Philem 25.

(vv.42-43): in either case it is a *soma* (body), but it is now *psykhikon*, that is, characteristic of and controlled by a *psykhe*, a human soul. What it will become is *pnevmatikon*, characteristic of and led by God's *pnevma*, his Spirit, just as the risen Lord is (v.44). Moreover, this order cannot be reversed: just as only a seed that has died can produce fruit, so the death of the *psykhikon* body must precede the transformation into the "spiritual" one (vv.45-49). The Corinthians' understanding has reversed that order, for they consider themselves to be "spiritual" already, without having experienced death and resurrection—and yet they are on their way to dying at some later point. Paul adds a chilling conclusion with special emphasis:[66] if they end up remaining "flesh and blood" (their bodies still *psychikon*) even by the day of the Lord's coming, they will not join him, for "flesh and blood cannot inherit the kingdom of God" (v.50).

He continues on the same subject by saying that it is the sequence of perishable followed by imperishable (vv.52-53), and not so much death itself, which is of essence in the matter of the resurrection from the dead, since "we shall not all sleep, but we shall all be changed" (v.51). Only then will there be resurrection from the dead, a final annihilation of death itself (vv.54-57), and a final judgment of everyone, including the Corinthians, by God. The Corinthians need to be prepared for that, and they can rest assured that whatever efforts they do expend will be remembered by the Lord (v.58).

Chapter 16

The letter ends with a request for the monetary collection for the "saints" in Jerusalem (vv.1-4), some information about travel plans of Paul and his companions (vv.5-12), some greetings (vv.13-24), and finally yet another exhortation to give thought to the Lord's coming (v.22).

---

66 Notice the apostolic authority in "I tell you this, brethren." (v.50a)

6

The Second Letter to the Corinthians

In this letter an editor has brought together several of Paul's messages to the Corinthians that deal with his apostleship. They show him on the defensive and confirm that here too, as in Thessalonica and Galatia, his opponents' main tactic was to question his authority.

Blessing Instead of Thanksgiving (1:3-11)

Since for Paul the incontrovertible sign of true apostleship is the suffering an apostle endures for the gospel's sake,[1] and given that this letter deals essentially with his apostolic authority, he jumps right into that subject at the very start of the letter. Instead of opening with the usual thanksgiving he inserts a liturgical blessing formula ("Blessed be the God and Father of our Lord Jesus Christ," v.3a), using it to introduce, not the usual reference to God's great and glorious salvific deeds, but rather God's deeds as mediated through the apostle's afflictions and sufferings *in which* God's abundant consolation is revealed.[2] The theme of comfort is nothing new; it can be traced back to the "gospel" of Second Isaiah, which opens with the words:[3]

> Comfort, comfort my people, says your God. Speak tenderly to Jerusalem, and cry to her that her warfare is ended...Behold, the Lord God comes with might, and his arm rules for him; behold,

---

1 1 Thess 1:6.
2 Notice the frequent use of *parakalo* (to comfort, console; 4 times in vv.4 and 6) and *paraklesis* (comfort, consolation; 6 times in vv.3-7) in this passage.
3 See the chapter "Paul and His Letters" regarding the centrality of the book of Isaiah for Paul's understanding and formulation of the gospel.

his reward is with him, and his recompense before him. He will feed his flock like a shepherd, he will gather the lambs in his arms, he will carry them in his bosom, and gently lead those that are with young. (Is 40:1-2, 10-11)

After this introduction Paul follows a pattern he set in 1 Thessalonians,[4] inviting the Corinthians to share in the sufferings without which there is no consolation from the true God (v.7), the God who raises from the dead (v.9b). At this point he tells them of a mortal affliction he suffered in Asia (vv.8-9), emphasizing that such an experience of being rescued from sure death taught him to give thanks to God and be reliant upon him (v.10-11). Paul, though having been under judgment of a death sentence, and expecting to experience it again in the future, is nevertheless speaking with authority, drawing his authority from the only source of authority for believers, that of the crucified Lord.

The Reason behind Paul's Change of Plans (1:12-2:13)

Paul then explains that if he postponed his visit to Corinth (1:15-17), it was not due to a change of mind regarding the gospel, i.e., a fear that he might be proven wrong in the presence of his church at Corinth. His gospel to them has always been what it is now (vv.18-20), and so is his understanding of his apostleship and the authority it gives him over them (vv.21-22). Actually the visit's postponement was meant to spare them (vv.22-23) since, if he came and found them failing, he would have to "use the rod"[5] and cause them pain (vv.2:1-4).

And how does he advise them to resolve their difficult situation? One would expect Paul, who is defending his gospel and apostleship, to ask the Corinthians to take a position with him against the perpetrator of the pain caused to Paul (most probably

4   1 Thess 1:6.
5   1 Cor 4:21

an insult; v.5). However, he unexpectedly teaches them that the best solution is to forgive and comfort the guilty one (v.7)! In such a way the Corinthians would be confirming that they are Paul's children in the gospel of God's consolation and, by the same token, defeating the real enemy, Satan (vv.8-11).

The Ministry of the New Covenant (2:14-5:15)

The apostle, through his preaching the gospel of the risen Lord, functions as though he were already part of the Lord's victorious procession (2:14). And since the victorious Lord is coming to judge, then one and the same event will be welcomed as the gift of life by those being saved and feared as the coming of death by those who are perishing (vv.14-16).[6]

Paul is a true apostle (v.17). Why should he even bother commending himself to the Corinthians who, by the mere fact of their being believers, are themselves his letter of recommendation (3:1-3)? And as a true apostle he is a minister of the new covenant spoken of in Jeremiah,[7] the same one that brings the gift of God's spirit as described in Ezekiel[8] (vv.4-6). While in the land of Canaan the biblical Israel had the Mosaic Law and ended up breaking it and being chastised through exile, even unto death. It is in the land of exile, among the Gentiles, that the same biblical Israel was offered the new covenant through the Spirit, and this Spirit's Law is written on the heart and thus unbreakable. That is what is being offered to Paul's Jewish contemporaries in his gospel. Their rejection of it is portrayed as a veil over their minds, a veil that could only be lifted by the Spirit as revealed in Paul's gospel (vv.7-18).

The real glory of God is reflected in the face of the crucified Christ, who is the content of this gospel (4:1-6). Consequently, the true apostle reflects this same Christ, and Paul has been doing

---

6   Compare with 1 Cor 1:22-24. See also 2 Thess 2:9-15.
7   31:31-34.
8   11:19-20; 36:26-27.

just that in his daily ministry:[9] he is himself "delivered unto death" every day so that his hearers may have fullness of life (vv.7-12) at the Lord's coming (vv.13-15) which will eventually bring about the yet unseen glory of God (vv.16-18). Until then the believers are to wait (5:1-4), concerning themselves only with their responsibility to always try to please the Lord who will judge them (vv.6-10). And the apostle is bound to this responsibility even more than anyone else since it is his duty to proclaim the gospel to others (vv.11-15).

The Apostle's Entreaty (5:16-7:16)

Having reestablished in the Corinthians' mind the validity of his apostleship and thus his authority over them, Paul entreats them to abide by the tenets of the gospel he has taught them. First and foremost, they are to view Christ from the perspective of the Spirit, not the flesh: the members of the Messianic community are a "new creation" (vv.16-17) not bound by the "fleshly" differentiation between circumcision and uncircumcision.[10] Christ himself is bound only by the scriptural God who raised him from the dead as first fruits of the resurrection from the dead and through him God will establish his *universal* kingdom—over Gentiles as well as Jews. In the same way, the Corinthians are bound by the same God and not by the "pillars," the "fleshly" kinsmen of Jesus who now lead the Jerusalem church. Christ reconciled the entire world, *all* human beings, Jews and Gentiles, to God (vv.18-20); the only classification of people who remain in need of reconciliation is that of *sinners*. In fact, the Christ preached in the gospel as "the word of reconciliation" (v.19) was crucified and as such he himself appears to be a guilty one, a sinner (v.21a), though he had committed no sin since he was God's Christ, the "holy one" of God. And since whenever a sinner is pe-

9   See 1:8-11.
10 See Gal 5:6 and 6:15.

nalized God's righteousness is revealed through the implementation of the "righteous" penalty, those who have endorsed the "word" relaying this reality are themselves witnesses to, and thus signs of, this righteousness (v.21b). They are to be as much portents of this reconciliation as is the apostle who brought it to them (6:1-10). His real consolation and comfort is their continued determination to follow that path of reconciliation by forgiving the one who insulted Paul (7:2-13a), and the matter is so important that he is sending Titus to make sure that they follow this apostolic directive (vv.13b-16).

The True Way of Apostleship and Its Test (10:1-12:10)

In chapters 8 and 9 Paul asks the Corinthians to share in the collection he is about to take up to Jerusalem as a last call to the leaders there to fully endorse his gospel and partake in God's kingdom. There follows a lengthy apologia, or rather explication, of what true apostleship in general is all about. First Paul reminds the Corinthians (10:1-11), and through them his opponents (v.12), that he differentiates between a personal insult, like the one he dealt with in chs.1-7, and an insult against him *as apostle*. In the latter case, it is the gospel itself that is at stake and he *must* defend the honor of the Lord who commissioned him:

> For though we live in the world we are not carrying on a worldly war, for the weapons of our warfare are not worldly but have divine power to destroy strongholds. We destroy arguments and every proud obstacle to the knowledge of God, and take every thought captive to obey Christ, being ready to punish every disobedience, when your obedience is complete. (10:3-6)

And, if he is about to boast, let it be known that he does so "in the Lord," i.e., within the limits assigned to him by the Lord himself, namely within the churches he himself founded through the gospel. He does not intrude in anyone else's turf, which would disturb the peace of an established community (vv.13-18). Rather, he defends the peace of his own communities, and hopes to see them grow both themselves and through his own continued efforts: "our hope is that as your faith increases, our field among you may be greatly enlarged, so that we may preach the gospel in lands beyond you." (vv.15b-16a) This too is a reminder to the Corinthians to stick with Paul and his gospel and reject the intruders.

With this in mind and before he starts "boasting," Paul puts the Corinthians to shame by exposing their "harlotry": they let themselves be deceived by a phony newcomer (vv.1-6). They misunderstood Paul's meekness and gentleness as being an expression of his lesser value, when in reality those qualities stemmed from his love for them (vv.7-11). And in order to drive his point home once and for all, he openly levels the serious charge that his opponents are in fact "servants of Satan," the archenemy of the gospel of Christ[11] (vv.12-15).

Then comes the "boasting." He claims he is not only a true apostle, but a better one than his kinsmen, and as proof he lists his hardships rather than his accomplishments for the gospel's sake (vv.16-33). For Paul this approach is not simply a literary device to soften up the Corinthians, but a logical conclusion of his gospel. Until he comes, Jesus Christ is the crucified Lord; this is the last recordable glimpse that anyone has had of him. Although he appeared to his apostles as risen from the dead in order to embolden them in their mission, the actual content of the gospel they, as his faithful servants, can offer *until he comes* is the proclamation of Christ crucified. Whoever would believe in him must accept that image of him. Consequently, the more this shameful weakness is mirrored in the life of a follower of Christ, the more faithful a servant he is, or at least appears to be. If he is an apostle, then he is that much better or greater an apostle. The difference between genuine being and mere appearance is irrelevant here since Paul's argument is *ad hominem* with the intention of exposing the "foolishness" of his opponents' attacks against him (vv.16-21).

11 See 1 Cor 7:5; 2 Cor 2:11; 1Thess 2:18.

What really matters is what happens *before the Lord himself.* So, after the digression into "foolish boasting," Paul refers to what goes on between him as slave/servant and Christ as his lord/master. The Corinthians being susceptible to flashy experiences,[12] the opponents must have tried to impress them by boasting about their own "visions and revelations." So, as he did regarding the speaking in tongues,[13] Paul informs them that he too had such experiences (12:1-6). But he immediately adds: "To keep me from being too elated by the abundance of revelations, a thorn was given me in the flesh, a messenger of Satan, to harass me, to keep me from being too elated." (v.7) His Lord decided to keep him under control so whatever power might flow through Paul would be recognized as the power of the Lord himself; and the simplest way to ensure this was to have Paul remain weak and look weak at all times (8-10).

A Final Stern Warning before Paul's Upcoming Visit (12:11-13:14)

In order to prepare the Corinthians for his coming "with the rod," Paul again reminds them of the real meaning of his gentle behavior toward them (12:11-18). Then he points out that, in Corinth, he cannot possibly be dishonored by any human being since he is *the* apostle of that church and an apostle is due all honor and respect. His only dishonor comes from his own master if he is found unfaithful, and he will be found unfaithful as an apostle if ultimately he winds up with only a "sinful" church in Corinth. Thus, he ironically tells them that, should they want to continue humbling him, the only way to do so is to persevere in their wicked behavior (vv.19-24)! But humbling *him* in this way will cost *them* God's kingdom.

12 See 1 Cor 12 and 14.
13 1 Cor 14:18.

Continuing on the same path, he threatens them with his own weakness! In it, after all, lies all power. Indeed, just as God's power was revealed in Christ's weakness on the cross, so will the Lord's power and authority be enacted in Corinth through Paul's weakness (13:1-5). Here again is another telling proof that the only reality of God's power in Christ lies exclusively in the apostle's *word*, which conveys the weakness of the crucified Christ.

No, Paul has not failed, precisely because he is weak. His visit is going to be a test for them, not him. And they better take this test seriously (vv.5-9), since "I write this while I am away from you, in order that when I come I may not have to be severe in my use of the authority which the Lord has given me for building up and not for tearing down." (v.10) Paul does not want to tear down unless he has to, for the sake of their salvation.[14] Until they meet he prays that they again find life in God's love and peace (v.11).

---

14 Compare with 1 Cor 5:1-5.

7

The Letter to the Romans

After having consolidated the collections from all his churches Paul is about to go up to Jerusalem with the proceeds as "the Gentiles' offerings" to the Savior, the Lord of Zion. His only problem is the "pillars" who may decide to decline Paul's offer, thus expressing their disagreement with him regarding God's gospel and, in his estimation, actually undermining it by perverting it.[1] Since they did decline once already, Paul had every right to expect they might do so again. But why should such a refusal concern him? He knew he was right and that if they refused it would be their loss. He would continue his work among the Gentiles and soon their numbers would overwhelm the few Judean Jewish believers. Although this reasoning seems valid, it proceeds from a false presupposition about how these numbers would actually have added up in Paul's time. We are accustomed to visualizing him as a religious Alexander the Great, a crusader conquering the world for the cause of Christ. But the "foolishness" of his gospel did not immediately attract great hordes, and the actual number of his converts within his lifetime was actually modest, practically negligible.[2] Thus Gentile Christianity's ultimate "overwhelming" of Jewish Christianity would hardly appear inevitable to Paul.

Since Paul was the only apostle to the Gentiles with a stature similar to the "pillars," he was afraid that at his death his insignificant churches would have no sufficiently influential support to continue in the line of his gospel and would soon be overwhelmed by his opponents' teachings, or might simply vanish. He already began preparations for his eventual death by building his churches around a

---

1 See Gal 1:7.
2 See 1 Cor 9:22 and Rom 11:14.

double set of (scriptural) readings: scripture itself, i.e., the Torah, Prophets, and Writings, *and* his own letters as the official interpretation of scripture.[3] So he thought of killing two birds with one stone: trying to convince the "pillars" of the correctness of his gospel on the basis of God's word in scripture *and,* at the same time, leaving this magisterial interpretation of scripture as a "reading" for his churches. Even if his interpretive work failed to convince the "pillars," it would nevertheless itself guide his churches on the right path. This explains, by the way, the treatise-like form of his letter to the Romans.

But why write to the community in Rome? It was not his church, nor did he ever visit it. Moreover, by addressing it authoritatively he would be breaking his own rule of not treading on someone else's turf when it came to preaching the gospel. Actually, it is precisely *because* it was not his church that Paul decided to write to the Roman community. It was comprised of Jews and Gentiles. Although not without inner tensions, still it was managing this double constituency *without* Paul's direct input. Thus, it functioned as a living proof that his gospel was viable of itself and could serve as an example disproving Jerusalem's criticism and the opponent's attacks. Furthermore, it was located at the heart of the Roman empire and could serve as a flagship showing the viability of his gospel, if not the most reliable guide to the gospel's content. Last but not least, if the Roman church fully endorsed his gospel, he could use Rome as his headquarters for the Western part of the empire, just as Ephesus was functioning in the East; indeed, after having "fully preached the gospel" in the Eastern part of the empire (Rom 15:19) he had plans to go westward (v.28).

Paul and Scripture

Before embarking on my overview of Romans, let me once again reiterate what is often overlooked by biblical scholarship and many

---

3   See pp. 27-28, 35-36, 52-53.

of the faithful, Orthodox as well as others. For Paul the one God is none other than the one "canonized" in scripture, i.e., embedded in (or, described by) its words, and is for us no different from the way he appears in it. For Paul, there is no "experience" of God that is independent of scripture; that is to say, one may have an experience of the biblical God, but such an experience must be verified by checking and judging it against the scripture which is that God's "revelation" as *he* chose to reveal himself. Hence, whether discussing the truthfulness of his gospel in Galatians, or building the Corinthians up to live according to God's will, or explicating God's dispensation (*oikonomia*) to the Romans and, through them, to Jerusalem, Paul always refers to scripture as the foundation of all his assertions. Witness the very high incidence of biblical quotations and references especially in Galatians and Romans. So whenever we speak of Paul's thought regarding a certain matter, we are actually dealing with his exegesis of scripture and his explication of what *it* says regarding that matter. This is to be borne in mind throughout Romans which is, in Paul's own words, the exposition of

> the gospel of God which he promised beforehand *through his prophets in the holy scriptures,* the gospel concerning his Son...Jesus Christ our Lord, through whom we have received grace and apostleship to bring about the obedience of faith for the sake of his name among all the nations. (1:1-5)

Salutation (1:8-15)

Since the Romans did not receive the gospel from him, Paul does not consider himself as their apostle. Thus, although he openly declares that he is an apostle, he nevertheless introduces himself delicately, saying that he and they would benefit one another at their eventual meeting (v.12). However, since Rome lies at the heart of the Gentile world whose apostle he is, the Roman church is situated within the realm of his mission (vv.5-6),[4] and on that

---

4 The RSV has after "among all the nations," "including yourselves" which is the translation of the original Greek *en hois este kai hymeis* (among whom you also are).

basis he is entitled at least to "impart to you some spiritual gift to strengthen you" (v.11). In order to forestall any misunderstanding whereby they might consider him to be meddling in their affairs, he immediately explains his reason for writing:

> I want you to know, brethren, that I have often intended to come to you (but thus far have been prevented), in order that I may reap some harvest among you as well as among the rest of the Gentiles. *I am under obligation* both to Greeks and to barbarians, both to the wise and to the foolish: so I am eager to preach the gospel to you also who are in Rome. (vv.13-15)

Thesis of the Letter (vv.16-17)

> For I am not ashamed of the gospel: it is the power of God for salvation to every one who has faith, to the Jew first and also to the Greek. For in it the righteousness of God is revealed through faith for faith; as it is written, "He who through faith is righteous shall live."

This is one of the most remarkably concise, and yet multi-faceted, statements in the Bible. Power and salvation as well as gospel/good news are eminently part of Roman imperial terminology: the emperor is the divine power (*dynamis*) that ensures salvation (*soteria*) to his subjects; hence, his accession to the throne and even his birth[5] were viewed as good news (*euangelion*). Paul is asking the citizens of Rome itself, the emperor's city, to be ready to witness that *their* lord who grants *them* salvation through his power is that Judean who was crucified by the Roman authority. For this they are undoubtedly going to be shamed, which they will find hard to swallow especially since many of them are probably free or freed Roman citizens. So in order to prevent any reaction on their part, Paul—himself a Roman citizen—begins by saying: "I am not ashamed of the gospel." (1:16a)

There is no other way for the believers, who can secure for themselves God's life-granting righteousness only through such faith in the crucified Christ of the gospel (v.17). And let no one be misled by

---

5 Both events were looked upon as appearances, theophanies of the (divine) emperor.

Paul's well-known defense of his Gentile converts: the first in line for that righteousness is nevertheless the Jew in whose Torah God's righteousness is promised.[6] After that comes the Gentile (v.16b) since this righteousness is revealed in the "shameful" gospel (of the cross) and not "shameful" circumcision.[7] But the Jew's priority does not allow him to forego the shame of the cross in favor of the lesser shame of circumcision. And it was indeed a lesser shame: even with all its shortcomings in the eyes of the Roman Gentiles, Judaism was a licit religion in the empire and thus protected by the Roman emperor and Senate; one was not liable to persecution as a Jew. On the other hand, anyone whether Jew or Gentile found apostatizing from the Roman deities and emperor in the name of someone who was crucified according to their laws, would be viewed as joining in an insurrection against the Roman authorities, the penalty for which would be imprisonment, torture, or death. No! Paul emphatically says to the Jew who has accepted the gospel but wishes to play it safe and hide behind circumcision and the Mosaic Law, allowing by the same token the Gentile to be "ahead of" him in accepting the "greater shame" of the cross. The Jew is first and will remain so; he has no choice but to accept his status. The choice was already made for him by the biblical God who will not allow him to go back to Egypt once he took him out of there. Yes, says Paul, the Jew is always first even in Rome where a crime of *lese majesty* is more readily obvious and more immediately punishable than in any other corner of the empire; the Jew will be first even on death row. That has been all along the policy of the biblical God beginning with Amos:

> You only have I known of all the families of the earth; therefore I will visit/punish you for all your iniquities. (3:2)

> Woe to those who are at ease in Zion, and to those who feel secure on the mountain of Samaria, the notable men of the first of the

6 See 9:4.
7 See chapter 3.

nations, to whom the house of Israel come! ...Therefore they shall now be the first of those to go into exile, and the revelry of those who stretch themselves shall pass away. (6:1, 7)

This is Paul's thesis in Romans, and since its basis is scriptural he will explicate and defend it scripturally.

All Mankind, Gentile and Jew, Is Guilty before God (1:18-3:20)

Adopting a view common in the Judaism of this time, namely that the Gentiles are by definition or nature "sinners,"[8] Paul describes summarily their sinful status (1:18-32). He then reminds the Jew that being privy to the Law is of no avail if the Jew does not put its commandments into practice. The reason is that the Law is after all the rule according to which God is to judge Israel, as is crystal clear from Deuteronomy. The Law was to be the rule of life for Israel in Canaan: should Israel break the commandments, it would be exiled unto death. This notion of divine judgment is at the heart of the passage 2:1-3:8 where Paul addresses the Jew. Not only does the mention of God's judgment bracket this passage (2:2 and 3:3, 8), but also the notion of judgment pervades it entirely.[9] In fact, scripture testifies that there are none righteous in Israel (3:9-20). Consequently, Israel is like the nations since it acts like them.[10]

Righteousness through Faith (3:21-31)

However, the same scripture that tells us "there is no distinction [between Jew and Gentile][11] since all have sinned and fall short of the glory of God," *also* witnesses that righteousness is granted by God

8 See Gal 2:15 and *Gal* 81-84.
9 Notice, besides *krima* (judgment), the extremely high incidence of *krino* (to judge, 2:1 [thrice], 3, 12, 16; 3:4, 6, 7).
10 This is the basic thread of the biblical story as well as the prophetic writings.
11 See 10:12.

apart from the Law (3:21), through faith that God is capable to do so and that he has done so through his Messiah, Jesus (3:22-26). On this Paul and the "pillars" are at one.[12] But if so, then where does the problem between them lie? Obviously in the "how" of the matter: granted that God is capable of implementing righteousness through his grace, *how* does he go about doing it? Again, the sole criterion by which both parties can settle the matter is scripture, the sole valid source for them in matters pertaining to God.

The Promise to Abraham (ch.4)

The "pillars" maintained that the Gentiles had to become children of Abraham in order to qualify for God's grace in Jesus Christ. They also maintained that to become a child of Abraham one would have to undergo circumcision and abide by the precepts of the Law.[13] It is not so, counters Paul. Scripture tells us that it was through faith in God's promise that Abraham was granted God's righteousness, not because he was circumcised or did any works of the Law (4:1-10). Circumcision was merely the sign or seal of God's grace to him *while uncircumcised* (v.11a). Consequently, when it comes to God's grace it is faith that counts; and from the perspective of faith Abraham is the father of the uncircumcised and circumcised *faithful* alike (vv.11b-12). Indeed, scripture again, in the passage dealing with circumcision, declares that God promised Abraham to make him "father of a multitude of nations"[14] (vv.13-18). Moreover, the call of Abraham, God's promise to him that he would be father of many, Abraham's faith, and the sealing of that faith with circumcision, all took place while Abraham and Sarah were beyond the point of begetting, when it seemed impossible that the promise could be fulfilled (v.19). Yet, Abraham *believed*

12 See Gal 2:15-16.
13 See Galatians.
14 Gen 17:5. Notice that the Greek word for "nations" is *ethne*, which also translates as "Gentiles."

(v.20) and through his faith was "fully convinced that God was able to do what he had promised" (v.21). Consequently, his children are to follow his example and believe that God realized his promise to Abraham to make him father of a multitude of nations, by resurrecting Jesus from the dead, thereby granting his righteousness to all (vv.22-25).

The Road from Righteousness to Eternal Life (5:1-7:6)

Having all, Jews and Gentiles, been made righteous through Christ, the believers are living within the realm of God's rule of peace (5:1). However, they still live within and are subject to the earthly realm in which they live until God implements his rule over those who have not yet believed (v.2). Until then, the believers must accept the crucified Messiah as their example and patiently bear sufferings, boasting[15] in them rather than feeling ashamed (vv.3-5), since their savior himself underwent such shameful sufferings in order to bring them to the state they are in (vv.6-11). The real enemy of the believers is sin: Christ secured life for them by being raised from the dead, but, according to scripture, the cause of death is sin (v.12). Sin has existed since Adam, although it is the Mosaic Law that makes clear the connection between death and sin (vv.13-14).[16] Thus, God's grace through Jesus Christ is a summons to stop allowing the sin that leads to death rule our lives, replacing it with the righteousness grace has granted us and which leads to life eternal (vv.15-21). The believer who refuses to do that makes God appear false, for it appears as though God's will (for us not to sin) is in fact not ruling those whom he has saved and whom he declared righteous. In baptism, which is the symbol of our communion with Christ, we

---

15 The RSV's translation of *kavkhamai* (to boast) as "rejoice" (in vv.3, 4, and 11) is misleading because it obscures the link in Paul's mind to the notion of shame, the opposite of boasting, connected with Christ's crucifixion (see Gal 6:13-14). This link is further obscured by its translation of *kataiskhyno* (put to shame) as "disappoint" in v.5.

16 Deuteronomy clearly states that it is God who exiles unto death his people if and when they sin against him by not obeying him.

die to sin (6:2) in order to live a new life (v.4). We leave one master to become servants of another (vv.6, 12, 16, 18, 20, 22);[17] we
exchange one servitude for another. However, the outcome of the
one is death (vv.21, 23a), whereas the result of the other is life
eternal (vv.22, 23b). Yet the latter is not an immediate, magical
result; its condition[18] is the believers' sanctification (v.22).[19]
Thus, it is up to the believers to take God's word in Christ seriously; Paul tells them: "So you also *must consider yourselves* dead
to sin and alive to God in Christ Jesus." (v.11) That the baptized
are no longer bound by the Law is taught by the Law itself (7:1):
its precepts do not apply to someone who has died (vv.2-3). But,
what is the use of baptism since it boils down to merely switching
from one master to another, from being bound by the precepts of
the Law to following the Spirit (vv.3-6) that also has a law of its
own (8:1)?

The New Law and God's Kingdom (7:7-8:39)

Escape from the Law is essential because it is intrinsically bound
to the reality of sin (7:7)[20] and sin's consequence, death.[21]
Though the Law was granted to secure life, its followers dis-
obeyed and were punished with death (vv.8-12). Paul is here
merely rendering in a nutshell the content of scripture itself.[22] In
the first scripture, i.e., the Torah, just before entering into Canaan,
the people liberated from bondage and death were given the Law

---

17 The terminology is taken from the situation of slaves in the Roman empire: the believer is likened to a slave that has been bought by a new master from his previous
one (see 1 Cor 6:20a; 7:23a; also Rom 7:4).

18 Notice how in speaking of sin, Paul says that its end is death (v.21), whereas in
speaking of servitude to God, he writes: "the return (*karpon*, fruit) you get is sanctification and its end, eternal life" (v.22).

19 See also 1 Thess 4:7.

20 See also Gal 3:19 and *Gal* 146-153.

21 See 5:12.

22 Notice how Paul begins his argument: "Do you not know, brethren—*for I am speaking
to those who know the law*—that the law is binding on a person only during his life?"

as a seal of God's presence among them in order to make it possible for them to enjoy the new life he granted. Yet there was a pro-
viso: the people were to follow that Law; should they not do so,
they would be punished with exile and death.[23] And that is precisely what the second scripture, the scroll of the Prophets,[24] tells
us happened. In order to make this point more pertinent to his
addressees and make them "relive" this sad situation, Paul relates
the scriptural story in personal terms (vv.13-25).

The scriptural prophetic books, while relaying God's punishment, also speak of a future when he will establish his own kingdom where all fully abide by his will, when he will dispense his
Spirit that will secure for them eternal life.[25] This is precisely what
took place through Jesus, God's Christ (8:1-30). And if God, the
judge, and his Christ, the prosecutor, are on the side of the baptized, then indeed no power of any kind, including death, can prevail against God's love for them in Christ (vv.13-39).

The Case of Paul's Jewish Kin (9-11)

Given this universal plan of God to invite and have all in his kingdom
of love and peace, Paul tries to find, always on the basis of scripture,
an explanation and, if possible, a meaning to the fact, painful for
him, that the majority of those who are the first to be invited[26] are
refusing to accept the gospel's message even as those who come after
them, the Gentiles, receive it gladly (9:1-5). The matter is of the
utmost seriousness. Indeed, the corollary of the Jews' refusal
could be that God's word of promise has failed (v.6a) and, if so,
then the Gentiles themselves could start questioning the veracity

23 See the book of Deuteronomy.
24 This second scripture comprises the Former Prophets (the Deuteronomistic History—Joshua, Judges, Samuel, and Kings) and the Latter Prophets (Isaiah, Jeremiah, Ezekiel, and the Twelve Minor Prophets).
25 Is 42:1; 44:3; 48:16; 61:1-4; Ezek 11:19-21; 18:30-32; 36:26-27; 37:14; 39:29; Joel
   2:28-29.
26 1:16; 2:9, 10.

of the gospel of salvation offered them. An emphatic "No!" is Paul's reply to the thought that God's word has failed. God's word has not failed because the Jews who reject the scriptural gospel are in fact *not* the scriptural Israel; when scripture speaks of "Israel" it does not mean the totality of the Jews of Paul's time. On the contrary, in scripture "Israel" is the totality of those among God's people who have been taken into his mercy.[27] Indeed, from the very beginning Israel was never a biologically defined and governed entity but rather the outcome of God's word of promise that is free from any bounds other than his own will (vv.6-17). This word of promise that began with Abraham has always included *all* his children from *all* nations.[28] It is this utter freedom of God that has always been a "stumbling stone" for Israel (9:19-10:4): the scriptural word is always God's word, even when entrusted to Israel.[29] The latter is bound by it and judged by it if it does not heed it.[30] The same applies to God's word of promise: when realized, it has to be accepted (10:5-17). Yet the Gentiles are doing so, while the majority of Israel, having heard the gospel, is refusing it (vv.18-21). Not all Israelites, though, are being stubborn: Paul himself is a telling example, and this is sufficient since the eschatological Israel in scripture is after all a "remnant, chosen by grace" (11:1-10).[31] And anyone who considers himself an Israelite is invited to avoid being "purged out"[32] by joining this remnant of all who are being saved according to God's promise to Abraham (vv.11-24; 28b).

---

27 See for instance Ezek ch.20 where although God purges the house of Israel (vv.31-39), it is still *all* the house of Israel, *all of them,* that will be accepted by him on his holy mountain (v.40).

28 See 4:13-25.

29 "They are Israelites, and to them belong the sonship, the glory, the covenants, the giving of the law, the worship, and the promises..." (v.4).

30 See the previous section.

31 See footnote 27

32 Ezek 20:38.

A Final Appeal to James and His Followers (11:25-36)

Paul is coming up to Jerusalem with the Gentiles' offering, especially from Macedonia and Greece, the lands of the "nations" par excellence (15:25). This is a golden opportunity for James to soften his heart to the message of the gospel. By accepting the offering he will acknowledge the full validity of Paul's gospel, namely that the Gentiles who accepted it are allowed to "enter" without hindrance into God's city (11:25). This in turn will corroborate from the mouth of the senior "pillar," God's mouthpiece,[33] that God's word of promise in Isaiah[34] has been indeed realized: God has indeed worked salvation in his city and has attracted the nations to it.[35] Then, according to the same Isaiah, this news will go forth (vv.26b-27) as an invitation to the rest of the Jews, both in Jerusalem and outside it throughout the Roman empire, who will hopefully follow the lead of James, an eminent Jerusalemite figure. Then God's plan to engulf *all*, both Jews and Gentiles, in his abundant mercy will have been realized (vv.28-32), an impossible feat in men's eyes, but possible for God (vv.33-36).

An Appeal and Advice to the Church in Rome (12-15)

Nevertheless, the success of Paul's mission to Jerusalem is not a foregone conclusion. James might still reject Paul's gospel, and if the Roman church refuses it now, rejection by Jerusalem would become that much more likely.[36] In the short term a rejection would not be disastrous; there would be in fact little change and Paul would merely continue his own efforts on behalf of his gospel. But the long-term consequences—after Paul's death—would be more serious. If after Paul's death the tradition of his gospel in the church of Rome were to die out, its survival anywhere would

33 See p. 9
34 See p. 9
35 See pp. 6, 9.
36 On the importance of the church of Rome for Paul's case, see the beginning of this
   chapter.

be in jeopardy. With this in mind, and assuming his letter would be received positively, he proceeds to give sundry practical bits of advice that would help ensure the perpetuity of his gospel there. Its survival there would even offset to a great extent its possible rejection by James for two reasons: Rome is the capital of the empire, and it would serve as a base for him to implant his gospel in its western reaches (15:28) after having done so in the East (v.19).

Final Greetings (ch.16)

The letter concludes with a lengthy series of greetings. The intention behind it may have been to include as many names as possible of Jews and Gentiles living in communion according to the "standard of teaching"[37] set by the Pauline gospel.

---

37 6:17.

8

Philippians

The Purpose of Philippians and the Pauline Legacy

This letter is to be considered as Paul's testament written from either Ephesus or Rome, depending on which of the two one considers to be the place of his death.[1] Several of its features, especially when considered together, bear strong testimony to its character as a testament:

1) It is written to the church where the gospel "originated" (4:15).[2]

2) It is addressed "to all the saints in Christ Jesus who are at Philippi, *together with the bishops and deacons* (1:1), meaning it was intended not only to be read publicly at church gathering(s) but also to be received as authoritative by the leaders themselves, to function as scripture for them.

3) In Paul's repeated mention of both his presence and absence within the same sentence (1:26-27; 2:12), reference to his absence may be an oblique reference to his impending death. This impression is confirmed by the immediate context of the earlier example, since the passage leading up to it reads:

> Yes, and I shall rejoice. For I know that through your prayers and the help of the Spirit of Jesus Christ this will turn out for my deliverance, as it is my eager expectation and hope that I shall not be at all ashamed, but that with full courage now as always Christ will be honored in my body, whether by life or by death. *For to me to live is Christ, and to die is gain.* If it is to be life in the flesh, that means fruitful labor for me. Yet which I shall choose I cannot tell. I am hard pressed between the two. My desire is to depart and be with Christ, for that is far better. But to remain in the flesh is more necessary on your account. (1:19-25)

1 See p. 16.
2 See pp. 11-13.

4) At the beginning of the same passage where Paul speaks of his absence, and which follows one speaking of his death, he speaks of his "coming" with the term *parousia* which due to its frequent use in connection with the Lord's coming suggests that Paul means to say here that he will come to them with Christ at that time:

> Convinced of this, I know that I shall remain and continue with you all, for your progress and joy in the faith, so that in me you may have ample cause to glory in Christ Jesus, because of my coming (*parousia*) to you again. (1:26)

5) In 3:17-21 Paul gives himself as an example to the believers saying:

> But our commonwealth (citizenship) is in heaven, and from it we await a Savior, the Lord Jesus Christ, who will change our lowly body to be like his glorious body, by the power which enables him even to subject all things to himself. (vv.19-20)

The words are reminiscent of political terminology in the Roman empire: citizenship, savior, lord, and "subjecting all things" are all frequently related to the person of the Roman emperor. Paul, though imprisoned and thus at the sole mercy of the emperor, openly confesses Jesus Christ, not the emperor, as his master. The very kind of talk that is likely to make his release impossible and his death likely is what he engages in here. One should remember that the letter is addressed to inhabitants of a Roman colony.[3]

6) The letter's superscription paves the way for Timothy as his successor. Beginning with Galatians Paul started differentiating between himself as apostle and his helpers[4] even when mentioning Timothy by name (1 Cor 1:1). Yet here not only does he not make such differentiation, but he even refers to both himself and Timothy as (equally) "servants of Christ Jesus" (1:1). That the letter serves as an introduction to Timothy as the heir to Paul is also suggested by the following statement:

> I hope in the Lord Jesus to send Timothy to you soon, so that I may be cheered by news of you. I have no one like him, who will be genuinely

3   See pp. 11-12.
4   See chapter 4.

anxious for your welfare. They all look after their own interests, not those of Jesus Christ. But Timothy's worth you know, how as a son with a father he has served with me in the gospel. I hope therefore to send him just as soon as I see how it will go with me; and I trust in the Lord that shortly I myself shall come also.[5] (2:19-24)

The Content of Philippians

After having recapitulated "the gospel from the first day until now"[6] Paul calls upon his addressees to proceed on this path until "the day of Christ"[7] (1:1-11). Then he boldly invites them to get used to his absence since his death may well be imminent, and to concentrate on the gospel he has preached to them (vv.12-30). Since the content of the gospel is Christ, not Paul, he draws their attention toward Christ in a passage (2:1-11) at whose center is a marvelous christological hymn that he has pieced together for the occasion (vv.6-11). Given Paul's absence (v.12), and possible death,[8] the Philippians themselves are to become "luminaries in the world"[9] as he has been (vv.13-18). Their examples are to be Timothy, his heir (vv.19-24), and Epaphroditus (vv.25-30).

Paul then recapitulates his gospel: righteousness is through Christ, not the Law (3:1-11).[10] The believers are still on their way toward the kingdom and must persevere until Christ's coming (*parousia*; 3:12-4:1).[11] And his gospel teaches the oneness of Jews and Gentiles in Christ, so he asks both, represented by the symbolic names Euodia[12] and Syntyche,[13] to be of the same mind (*to*

5   See my comments above on 1:26.
6   1:5.
7   1:10.
8   See my comments above.
9   2:15.
10 Compare with Gal 1-4 and Rom 1-5.
11 Compare with Gal 5-6 and Rom 6-8; also 1 Cor.
12 The Greek *Euodia* is composed of the prefix *eu*, meaning right, and the noun *hodos* (way). It refers to the Jewish followers of the "way" (see Acts 16:17; 18:25-26; 19:9, 23; 24:14, 22; and *Gal* 54-55) as defined by Paul (see Gal 6:16 and *Gal* 326-327).
13 The Greek *Syntykhe* is composed of the prefix (preposition) *syn*, meaning (together) with, and the noun *tykhe* (fate). It refers to the Gentiles who believed in the gospel of Jesus, the Christ of (Jewish) scripture.

avto phronein)[14] in the Lord under the guidance of Paul's true yokefellow, Timothy (4:2-3), until the Lord comes (v.5). The Lord is near and God will soon establish his peace (vv.6-9). Before bidding them farewell (vv.21-23), Paul again recalls how the church in Philippi is tightly linked in his mind to the gospel (vv.10-19).

The Final Break with Jerusalem

Romans contained an open invitation to James and Jerusalem to endorse the *sole* gospel of salvation, Paul's gospel, in order to avoid being cut off from the olive tree of the fathers and remain instead part of the "remnant, chosen by grace" of which Paul himself is the prototype.[15] Negative remarks about Jews in Philippians constitute clear signs that the offer was declined. They are addressed as "dogs" (3:2), a term used in Judaism to refer to Gentiles as outsiders.[16] By not accepting the gospel, which is God's word,[17] James and his followers have been cut off from the olive tree;[18] they are the "enemies of God"[19] because they are "enemies of the cross of Christ" (3:18). On the other hand, Gentiles who accepted the gospel have been grafted into the same olive tree and thus are "the true circumcision, who worship God in spirit, and glory in Christ Jesus, and put no confidence in the flesh" (3:3). They are the true citizens of the "heavenly" city of God (3:20).[20]

14 Compare with 2:2.
15 See comments on Rom 11.
16 See Mk 7:27-28//Mt 15:26-27; Mt 7:6; Rev 22:15.
17 See Rom 1:1-4.
18 Nowadays many Christians as well as Jews are scandalized by this terminology. The reason is that both, each in their own way, consider that they *are* God's Israel by the mere fact that they are Jews or Christians. This was not how people thought in the first century and it does not reflect the viewpoint expressed in scripture (see, e.g., Ezek 20:33-40). The Essenes and the Pharisees did not consider other first century Jews to be members of God's Israel; hence Paul's expression "the Israel of God" in Gal 6:16 (see *Gal* 326-7).
19 Rom 11:28.
20 See also Gal 4:24-27.

9

Paul's Immediate Legacy

Colossians

It is safe to assume that Paul died before the start of the Judean Jewish revolt in 66 A.D. which was a harbinger of the end of Jerusalem; otherwise, he would have touched on this matter when he referred to the heavenly and earthly Jerusalems in Phil 3:19-20. At his death his main followers congregated around Timothy, his "son in the gospel" (2:22), in Ephesus (or its surroundings) which had become the Pauline headquarters.[1] There Timothy built upon Paul's compendium of the gospel as expounded in Romans and Philippians, writing Colossians as the charter for all the Pauline churches (4:16). Out of deference for Paul who included him as a co-servant in his testament letter to the Philippians, Timothy reverts to Paul's earlier correspondence[2] and differentiates between Paul as apostle and himself as only a brother (1:1).[3]

The letter reflects the notion of a new beginning based on Paul's gospel, the word of truth, that is bearing fruit and growing in the whole world (1:5-6); the addressees themselves are asked "to lead a life worthy of the Lord, fully pleasing to him, bearing fruit in every good work and increasing/growing in the knowledge of God" (1:10). The radicalism of this new beginning can be detected in the vocabulary used to describe it: it is reminiscent of the creation story in Gen 1.[4] The wisdom terminology connected

1 See p. 15.
2 Gal 1:1-2; 1 Cor 1:1; 2 Cor 1:1.
3 See *Gal* 22-23.
4 Gen 1:11, 12, 22, 28, 29. The verb *auxano* (grow/increase) occurs also in Gen 8:17; 9:1, 7; 17:6, 20; 28:3; 35:11.

with the gospel in this letter[5] brings to mind a passage from the
Wisdom of Solomon:

> Wisdom rescued a righteous man when the ungodly were perishing;
> he escaped the fire that descended on the Five Cities. Evidence of their
> wickedness still remains: a continually smoking wasteland, plants *bear-
> ing fruit* that does not ripen, and a pillar of salt standing as a monu-
> ment to an unbelieving soul...When a righteous man fled from his
> brother's wrath, she guided him on straight paths; she showed him *the
> kingdom of God,* and gave him *knowledge* of angels; she prospered him
> in his *labors,* and increased the fruit[6] of his *toil.* (10:6-7, 10)

What is striking is that the words I italicized in v.10 are used by
Paul in reference to his apostolic activity.[7] Notice also how the
quoted verses that refer to the "righteous one" under attack by the
wicked and his "brother" fits what happened to Paul himself.

This new creation is nothing else but the church whose head is
Christ (Col 1:18). This Lord, however, abides not with the
"thrones or dominions or principalities or authorities" (v.16),
whether in Rome or Jerusalem, but as crucified (v.20) "among the
Gentiles" who accepted Paul's gospel (v.27). They were circumcised through baptism in the circumcision of Christ, not made by
human hands (2:11); and though they live in the Roman empire,
their "lord" is not the emperor, but Christ crucified (3:17-4:1).

2 Thessalonians

The Judean Jewish war (66-70 A.D) polarized attitudes toward
the coming of the Messiah, God's representative. Since Paul had

5 *sophia* (wisdom; 1:9, 28; 2:3, 23; 3:16; 4:5); *gnosis* (knowledge; 2:3); *epignosis*
   ([full/complete] knowledge; 1:9, 10; 2:2; 3:10); *epiginosko* ([fully/completely]
   know; 1:6).
6 "Increase the fruit" is the translation of the Greek *plethyno* which occurs in conjunction with the verb *avxano* (grow/increase) in Gen 1:22, 28; 8:17; 9:1, 7; 17:20;
   28:3; 35:11.
7 See 2 Cor 11:27 and 1 Thess 2:9 (also *I Thess* 92-94) on *mokhthos* (labor). Moreover, besides Rev 16:10, 11; 21:4, *ponos* (toil) occurs only in Col 4:13 in the entire
   New Testament.

repeatedly stressed the Lord's coming as an important feature of his gospel, his opponents took this opportunity to disturb his churches by spreading the rumor that Paul's Messiah was coming in conjunction with the Jewish war. Timothy sent a corrective circular underscoring that no other teaching concerning this matter is valid save Paul's teaching in his gospel that was delivered once and for all:

> Now concerning the coming of our Lord Jesus Christ and our assembling to meet him, we beg you, brethren, not to be quickly shaken in mind or excited, either by spirit or by word, or by letter purporting to be from us, to the effect that the day of the Lord has come...But we are bound to give thanks to God always for you, brethren beloved by the Lord, because God chose you from the beginning to be saved, through sanctification by the Spirit and belief in the truth. *To this he called you through our gospel,* so that you may obtain the glory of our Lord Jesus Christ. *So then, brethren, stand firm and hold to the traditions which you were taught by us, either by word of mouth or by letter.* (2:1-2, 13-15)

This statement seals Paul's teaching as expounded in his letters, thus making of them at one and the same time both the official interpretation and the source of his gospel.

That Timothy opted to address this letter to the Thessalonians had to do with the fact that Paul's letter to that church dealt extensively with the Lord's coming (1 Thess 4:13-5:11) in response to worries regarding this matter, that had arisen among its members. By making its senders the same as those of 1 Thessalonians (Paul, Silvanus, and Timothy) he bestowed upon its content the seal of Paul's voice and signature (2 Thess 3:17).

Excursus: Pseudepigraphy

Unlike our times where there is stress on and interest in the actual author of a book or a text, in Paul's time as well as earlier the interest was much more on the content or teaching of the book or text. For instance, it is hard to tell to what extent the Socratic dialogues ascribed to Plato go back to Socrates himself or are totally Plato's work; and some of the dialogues may have been written by Plato's disciples after the manner of their master's original works. Similarly, it is difficult to know for sure the extent to which teachings ascribed to Plotinus, Buddha, or Confucius go back to them personally or to their disciples. This phenomenon is easily detectable in the Old Testament where the entire tradition connected with the Law is ascribed to Moses,[8] the Psalms are said to be of David,[9] Solomon is the patron of Wisdom writings,[10] and the entire thought of the Isaianic school spread over centuries was gathered under the aegis of Isaiah himself.[11] In this way the *oneness* of a given tradition of teaching was ensured; furthermore, by putting the entire process of thought originated by the master under his name, his school expressed the honor in which he was held.[12] Thus, it is always the master's pristine voice that is heard throughout the centuries and that brings together his diverse following into *one* community. The phenomenon is similar to what we encounter today under such terminology as "Luther's legacy," "Kantian school," or "Marxist philosophy."

8   See *OTI 1* 84.
9   See *OTI 3* 98.
10 See *OTI 3* 127-8.
11 See *OTI 2* 108-10.
12 See previous note.

II

Mark

10

Introduction

The Old Testament as Scripture for the Gentile Churches

The consensus among scholars is that Mark is the earliest of the four canonical gospels and was not written until after 65 A.D.[1] This means the first communities of believers began and grew throughout their first three decades without a written "gospel." The only writings reflecting faith in Jesus as the Messiah and originating from this period are the letters Paul sent to the Gentile churches he had founded.[2] In these epistles the word "gospel" refers not to a written document but to Paul's teaching about the Messiahship (divine Sonship) of Jesus and its significance for both Gentiles and Jews. "The gospel" in this context is essentially a synonym for "the faith," as is most obvious in Galatians.[3] The agreement reached among Christian leaders at Jerusalem and described in this letter (2:1-10) bears witness to the fact that the lack of interest in a written gospel evident in Paul's epistles is not unique to him: no one during this early period spoke of "a gospel" or "the gospel" as a written document and thus as a part of scripture. There was in fact no "New Testament" as we now know it, and more importantly, *there was no discernible sense that something was amiss because of that lack*. Indeed, our term "Old Testament" presumes there is a "New" counterpart, but such was not the case at this time.

---

1 A few postulate an original Aramaic version of Matthew prior to Mark (but even they agree that the Greek version of Matthew, which is our canonical version, was written after Mark), and another small group believes John predates Mark.
2 The exception is Romans that was written to a church not founded by him.
3 1:23; 3:2, 5; see my comments in *Gal* 55, 100-101.

The Old Testament as scripture was considered complete and sufficient throughout those first 30 years.

This was no less true among Gentile believers than it was among Jewish ones; the scripture consisting solely of the Old Testament was considered applicable equally and directly to all believers, Jew and Gentile alike (though Paul's opponents interpreted certain portions of it differently than he did). That even Paul's Gentile converts had to adopt the Old Testament as their own no less than Jews did is clear from the way Paul's epistles assume his Gentile readers have thoroughly assimilated its content. And the Old Testament's authority extended even to practical issues in Gentile communities, as can be seen in 1 Corinthians: even when Paul addresses matters peculiar to the Gentile nature of those communities—matters which would not have been issues at all among Jews—he consistently appeals to the Old Testament writings as a final authority containing solutions to "Gentile" problems no less than strictly "Jewish" ones.

The Gospel and the Person of Paul

"The gospel" itself remained an oral proclamation, something outside of written scripture, and we find no evidence in Paul's epistles that oral preaching ever came to be considered inadequate as a vehicle to convey the content of this gospel. Nowhere in Paul's epistles does he hint at any sense of discomfort about the absence of a comprehensive or systematic written version of the content of his preaching. For Paul, the gospel was in its essence brief, and it always pointed back to the scriptures of the Old Testament, as can be seen from his summary of the Thessalonians' response to his preaching: they "turned to God from idols, to serve a living and true God, and to wait for his Son from heaven, whom he raised from the dead, Jesus." (1 Thess 1:9b-10)

So long as Paul was alive, his teaching was itself "the gospel" and was not replaced or supplemented by any written works that could be called "a gospel" or "gospels." Paul did offer defenses and explanations of his gospel in written form within his epistles, but there was no attempt at a systematic literary exposition, no attempt to create a writing that could itself be called a gospel.

Thus, for the Pauline Gentile churches all was well so long as Paul was alive. The shining hope of their faith was the "new Jerusalem," a vision of hope in the eschatological future that Paul himself created for them. While he lived, he alone stood as their tangible and secure link with that hope and that goal. The Old Testament books of Ezekiel and Isaiah had centuries earlier spoken of a "new Jerusalem," and those texts at that time had in a similar manner created that concept as a new and concrete reality in the minds of the readers and hearers of scripture. Likewise, Paul's eschatological "new Jerusalem" became a reality for those who accepted his gospel, and it became that because his hearers trusted his authority just as their predecessors trusted the authority of Ezekiel and Isaiah.

"The Jerusalem above" (Gal 4:26) is embedded in Paul's gospel, having been preached first to the communities he established, and preserved for us in written form in his letters. It was only through Paul that his converts learned about this "Jerusalem above" as their "free mother,"[4] but he drew it directly from the words of Isaiah;[5] he was simply proclaiming "God's gospel, promised beforehand" by God himself in the book of "his prophet" Isaiah.[6] In simpler terms, Paul was telling the Gentiles that Isaiah's promises had been fulfilled, and he was explaining how they had been fulfilled.[7] For Jews the prophetic texts themselves would already be familiar, but this interpretation of their intent and fulfillment

---

4 Gal 4:26. Indeed, Paul's Gentile believers had never seen—and possibly not even heard of—the city of Jerusalem except through his preaching, which presented it exclusively in biblical terms.
5 Gal 4:27. See my comments in *Gal* 249-50.
6 Rom 1:1-2.
7 See on this *OTI2* 214.

would not, and it was precisely this interpretation that was the essence of Paul's gospel. Thus, whatever Paul said to the Gentiles applied equally to the Jews since his gospel was the one and only true gospel and was addressed to both.[8] Nevertheless many or most Jews who accepted the Messiahship of Jesus rejected Paul's interpretation of the significance of that Messiahship, and while he lived Paul was constantly forced to defend his gospel against those who preached "another gospel" (Gal 1:6)

Consequently, throughout Paul's lifetime his gospel stood firmly on the basis of Paul's own personal authority, and only on that basis. After Paul's death his Gentile followers were left without root or anchor. Granted, both Jewish and Gentile believers still had their one common body of scripture, a collection of texts that served as the authoritative source for Paul himself when he preached his gospel. But the texts could be interpreted in many different ways, and the essence of Paul's gospel was his own interpretation of these texts, an interpretation which he claimed to be the sole correct one.[9] And only Paul's interpretation effectively secured the full membership of the believing Gentiles as equals alongside their Jewish counterparts in the *one* church of the *one* God. But who among the authoritative apostles dared to say so unequivocally besides Paul? None, to our knowledge. For the others, a Gentile would always be somehow secondary until and unless he would fully become a Jew by following the dictates of Jewish Law.

Thus, beginning with the break at Antioch between him and emissaries of the Jerusalemite Jewish Christian leadership (Gal 2:11-14), Paul realized that his Gentile churches would always be hounded by the camp of James and Barnabas. And, as early as that break and starting with 1 Thessalonians, he decided to seal his teaching in writing by sending letters to those churches, knowing that some day he would die and leave them orphaned, at the

---

8   Gal 1:6; 2:7-8; Rom 10:12; also 3:22-23. See *Gal* 69-70; also 37-39.
9   In *Gal*, especially chs.4 and 5, I show that Paul's interpretation was correct.

mercy of his opponents, who would tell them that they as Gentiles were *still* "separated from Christ, alienated from the commonwealth of Israel, and strangers to the covenants of promise, having no hope and without God in the world" (Eph 2:12). But a situation that could have ended in disaster for them was salvaged precisely because of the way Paul had always presented his gospel as a *word (logos)*. It was in effect Paul's gospel *word*—rather than Paul himself—that had proclaimed to them the new reality of their new faith and assured them of its truth. Throughout his mission to the Gentiles Paul had drilled into his converts' minds that what was of import was not his person, but rather his gospel teaching; he was merely passing on to others what the Lord had conveyed to him. Numerous texts testify to this view of himself as merely a servant and of the gospel he serves as not merely "his" but "*the* gospel," something with independent existence and a life of its own:

> Paul, a servant of Jesus Christ, *called to be an apostle, set apart for the gospel of God...* For God is my witness, whom I serve with my spirit in the gospel of his Son... But on some points I have written to you very boldly by way of reminder, because of the grace given me by God to be a minister of Christ Jesus to the Gentiles in the priestly service of the gospel of God... Now to him who is able to strengthen you according to my gospel and the preaching of Jesus Christ, according to the revelation of the mystery which was kept secret for long ages but is now disclosed and through the prophetic writings is made known to all nations, according to the command of the eternal God, to bring about the obedience of faith—to the only wise God be glory for evermore through Jesus Christ! (Rom 1:1, 9; 15:15-16; 16:25-27)

> For though you have countless guides in Christ, you do not have many fathers. For I became your father in Christ Jesus through the gospel... If we have sown spiritual good among you, is it too much if we reap your material benefits? If others share this rightful claim upon you, do not we still more? Nevertheless, we have not made use of this right, but we endure anything rather than put an obstacle in the way of the gospel of Christ... I do it all for the sake of the gospel, that I may share in its blessings. (1 Cor 4:15; 9:11-12, 23)

And even if our gospel is veiled, it is veiled only to those who are perishing. In their case the god of this world has blinded the minds of the unbelievers, to keep them from seeing the light of the gospel of the glory of Christ, who is the likeness of God... Under the test of this service, you will glorify God by your obedience in acknowledging the gospel of Christ, and by the generosity of your contribution for them and for all others... For we are not overextending ourselves, as though we did not reach you; we were the first to come all the way to you with the gospel of Christ... For if someone comes and preaches another Jesus than the one we preached, or if you receive a different spirit from the one you received, or if you accept a different gospel from the one you accepted, you submit to it readily enough... Did I commit a sin in abasing myself so that you might be exalted, because I preached God's gospel without cost to you? (2 Cor 4:3-4; 9:13; 10:14; 11:4, 7)

I thank my God in all my remembrance of you, always in every prayer of mine for you all making my prayer with joy, thankful for your partnership in the gospel from the first day until now... It is right for me to feel thus about you all, because I hold you in my heart, for you are all partakers with me of grace, both in my imprisonment and in the defense and confirmation of the gospel... I want you to know, brethren, that what has happened to me has really served to advance the gospel... The latter do it out of love, knowing that I am put here for the defense of the gospel... Only let your manner of life be worthy of the gospel of Christ, so that whether I come and see you or am absent, I may hear of you that you stand firm in one spirit, with one mind striving side by side for the faith of the gospel... But Timothy's worth you know, how as a son with a father he has served with me in the gospel... And I ask you also, true yokefellow, help these women, for they have labored side by side with me in the gospel together with Clement and the rest of my fellow workers, whose names are in the book of life. (Phil 1:3-5, 7, 12, 16, 27; 2:22; 4:3)

...for our gospel came to you not only in word, but also in power and in the Holy Spirit and with full conviction. You know what kind of men we proved to be among you for your sake... For you yourselves know, brethren, that our visit to you was not in vain; but though we had already suffered and been shamefully treated at

Philippi, as you know, we had courage in our God to declare to you the gospel of God in the face of great opposition. For our appeal does not spring from error or uncleanness, nor is it made with guile; but just as we have been approved by God to be entrusted with the gospel, so we speak, not to please men, but to please God who tests our hearts... So, being affectionately desirous of you, we were ready to share with you not only the gospel of God but also our own selves, because you had become very dear to us. For you remember our labor and toil, brethren; we worked night and day, that we might not burden any of you, while we preached to you the gospel of God... we sent Timothy, our brother and God's servant in the gospel of Christ, to establish you in your faith and to exhort you. (1 Thess 1:5; 2:1-4, 8-9; 3:2)

I would have been glad to keep him with me, in order that he might serve me on your behalf during my imprisonment for the gospel. (Philem 13)

The Pauline Corpus as Scripture

The emphasis on the gospel is so strong as to overshadow any image one might gain of Paul's person; it is as though he rendered himself transparent so that his readers and hearers would see in him only the gospel itself. As he eloquently stated as early as in 1 Thessalonians (2:8) and as late as in Philippians (1:3-5, 27), the gospel was the only possible bridge of communication between him and them, the only prism through which he and they would view one another. Thus, whenever Paul spoke of himself, it was in regard to his own authority as an apostle of the gospel, and the purpose of such remarks was to aid his defense of the gospel. He trained his flock to view him exclusively as an apostle, and specifically as *their* apostle (1 Cor 9:2; 2 Cor 3:1-3), and the authority over them that this gave him he used strictly to promote the gospel among them. This authority was particularly useful because it could be exercised from afar as well as while physically present:

For though absent in body I am present in spirit, and as if present, I have already pronounced judgment in the name of the Lord Je-

sus on the man who has done such a thing. When you are assem-
bled, and my spirit is present, with the power of our Lord Jesus,
you are to deliver this man to Satan for the destruction of the
flesh, that his spirit may be saved in the day of the Lord Jesus.
(1 Cor 5:3-5)

His ability to exercise authority in this manner rendered his physical presence immaterial since he effectively made himself present
through his words; in a sense he sent to his churches an incarnation
of himself in words. It was in recognition of this power in Paul's
words that his co-workers, under the leadership of Timothy, gathered the letters he wrote to his churches into a corpus that became
their authoritative reference for his gospel.[10] This corpus ensured
that the ongoing opposition to Paul's gospel could not take advantage of Paul's absence, for in these epistles Paul remained power-
fully present even after his death. The act of collecting Paul's
epistles for this purpose was the first step toward the creation of a
"fourth (and last) scripture"[11] of the "Israel of God" (Gal 6:16), the
birth of what came to be known as the New Testament.

    In creating this new body of scripture the Pauline leaders of
the emerging Gentile churches were merely following in the footsteps of their predecessors, Ezekiel and the priestly writers of the
Old Testament who began to gather the "words" of Amos, Hosea,
Isaiah, Micah, and Jeremiah.[12] The same process repeated itself in
the first century A.D. The Pauline school took the first step by
putting together the master's epistles into a corpus, and it aug-
mented that corpus with a series of additional letters composed
along the line of his teachings and, as was usual in those times, su-
perscripted with his name out of deference to him (the first of
these being Colossians and 2 Thessalonians). Thus, both Paul's

---

10 See p. 107.
11 See also my discussion of the NT as the "fourth scripture" in *OTI3* 157, 181-86,
   187-91. See *OTI1* 143-45 on the Pentateuch as "first scripture," *OTI2* 201-205 on
   the "Prophets" as "second scripture," and *OTI3* 151-52 on Wisdom literature as
   "third scripture."
12 See *OTI2* 161, 201-2.

disciples and his predecessors the Old Testament prophets created a set of authoritative scriptures that would define the very character and nature of God's Israel.

A More Systematic Charter

The second step undertaken by the Pauline school was much more complex. Here one must recall that, besides editing the prophets' words into scrolls as scripture, the school of Ezekiel proceeded to produce its own writings, the *Torah* (Pentateuch), in order to present a more systematic view of their teaching.[13] The Pentateuch is the story of the origins of God's people revisited in the light of the prophetic teaching that identified and defined the true God for nascent Judaism.[14] The gospel of Mark was produced along similar lines. It revisited whatever stories regarding Jesus were still alive in the memory of the early church leaders, in the light of the Pauline gospel teaching. In Paul's preaching and teaching, Jesus the Messiah and Lord was co-extensive with the gospel taught and preached by the apostle. The gospel of Paul to the Gentiles carried Jesus for them; the only Jesus they knew, beginning with Timothy and Mark who had never personally seen him, was the reality engraved on their minds and hearts by Paul's apostolic words.[15] They—probably leaders such as Timo-

---

13 See *OTI2* 160-61.
14 See *OTI1* and *OTI2*. The key word here is "define." The authoritative writings of nascent Judaism were the product of a minority faithful to the teaching of those who came to be recognized as the true prophets, bearers of the divine word. The biblical Israel did not "exist" anywhere outside the minds of these prophets; they created the understanding or idea of Israel which we now speak of as the "biblical Israel." In other words, our vision of what Israel was or is has been shaped by the writings of these prophets; many *or most* of their contemporaries may have had a vastly different view of "Israel," its history, and its nature or character. The same is true of "early Christianity": what for us has become normative may well have been—and in fact was—a small minority fighting for its very life at the time.
15 Besides the already-mentioned passages regarding the primacy given by Paul to the gospel over his own person, see also: Rom 1;1-4; 10:16-17; 1 Cor 3:10-11; 4:17; 15:1-5; 2 Cor 2:12; Gal 1:6, 11-12, 15-16; 4:13, 18.

thy and Mark—must have decided that Paul's written legacy was
inadequate, even supplemented as it was by works such as Colossians. They concluded that a more systematic view of Christ, the
subject and content of Paul's preaching, had finally become necessary. But why? What would have triggered in their minds the
idea of embarking on such a monumental project? What was the
purpose? Whom would it benefit? And was it absolutely necessary
or merely beneficial, a nice-to-have extra?

The event that led to the decision to write a gospel book was
Paul's death. This left the Gentile churches in a very precarious
position with no apostle supporting them and necessitated finding a different, yet equally authoritative, means of support. Paul's
epistles were being collected, and Timothy did provide a new
charter (Colossians) based on Paul's apostolic authority, but despite everything said above about the importance of Paul's apostolic word over his person, that written word in these collected
epistles still did not carry the same weight as a living apostle. The
remaining living apostles were associated with the Jerusalemite
leadership, which had openly rejected the believing Gentiles' freedom from circumcision and the Mosaic ordinances. The only
hope was to sway one of these leaders into the Pauline camp.
James himself (or his following) might be too difficult to persuade, but Peter (or his following) was apparently less adamant on
this position than James and seemed a possible convert to the
Gentile cause. Moreover, he was an apostle, and officially Paul's
counterpart among the Jews for that matter (Gal 2:7-8), so he
would also have substantial influence with James (v.9) and the rest
of the Jerusalem leadership.

Mark

The Pauline following included among its membership a natural
bridge to the Petrine group in the person of Mark. He was part of
Paul's entourage during the apostle's last days: "Epaphras, my fel-

low prisoner in Christ Jesus, sends greetings to you, and so do Mark, Aristarchus, Demas, and Luke, my fellow workers." (Philem 23-24) And later on we find Mark still with Timothy (Col 4:10). What made him uniquely fit for this task, however, was his earlier close connection with Barnabas (Col 4:10; see also Acts 12:25; 15:37) and, more importantly, with Peter: "She who is at Babylon, who is likewise chosen, sends you greetings; and so does my son Mark." (1 Pet 5:13; see also Acts 12:12) For a while, his relation to Barnabas made him suspect in the eyes of Paul's colleagues, to the extent that Timothy had to add an extra note vouching for his trustworthiness: "Aristarchus my fellow prisoner greets you, and Mark the cousin of Barnabas (concerning whom you have received instructions—if he comes to you, receive him)." (Col 4:10) Thus, Mark was someone who actually shifted allegiance from Barnabas (and Peter) to Paul, i.e., he himself had done what was about to be asked of Peter or his successors.

Authorship

The fact that Mark was the bridge to the Petrine following must have sealed the tradition that the gospel was named after him; and he may well have actually been the author. However, the gospel text seems to allude to Mark as part of the gospel story.[16] Another candidate would be the author of Luke-Acts, who shows a mastery of the Greek language essential for anyone contemplating an undertaking of this sort. Moreover, this would explain the liberty Luke took in rewriting the first gospel into his monumental two-volume work, Luke-Acts. At any rate, if Luke was the author, he would have written "Mark" under the scrutinizing eye of both Timothy and Mark, given the delicacy of the matter. Since the appeal to Peter was either written by Mark himself or used Mark as an example, or both, this book is in a sense a "Markan" message

16 Refer to my comments on Mk 11:2; 14:51; 16:5

to the Petrine following, and since Luke's name brings to mind Luke-Acts, I shall henceforth refer to this gospel and its author as simply "Mark."

The Written Gospel

Still, one does not embark on an impossible mission. One needs to have some realistic hope of success before investing an immense effort in such a grandiose undertaking. What would have been the sign that the endeavor might succeed? It lay in the situation in and around Jerusalem at that time. A Jewish rebellion against the Roman authorities started in Jerusalem in 66 A.D. and triggered a war that ended with the siege and the fall of the city to the Roman armies in 70. As is typical of such rebellions, the situation was polarized, and the Judean Jewish believers in particular were in a difficult predicament. As Jews they would be considered traitors if they did not openly side with their fellows by taking up arms to defend Jerusalem. As followers of Jesus, their doing so would constitute betrayal of their faith in him as the Messiah who had already secured for them the kingdom of God and guaranteed them the freedom their Jewish fellows were militantly fighting for. In other words, the Jewish revolt of 66 forced the Jerusalemite church to realize the depth of the chasm between it and contemporary Judaism. The Jews' conception of God's city as the physical, earthly city of Jerusalem had not changed since the time of Jeremiah and Ezekiel, at which time it had been opposed to those prophets' views also.[17] Those two prophets taught that it is the word of God that matters, not an earthly city. Indeed, Jeremiah, as bearer of the Lord's word (Jer 1:1-9), in a sense became *himself* the Lord's city and as such *opposed* the Jerusalemites and Judahites (vv.18-19). Ezekiel too became the abode of the divine word (Ezek 3:1-3) and spoke *against* the rebellious

17 See e.g. Jer 7; 21; 25:1-13; 26; 28; Ezek 2:1-3:11; 20.

house of Israel (2:1-7; 3:4-11), and he did so from Babylonia, the land of the Gentiles who had exiled him there in 597 B.C. and were about to strike down Jerusalem a decade later just as the Romans did in the first century A.D. Through these two prophets, God's saving message to Jerusalem was directed against it and from outside its boundaries!

Mark capitalized on this situation and formulated his literary plan according to the scheme of Ezekiel. The divine word, now as Paul's gospel, summoned the Jerusalemite church to break with the insurgent Judaism of Judea, and it did so from outside Jerusalem—from Rome or Western Asia Minor. Moreover, it called upon that church to move away from Jerusalem and settle among the Gentile churches, from whom the divine word as gospel was now originating. And since this divine word was identified with Jesus himself, the crucified Messiah, Mark used whatever traditions about Jesus were at hand and presented them as a *story*, namely the story of Jesus from Galilee. The importance of his Galilean origin is that it means he came from outside Jerusalem and outside Judea. It was to this place relatively foreign to Judaism that Peter was called to leave Jerusalem in order to "see him risen" (Mk 16:7) and thereby to become a true apostle of Jesus.[18]

I strongly believe Mark went even further: he conceived and patterned this story of Jesus after the plan of the book of Isaiah. This means he intended it from the beginning to act as scripture, to be read in the Pauline Gentile churches as well as, hopefully, in the Jerusalemite church community in its eventual new location outside Jerusalem. Why would he have chosen the book of Isaiah to emulate? Two main reasons come to mind, one material and one formal. Materially, besides being the Messianic book par excellence[19] and consequently the most appropriate as a blueprint

---

18 See 1 Cor 9:1; 15:5-8 for the connection between "seeing the Lord" and being an apostle.
19 See *OTI2* 121-128; 166-185; 196.

for the story of Jesus the Messiah, the book of Isaiah is conceived as the "story of God's word" addressed to his city, Jerusalem. God's word judges the city and calls it to become truly his city, the place where he will fully execute his *mišpat* (righteous judgment) and to which all nations will flock to enjoy his *šalom* (peace).[20] The fact that this "story" is one of "continual faithlessness on Israel's part and equally unrelenting faithfulness on the Lord's part"[21] made it remarkably appropriate for Mark's purposes. His intention was to emphasize how "Israel," in the persons of Peter and James, was unfaithful to God's word as expressed in the (Pauline) gospel.

Formally, the one "story" presented in Isaiah is actually presented "as *a whole series of stories following one repeated pattern*."[22] The purpose of this arrangement is to underscore the people's faithlessness versus the Lord's faithfulness, for the repeating pattern is that "the people through their rebellions try to put an end to the story, but God, through his prophet(s), always has the last word."[23] This pattern, though particularly clear in Isaiah, is actually encountered throughout the Old Testament, making it effectively a "scriptural" as much as "Isaianic" pattern.[24] Mark, as we shall see, follows suit.

This scriptural pattern entailed another very important feature. Isaiah's "story" is presented more specifically as that of the city of Jerusalem from its beginnings up to its end as the "new" Jerusalem. Yet the city is viewed throughout *from the perspective of the end*, as is clear from Isaiah's opening "vision" of the divine "word": its subject matter is the eschatological Jerusalem where God's eschatological *šalom* (peace) is established and to which all the nations flock (2:1-4).[25] This "perspective from the end" is a

---

20 See *OTI2* 197-8.
21 *OTI2* 197.
22 *OTI2* 197 (italics are added).
23 *OTI2* 197.
24 *OTI2* 201-205; *OTI3* 99-104.
25 *OTI2* 197.

trademark of the Old Testament literature as well as Paul's gospel, for Paul's Christ is always the one who is coming, the risen Lord who will come to judge the world.[26] Consequently, when Jesus begins "preaching the gospel of God" (1:14) at the very beginning of Mark, that gospel is already focused on the end time: "The time is fulfilled, and the kingdom of God is at hand." (v.15) The Jerusalem of Isaiah's day was a real earthly city, but what he wrote about it was colored by his vision of its future glory; in the same way Mark wrote about the human person Jesus of Galilee but his presentation of that person was always colored by his vision of the risen Lord expected to return in glory.

The Written Gospel as Scripture

As I indicated earlier, Mark was not merely writing a dissertation or an appeal addressed to Peter and the Jerusalemite church such as what Paul did with his letter to the Romans. He was also writing a "scripture" for the Pauline Gentile churches based on Paul's gospel as it had been presented in Paul's preaching and teaching. He actually refers to his work as a "gospel" by placing that word in the very first sentence, which effectively acts as a title: "(The) beginning of the gospel of Jesus Christ, the Son of God."

Another indication that Mark intended to write a "scripture" is the remark "...let the reader understand..." in 13:14. That reference to *one* reader is telling. Nowadays, being children of the post-printing press era, our understanding of the meaning of "books" and even "reading" is quite different from that of the first century A.D. At that time, copies of any given manuscript were very few and their "reading" was done usually in gatherings. This is borne out by the meaning of the Hebrew verb *qara'* and the corresponding Greek *anaginosko*; both meant "to read *aloud*," and not just for oneself, as we understand it today. Thus, the very no-

---

26 See *OTI2* 198-205; 1 Thess 1:9-10; 1 Cor 11:26-34; also *Gal* 272-3.

tion of reading implied that it would be done aloud by one person, the "reader," in an official gathering at which the others present were the "hearers." Rev 1:3 offers another witness to this: "Blessed is *he who reads aloud* the words of the prophecy, and blessed are *those who hear,* and who keep what is written therein; for the time is near." Two things in this text are especially significant: a) the RSV translates the same Greek word once without and once with "aloud"; b) the original Greek of Revelation has "Blessed is *the reader* and the hearers of the words of the prophecy." Therefore if Mark was addressed to one reader, that person was "*the* official, public reader" of the gathered community.[27] And since scripture was read and commented upon at these gatherings, the reader or commentator is the one who had to understand the text, in order to explain it to the others.

My conclusion is that in Mark we have a "story" intended to be read in the Pauline gatherings as a prophecy would,[28] a "story" being offered as a "word," and more specifically as the "word of God." This is exactly how the "stories" of the Patriarchs, the exodus, and the kingdoms of Israel and Judah, are handled in the Old Testament. In other words, Mark was conceived as scripture.

The Content of the Story

So Mark decided to create a "story of Jesus" and intended it to serve as scripture, but what will have been the source for the overall outline of that story? Could he have created it from scratch, devising his own plan for fitting numerous short vignettes about Jesus into a cohesive whole? I am convinced that he in fact utilized a story outline that had already been known among the Gen-

27 The same understanding of "reading" still obtained in the 7th century A.D., when the scripture of Islam came to be known as *Qur'an* (reading/something to be read) whereas the public reader is a *mu'adhdhin* (one who causes [others] to hear), his (public) reading is *'adhan* (that which is heard), and the minaret from where the reading is done is *mi'dhanat* (the source of that which is made to be heard).
28 As in Rev 1:3.

tile churches. Earlier I referred to two essential points: the practical equivalence between the person of Jesus and the words of the gospel concerning him; and the fact that for the Gentile churches as well as for the Jews, Timothy and Mark, Paul was *the* apostle, the original authoritative bearer of this gospel. When one takes these two matters seriously into consideration, one can understand that in the minds of Paul's disciples and communities, the "gospel story" was already outlined: it followed the major contours of *Paul's* life and activity *as an apostle*. It is not difficult to determine those contours, for they are laid out in some detail in Paul's epistles. These letters were written by him *as an apostle,* that is, in conjunction with his explication and defense of his gospel. Of these letters, only in Galatians and Philippians is the argument itself closely interwoven with personal data about Paul as an apostle, thus making the author's own history and experiences a kind of "gospel story." The former deals squarely with Mark's immediate interest: Paul's gospel on the one hand, and Peter, James, and the Jerusalemite church, on the other. The latter is Paul's testament from his place of imprisonment prior to his death and reflects the fact that the Jerusalemite church authorities did not heed Paul's appeal to them through his letter to the Romans. It is along the lines of the arguments in these two epistles that Mark wrote his "gospel story."

The Old Testament Precedent

This whole process may seem strange to the contemporary reader, but it is precisely what had been done earlier in the Old Testament, and Mark was merely following an example set for him by scripture itself. The Pentateuch as a whole, as well as Deuteronomy and the Deuteronomistic History in particular, were "stories" conceived on the basis of the prophets' teachings.[29] One can

29 See *OTI1* 71-118; 124-126; *OTI2* 160-162.

even say that these same "stories" were actually woven from the prophets' personalities and lives. Scholars have long pointed out similarities between Moses and Jeremiah.[30] They have also noticed that the Pentateuch describes two Aarons: one subservient to Moses and even opposed to him,[31] the other his successor as high priest throughout the ages.[32] Whereas Moses led Israel during his lifetime, this second Aaron leads it throughout the generations.[33] This second Aaron bears a remarkable resemblance to Ezekiel, the exilic priest-prophet. Indeed, Ezekiel's eschatological Jerusalem is the blueprint of Aaron's temple in the wilderness.[34] Finally, Joshua, Israel's leader into Canaan, the land promised to Abraham, is patterned after Second Isaiah and, to some extent, Ezekiel. The names Isaiah and Joshua are from the same root in Hebrew meaning "the Lord saves," and Second Isaiah is the prophet who speaks of the return to God's city, Jerusalem, and at the same time presents Abraham as the one to whose progeny the promise is made.[35] On the other hand, the land's conquest by Joshua is done in a "priestly" manner: it is the Lord who leads Israel in a cultic manner into the land as though it is his holy of holies, exactly as Ezekiel's "new Jerusalem" is.[36]

Mark has created a similar mixture in his gospel; the life of Jesus here is reminiscent of the New Testament "prophet"[37] Paul. Mark's purpose is to call upon the Jerusalem church and Peter's followers—and ultimately through them, the Judaism of his time

---

30 Compare e.g. Jer 1:6 with Ex 4:10; also Jer 5:19; 16:10-11; 22:8-9 with Deut 28:47-48; 29:23-24; also Jer 7:16; 11:14; 14:11; 15:1; with Ex 32:11-14; 30-32; Num 11:2; 14:13-19; 16:22; 21:7; Deut 9:25-29.

31 Ex 4:10-17, 28; 7:1-2, 9, 19; 8:16; 16:9, 33; 32:1-6, 21-25, 35; Num 12:1-9.

32 Ex 28-31; 39; Num 17:16-26.

33 Leviticus, passim.

34 Ezek 40-48; Ex 35-38.

35 Is 41:8-9; 51:1-3.

36 Josh 3-4; 6:1-21; Ezek 48:30-35; OTI2 159-160.

37 Indeed, as I show in my comments on Gal 1:15-16 in Gal 42-46, Paul himself saw his own life and his apostleship as a reflection of Jeremiah's life as a prophet.

as a whole—to relinquish the earthly Jerusalem that is bound to destruction, and follow the prophetic call arising from the "wilderness of the Gentiles," into the new, heavenly Jerusalem. This prophetic voice was none other than Paul's, "an apostle, set apart for the *gospel* of God which he *promised beforehand through his prophets in the holy scriptures.*" (Rom 1:1-2) And consequently, the image of Paul shows through in Mark's portrayal of Jesus, just as the image of Jeremiah shows through in the Pentateuch's depiction of Moses.

The Structure of Mark

The literary structure of Mark can best be discerned precisely by paying attention to the way Paul and the issues facing his Gentile churches show through in the story of Jesus. The story is built around a framework that begins with a preamble (1:1-15) followed by three cycles of calling/invitation (1:16-3:12; 3:13-6:6a; 6:6b-8:21) and three cycles of teaching (8:27-9:29; 9:30-10:31; 10:32-45). Then there is a pivotal pericope[38] where Timothy's leadership as Paul's successor is introduced (10:46-52), and that is followed by two long sections, one offering the gospel for the last time to the Jerusalemite Christian leadership (chs.11-13) and one recounting their refusal of it (chs.14-15). Finally there is a short text indicating the door is still open for Peter and his following (16:1-8) to accept Paul's gospel.

The following list breaks this structure down into some more detail and indicates how these sections reflect Paul himself, his gospel, or specific issues faced by adherents to his gospel. It is offered here less as an initial overview than as a "quick reference" that may help the reader to visualize more easily the flow of the

---

38 The Greek noun *pericope,* from the verb *perikopto* (to cut around), means a given item that has been cut out of a larger bulk. It has become usual in biblical scholarship to refer to a literary passage (within a book) that encompasses a contained story or statement.

Markan story while following the main text of this book. It is placed here merely to make sure that the reader is aware of its availability; to anyone who is reading the book for the first time I suggest that this list be skimmed quickly or skipped entirely.

Preamble (1:1-15)

Paul's conversion from the Judaism of his time to the crucified Christ, and the beginning of the gospel.

Three Cycles in Which the Other Apostles Are Invited to Accept Paul's Gospel (1:16-8:21)

First cycle (1:16-3:12): up to the Jerusalem meeting.

Introduction: Call to the "pillars" (1:16-20).

A. The essence of all subsequent stories in a nutshell: three basic stages of the propagation of the gospel (1:21-39).

    1. Pauline activity before the Jerusalem meeting (1:21-28).

    2. The meeting with the pillars (1:29-34).

    3. The reaching out to the Gentiles (1:35-39).

B. Expanded version of the Pauline gospel story (1:40-3:12).

    1. Paul's conversion (1:40-45).

    2. Confrontation with the pillars (2:1-3:6).

    3. The gospel is preached throughout the Roman empire (3:7-12).

Second cycle (3:13-6:6a): from the incident at Antioch until the writing of Romans.

Introduction: Call to the apostles (3:13-19).

A. Confrontation with (3:20-30) and separation from (3:31-34) the "brothers," corresponding to Gal 2:10-14.

B. Content of the gospel (4:1-34).

C. Invitation to go out of the realm of Judaism (4:35-41) and preach the gospel also to the Gentile world (5:1-20).

D. The gospel to the Gentiles is also offered to the Jews (5:21-34), corresponding to the thesis of Romans.

E. The Jewish leadership refuses the gospel (6:1-6a).

Third cycle (6:6b-8:21): after Paul's death.

    Introduction: Call to the apostles to reach outside the realm of Judaism (6:6b-13).

    A. The death of Paul (6:14-29).

    B. The apostles are called to carry on his teaching of table fellowship (6:30-44).

    C. They are called to go out to the Gentiles (6:45-52).

    D. They are shown the way: the gospel is offered to the Gentiles (6:53-56).

    E. Criticism and correction of the judaizing teaching of the pillars (7:1-23).

    F. The gospel is to go unhindered to the Gentiles (7:4-30) throughout the Roman empire (7:31-37) to the extent of full table fellowship with them (8:1-10).

    G. Refusal by the Jewish leadership (8:11-21).

Timothy, an Example for the Pillars in That His Eyes Were Opened to the Gospel (8:22-26)

This passage serves as a hinge between the sections comprising the two sets of cycles. Timothy is the prime Jewish follower of Paul and thus is the best emissary from him to the Jews. He is also the one who carried the teaching of Paul's gospel after the latter's death.

Three Cycles Detailing the Gospel of the Crucified Messiah (8:27-10:45)

    Introduction: the beginning of the gospel is linked to Philippi (8:27-30)

First cycle (8:27-9:29)

    A. First announcement of Jesus' death (8:31).

    B. Teaching Peter the gospel of the cross (8:32-9:1).

    C. Teaching the pillars the same gospel (9:2-13).

    D. The one community created by the gospel includes the Gentiles (9:14-29).

Second cycle (9:30-10:31)

    A. Second announcement of Jesus' death (9:30-32).

B. Teaching of the pillars (9:33-50).

C. The gospel includes the Gentiles on the same footing as the Jews (10:1-31).

Third cycle (10:32-45)

A. Third announcement of Jesus' death (10:32-34).

B. Presentation of the gospel to the pillars (10:35-45).

Timothy Heads the Pauline Community (10:46-52)

Timothy Comes to Jerusalem with Paul's Message as It Is Conveyed in Romans (11-12)

A. The Entry into Jerusalem (11:1-11).

B. Jesus' Authority (11:15-33).

C. Last Words of Teaching before the Announcement of the Last Test (ch.12).

Last Call to the Pillars before the Lord's Coming (ch.13)

Refusal of Timothy's Message (14-15)

A. Jerusalem's First Refusal of the Gospel (ch.14).

B. Jerusalem's Second Refusal of the Gospel (ch.15).

Mark's Offer to the Petrine Community (16:1-8)

11

Preamble (1:1-15)

"The Beginning of the Gospel"

The expression "(the) beginning of the gospel" was most probably borrowed from Phil 4:15, the only other place it occurs in the New Testament. There Paul defines this "beginning of the gospel" in chronological terms by saying the gospel "began" when he departed from Macedonia. But he had been preaching the same gospel for many years prior to that; why would he consider it to have started only then? The best explanation is that he means to say this was the first time he exercised the authority given him by the Jerusalem council as "apostle to the Gentiles" (Gal 2:7-10).[1] Mark will have found this reference to "the beginning of the gospel" appropriate because it could describe the beginning of his own "apostolic" work—the creation of a written "gospel"—in the same way that Paul's Macedonian preaching marked the beginning of his apostolic work. The word "gospel" was thus used similarly in reference to each writer's relationship to the gospel, and the word "beginning" was likewise used in a relative rather than absolute manner, for Mark also did not mean to imply that "the gospel" did not in any way exist prior to the "beginning" he described.

John the Baptist as an Image of Paul the Apostle

While "the beginning of the gospel" and other parts of Mark appear to be drawn from Paul's writings, the figure of John the Baptist in Mark's gospel bears a remarkable resemblance to Paul himself. That Mark's portrayal of a historical character such as John the Baptist

---

1   See pp. 12-13.

might reflect a greater interest in conveying a message than in reporting a kind of "literal history" should not be surprising, for this is consistent with the way Jesus Christ himself is portrayed. As I will show below, while portraying the events of Jesus Christ's earthly life, the focus of Mark's gospel is really on the post-resurrection Lord who has ascended and will return. In the same way, the portrayal of John the Baptist as forerunner of the pre-resurrection Jesus has been inspired and influenced by the example of Paul, who at a later time became a forerunner of the risen and returning Lord. For evidence of this we can start by analyzing the three Old Testament texts Mark applies to John the Baptist.

These texts are presented as a single quotation from Isaiah, but the first part of that quotation (1:2) does not come from there. Instead, it appears to be a condensed combination of two other texts, one from Ex 23:20 ("Behold, I send an angel before you, to guard you on the way and to bring you to the place which I have prepared. Give heed to him and hearken to his voice, do not rebel against him, for he will not pardon your transgression; for my name is in him.") and one from Mal 3:1 ("Behold, I send my messenger to prepare the way before me, and the Lord whom you seek will suddenly come to his temple; the messenger of the covenant in whom you delight, behold, he is coming, says the Lord of hosts."). The Exodus text introduces the forerunner as "an angel" (an allusion to Moses) who is leading Israel into the *wilderness*, which as we shall see is a recurring theme in Mark. The passage in Malachi, after repeating the reference to "angel" (here translated "messenger"), mentions the coming Lord, another prominent theme in Mark. Both texts identify the forerunner as *angelos* (angel/messenger), which calls to mind Paul's characterization of himself as *angelos theou* (angel/messenger of God; Gal 4:14).

The continuation of Mark's Old Testament quotation in v.3 is indeed from Isaiah, from ch.40 of the Septuagint version. Here again we find that the message originates in the desert or wilderness.

Also of interest is the use of the term "way" (*hodos*), a technical term in Pauline circles for both the gospel message and those who follow it.[2] Of the three Old Testament texts, this was most important in Mark's mind, as is clear from the fact that he ascribed all three to "Isaiah the prophet" (1:2-3).

The relative importance of the passage from Isaiah becomes even clearer when one realizes that a text with the word *eutheias* (straight) in it was the perfect choice for Mark due to his remarkably frequent use of other forms of the same word, especially the adverb *euthys* (straightaway/immediately). The latter appears no less than 42 times in this short book, compared to only 12 times throughout the rest of the New Testament—so often that English translations ignore many of these 42 instances of the word because it is so repetitive and would not sound natural in English.[3] But the word should not be written off so lightly, as if Mark sprinkled his carefully planned gospel text with accidental and superfluous extras. In fact, the connection between the adverb *euthys* and the adjective *eutheias* found in 1:3 will have been unmistakable for Mark's hearers. The two words sound alike and are closely related in meaning.[4] Given the fact that the other form of the same adverb, *eutheos,* occurs 34 times in the New Testament but never in Mark, one may conclude that the choice of *euthys* was deliberately made because its link to the *eutheias* of Isaiah would be more apparent. Each of the 42 times Mark repeats this word he is effectively pointing out how this prophecy of Isaiah's is fulfilled. But why would he have chosen this particular word for such heavy emphasis? Here again, his apparent source is Paul who uses *eutheos* to describe his prompt obedience when God called him to

---

2 As in "way of the Lord"; see *Gal* 54-55.
3 Mk 1:10, 12, 18, 20, 21, 23, 28, 29, 30, 42, 43; 2:8, 12; 3:6; 4:5, 15, 16, 17, 29; 5:2, 29, 30, 42 (twice); 6:25, 27, 45, 50, 54; 7:25, 35; 8:10; 9: 15, 20, 24; 10:52; 11:2, 3; 14:43, 45, 72; 15:1. The other occurrences are in Mt 3:16; 13:20, 21; 14:27; 21:2, 3; 26:74; Lk 6:49; Jn 13:30, 32; 19:34; Acts 10:16.
4 In fact the masculine singular form of the feminine plural adjective *eutheias* is *euthys*, identical to the adverb.

preach the gospel of his Son to the Gentiles.[5] The word appears only once in Paul's correspondence, in Gal 1:16 (and many English translations ignore it here too, as they do *euthys* in Mark); all the other New Testament instances are found in books written after Mark. While adopting Paul's stress on the importance of "immediate" response to God's call from Paul, Mark chose a different form of the word Paul used in order to make his intended link to Isaiah 40:3 more apparent.

Further confirmation that the story of John preaching a baptism of repentance for the forgiveness of sins has been modelled after the story of Paul preaching a baptism into Christ can be found in parallels between the two individuals and their work. Paul described the central aspect of his own work as "preaching" (*kerysson*) and Mark uses the identical word for what John does. The focus of Paul's preaching was on baptism, and Mark presents that as so important for John that he gets the nickname "baptizer." Paul began his ministry in the "wilderness of the Gentiles,"[6] and Mark describes John's origins in the wilderness at length, supplementing his own account with scriptural quotations. Indeed, John's baptism and its very character as a new beginning for those baptized can be seen as reminiscent of the work of Paul in promoting baptism into Christ.

Of these similarities, the theme of the wilderness is a particularly significant one. For all ancient city-dwellers, the wilderness was the domain of punishment, exile, and death; and for Jews in particular it was the domain of the "nations," i.e., the Gentiles, who are sinners by definition and thus estranged from the true God and in need of repentance to find him.[7] But in the Old Testament the wilderness also became the place from which God proclaimed sal-

---

5   See the discussion of this adverb in *Gal* 6-7.
6   See below.
7   See *Gal* 83-84. The same Hebrew verb *šub* (return) is used to render the notion of repentance and coming back (to God). See also 1 Thess 1:9.

vation to Jerusalem, and to which he called the Jerusalemites to come for cleansing and rejuvenation.[8] And this is what we see happening in John's case, for "there went out to him *all the country of Judea, and all the people of Jerusalem*; and they were baptized by him in the river Jordan, *confessing their sins*" (1:5). Thus we can discern in John's location and in the remarks about who came to him an intent to invite the Jews to go out of Jerusalem and Judea in order to meet in the "wilderness (of the Gentiles)" the gospel that will unite them to God. And everyone whom John baptized accepted that baptism in order to gain a new beginning, just as the baptism preached by Paul was connected with acceptance of the gospel for the purpose of a new beginning.[9]

A synopsis of John's message will show more clearly the parallel between him and Paul. John's preaching is a call to *all* Judeans and Jerusalemites to await the Christ who comes from (Nazareth of) Galilee (v.9). It is consequently also a reminder to them that they are bound by a duty of obedience to this coming Christ, and only to the Christ specifically introduced by John; someone other than Jesus of Nazareth could call himself the Christ but would not be the one proclaimed by John.

In vv.6-7 John is equated with Elijah, whose reputation was well-established as representative of the Old Testament prophetic writings and as the forerunner of the Lord.[10] This is just as Paul perceived himself—as a messenger proclaiming the coming of the Lord. Also, John here proclaims, "After me comes he who is mightier than I, the thong of whose sandals *I am not worthy (ouk eimi hikanos)* to stoop down and untie." The italicized phrase is taken verbatim from 1 Corinthians (its only occurrence in a text earlier than Mark) where the context is an expression of humility

---

8 See e.g. Is 35:1-2; Jer 2:2, 6; 31:2; Ezek 34:25; Hos 2:14; 9:10; 13:4-5; Joel 2:22.
9 1 Cor 1:13-17. Its end or ultimate goal being the eschatological kingdom of God brought about by the risen Christ through the Holy Spirit; Rom 6 and 8.
10 See 2 Kg 1:8. See also below on Paul and Elijah, and *OTI2* 203-5.

by Paul similar to John the Baptist's declaration in Mark: "For I am the least of the apostles, unfit (*ouk eimi hikanos*) to be called an apostle, because I persecuted the church of God." (15:9)

Hints of the Future in Christ's Baptism

I mentioned earlier that in his portrayal of Jesus, Mark is more interested in conveying a message about Jesus as the Returning Lord than in presenting a "literal" history of his earthly life. As one example of this emphasis, consider the phrase "in those days" which in v.9 introduces Jesus' first appearance. This phrase is typical of the prophetic literature when reference is made to the Lord's coming and does not occur again in Mark until ch.13, whose subject matter is Christ's coming in glory. Moreover, Jesus' baptism is sealed by the descent of the divine Spirit, the evidence of Jesus' divine sonship and lordship.[11] Finally, the divine statement made to Jesus (v.11) is cast in the form of a protocol from Ps 2:7 used at the enthronement of a king, in which the king is given the title "Son of God." Mark's language, however, does not merely borrow from Ps 2:7 but also resembles portions of Gal 1:16 where Paul states that God "was *pleased* to reveal his Son *in me*" (Gal 1:16). The impression that Galatians was a source for Mark is strengthened by another phrase Mark uses at this point: "my beloved Son" (*ho huios mou ho agapetos*). This appears three times, exclusively in reference to Isaac, in the entire Old Testament (LXX Gen 22:2, 12, 16), all in the story about God's command that Abraham sacrifice him. It can hardly be a coincidence that in Galatians Paul discusses Isaac, presenting him as the image of true sonship to God and of innocent suffering (4:28-29). Since Paul viewed himself as a son of Abraham and of God after the manner of Isaac, and since this sonship to God was both made possible and put into effect through the agency of Christ (4:4-7), Mark

11 See Rom 1:4.

presented the sonship of Jesus, the unique[12] Son of God, in the same terms. The scene was thus set for the suffering of this unique son, which is a—if not *the*—central theme of Mark's gospel.

The Battle in the Wilderness

Just as Paul went to Arabia rather than Jerusalem immediately after the divine revelation that made him an apostle to the Gentiles (Gal 1:16), Jesus was "driven out" by the Spirit into the wilderness, away from Jerusalem (in whose proximity he was at the Jordan river).[13] And there, in the wilderness where the true God really appears,[14] takes place the eschatological battle between the Lord and his angels against Satan and the apocalyptic "beasts" (*theria*). The English "beasts" does not convey the apocalyptic connotations of the Greek word. In the New Testament, by far its most common usage (37 times) is in the singular *therion* in the apocalyptic book of Revelation where it refers to Satan or his representative. And the context of Acts 28:4, 5 where *therion* refers to a "creature" that Paul "shook off in the fire, and suffered no harm" after his escape from the "raging sea," is very close to that of Revelation and thus also has apocalyptic overtones.[15] The fact that in Mark 1:12-13 neither Satan nor the beasts could defeat Jesus shows that God indeed "put all things in subjection under his feet" (1 Cor 15:27), and it is thus as a victor that he then proceeds to Galilee in v.14.

The Journey to Galilee

The observation that Jesus' journey to Galilee did not take place until *after* the arrest of John the Baptist that led to his death (v.14) is

---

12 The LXX *agapetos* of Gen 22:2, 14, 16 is the translation of the Hebrew *yahid* meaning "unique; only."

13 See my comments in *Gal* 51 on the proximity of Arabia to Jerusalem.

14 "Forty days" is a clear reference to Israel's wandering after exodus in the wilderness where God appears to Moses.

15 There are four other occurrences. Tit 1:12 and Heb 12:20 are quotations. In Acts 11:6 and Jas 3:7 it is part of an enumeration of animals and so does mean simply wild animals.

not offered merely to give chronological information about these two events. Indeed, the remark seems out of place here since the actual arrest and death of John are related five chapters later, in 6:14-29. But the otherwise curious comment makes sense if one understands it as an oblique reference to Paul's death and an assertion that Christ's return would come soon after that, which precisely fits the historical background for the writing of Mark's gospel.

This interpretation can be carried a step further. Jesus preached a gospel of repentance and faith in Galilee (1:14-15), just as Paul did among the Gentiles. However, one aspect of Jesus' preaching in these verses is unique: the fact that its hearers are called to have faith, not in "God" or "Christ," but in *the gospel*. The phrase "believe in the gospel" is definitely not Pauline—Paul speaks of faith in Christ—and cannot be found anywhere else at all in the New Testament. The only way to make sense of it is to understand it as a reference Mark is making to his own written gospel. In other words, since Christ is not physically present, and now that Paul himself too is gone, the Christ in whom believers are to believe can only be found in the gospel Paul preached, and this gospel, *the* gospel, is now accessible in this writing of Mark which he has explicitly dubbed "the gospel" (1:1). Thus, the hearers of Mark's words are asked to believe in these words that carry Paul's gospel for them. My understanding is corroborated by the fact that only in Mark do we find full parallelism—in fact, functional identity—between the person of Jesus and the gospel: "For whoever would save his life will lose it; and whoever loses his life for my sake and the gospel's will save it;" (8:35) "Truly, I say to you, there is no one who has left house or brothers or sisters or mother or father or children or lands, for my sake and for the sake of the gospel..." (10:29) What Mark has done here is similar to what was done in the Old Testament, where God was made into a word.[17] Mark is transforming Paul's Christ into a writ; he is scripturalizing, canonizing Paul's teaching.

17 See *OT12* 87-90, 127-8; 132, 213-4; also Deut 30:11-14 and Ps 119.

12

The First Cycle of Calling (1:16-3:12)

The Call to the Pillars

The first part of Mark's gospel (1:16-8:20) comprises a series of stories of apostolic calling by Jesus, all of which follow the historical sequence of events in Paul's life that we learn about from Galatians. The first cycle begins with Jesus "passing along by the Sea of Galilee," which in Mark symbolizes the Roman (Mediterranean) sea, the domain of the Gentiles.[1] It is there that he encounters Simon and Andrew "*amphiballontas* in the sea" (v.16). There is a play on words in the Greek here. English translations render the word by "casting a net" or something similar, based on the literal meaning of the verb as "to throw around," its frequent use in reference to nets, and the following phrase "in the sea"—but in fact there is no noun for "net" in the Greek text. The omission of "net" is not to be ignored, for the verb *amphiballo* without an object also carries the meaning "to vacillate/to be doubtful," which would make it a particularly apt allusion to the apostles' behavior in regard to Paul and his gospel, especially to that of Simon/Peter/Cephas as it is described in Gal 2:1-14.

As for Jesus' promise to make Simon and Andrew "fishers of men," the inspiration for the latter phrase comes from Ezekiel. This book was important for Mark due to its vision of the new Jerusalem, an eschatological vision that shaped Mark's own view of the future after Christ's return. In Ezekiel's view the future community of God's people would be based upon the temple

---

1   The bases for drawing this conclusion about the symbolic significance of the Sea of Galilee, are presented many times throughout my comments below.

(47:1-48:28),[2] and Jerusalem itself within the new community would be equivalent to the holy of holies (48:30-35). In a key passage located before the description of the land (47:13-23) and its division among the tribes (48:1-28), we read:

> Then he brought me back to the door of the temple; and behold, water was issuing from below the threshold of the temple toward the east (for the temple faced east); and the water was flowing down from below the south end of the threshold of the temple, south of the altar. Then he brought me out by way of the north gate, and led me round on the outside to the outer gate, that faces toward the east; and the water was coming out on the south side. Going on eastward with a line in his hand, the man measured a thousand cubits, and then led me through the water; and it was ankle-deep. Again he measured a thousand, and led me through the water; and it was knee-deep. Again he measured a thousand, and led me through the water; and it was up to the loins. Again he measured a thousand, and it was a river that I could not pass through, for the water had risen; it was deep enough to swim in, a river that could not be passed through. And he said to me, "Son of man, have you seen this?" Then he led me back along the bank of the river. As I went back, I saw upon the bank of the river very many trees on the one side and on the other. And he said to me, "This water flows toward the eastern region [LXX *into/toward Galilee* which is toward the eastern region] and goes down into the Arabah [LXX *Arabia*]; and when it enters the stagnant waters of the sea, the water will become fresh. And wherever the river goes every living creature which swarms will live, and *there will be very many fish;* for this water goes there, that the waters of the sea may become fresh; so everything will live where the river goes. *Fishermen will stand beside the sea;* from Engedi to Eneglaim *it will be a place for the spreading of nets; its fish will be of very many kinds, like the fish of the Great Sea...*" (47:1-13)

What Paul tried to do his entire life, Mark too is attempting to accomplish, by having Jesus invite the vacillating Simon to follow him out of Jerusalem into the land of the Gentiles, following the path of Ezekiel's life-giving waters and for the purpose of bringing the good news of Ezekiel's "new Jerusalem"[3] to the Gentiles.[4]

Jesus then does the same with James and John, whose names recall the "pillars" that met with Paul at the Jerusalem meeting (Gal 2:1-10). They too are immediately put in a negative light in that they are the sons of "Zebedee" and are together with the "hirelings" (*misthotoi*). The latter term is clearly intended to express something beyond mere historical fact; in the entire New Testament it occurs only here and in Jn 10:12-13 where it also carries a negative connotation: "He who is a hireling and not a shepherd, whose own the sheep are not, sees the wolf coming and leaves the sheep and flees; and the wolf snatches them and scatters them. He flees because he is a hireling and cares nothing for the sheep."

The name Zebedee strengthens the impression that "hireling" carries negative connotations here, for in Hebrew it is virtually the same name as Zabdi,[5] a name that in Joshua 7:1-26 belongs to a Judahite who acts in his own self-interest as a mercenary rather than fully and freely at the service of God. Thus James and John, the Jerusalemites and thus Judahites, are presented as "the sons of"—which is a Semitic expression meaning "of the same kind," "similar to," "of the party of"—the Judahite Zabdi.

A "Pauline" Tour with the Pillars

Having invited Simon, James, and John, "the pillars," Jesus takes them along Paul's path. First they go into Capernaum, into a syna-

---

3 Paul speaks of the "Jerusalem above" in Gal 4:26.
4 The appellation "son of man," so highly controversial in scholarship, was also most likely drawn from the book of Ezekiel. The first time that title occurs is in 2:1-12, where Mark draws a parallel between Paul's confrontation with the "pillars" in Jerusalem and Jesus' confrontation with the scribes in Capernaum (see below). This parallel is part of a broader scheme I point out in the Introduction: Mark is comparing Paul's bringing the gospel from the Gentile domain to Jerusalem with Ezekiel's proclamation of God's word to Jerusalem from Babylonia.
5 The Hebrew alphabet contains only consonants, and the consonants of these two names are identical.

gogue on a sabbath (1:21-28); this is what Paul usually did. Capernaum in Aramaic means "the village of grace," which to a Jew would connote Judaism itself, the domain of the Jews to whom God's grace was granted in the *torah*. Jesus challenges the teaching of their scribes, presenting them with a new authoritative teaching as only the Messiah, the Holy One of God, could offer. And yet, just as the Jerusalemite leaders did to Paul, they interpreted the teaching he offered them as an attempt to "destroy" them as a separate Judaic entity. After this, Jesus' fame spread everywhere throughout the surrounding region of Galilee, just as Paul's did among the Gentiles.

Then there is the encounter with the "pillars" at their own "house," an event reminiscent of Paul's journey to a council with the "pillars" at their "house" in Jerusalem (1:28-34). Paul too traveled to a "household"—the Jewish church headquartered in Jerusalem— that in his view lay sick and in need of healing. Why is it Simon's "mother-in-law" who is the sick person? The word "mother" would have been a more typical metaphor for a household in general. The reason is that in Aramaic as well as Hebrew there is assonance between *hamah* (mother-in-law) and *hommah* (fever); this is a play on words suggesting that Simon's household is not just coincidentally sick but fundamentally so, i.e., by its nature sick or headed in the wrong direction.[6]

After healing the sick Jesus "went out and went away" (*exelthen kai apelthen*) to a "place of wilderness" (*eremon topon*), and there he prayed. To make out of the wilderness (of the nations)[7] an acceptable "place of prayer" is precisely what Paul set out to do, beginning with Antioch, after the Jerusalem meeting. But before long Peter, and with him the rest of the Jews (Gal 2:13), took a

---

6 The image of the fundamentally sick household is continued by the healings of the sick and demon-possessed who gathered around Jesus from "the whole city" in vv.33-34.

7 Like the sea of Galilee, which throughout Mark represents the Roman sea (the Mediterranean) and thus the land of the Gentiles, the "wilderness" also throughout Mark—as will become clear below—is a reference to the land of the Gentiles.

stand against him, and ever after he was continually beset by his opponents. This is precisely what is reflected in 1:36-37: "And Simon and those who were with him pursued (*katedioxen*) him, and they found him and said to him, 'All are searching for (*zetousin*) you'." The verb *katadioko* means literally "to pursue (with the aim of hurting), to hunt down," and thus "to persecute," and is found only here in the New Testament. The parallel verb *zeto* carries similar connotations, which is confirmed by its use elsewhere in Mark: out of nine occurrences, five are connected with an intention to kill Jesus and two with the aim of challenging his teaching.[8] That *everyone* is after Jesus means they all had opposed or abandoned him, just as Paul's contemporaries did to him. But Jesus, like Paul and for the same reason, persisted in the face of opposition because "that is why I came out (*exelthon*), that I may preach (*keryxo*) there also" (v.38).

Paul's Conversion

The following set of stories (1:40-3:12) is a more developed rendition of the first one. It begins with the story of a leper, a member of the most abject class of outcasts in the Old Testament, who ends up becoming a broadcaster of "the (gospel) word."[9] This is none other than Paul's own story as told by Paul himself.[10] The leper was given the task of being "a testimony to them" (*eis martyrion autois*),[11] i.e., to "the priest" and those around him, which sounds like what Paul became to James and his entourage. But this leper did not go directly to the "city" of Capernaum,[12] a symbol

8 Mk 11:18; 12:12; 14:1, 11, 55; Mk 8:11, 12.
9 The RSV translates *ho logos* (the word) in 1:45 as "it," i.e., meaning his healing, but this does not fit the context and obscures the significance of "the word" as a technical term; see below.
10 See Gal 1:13-17; see also 2:15-16.
11 The RSV rendering "for a proof to the people" is a misleading paraphrase. The same RSV translates the same exact expression *eis martyrion autois* as "for a testimony against them" in 6:11 and as "to bear testimony before them" in 13:9.
12 The city is identified in 1:21 and 2:1; it is mentioned without the name also in 1:33.

of the domain of Judaism. Instead, he began by "proclaiming much and spreading the word, so that Jesus could no longer openly go into (the) city but stayed outside in places of wilderness, and people came to him from all over."[13] The combination here of the words and phrases "go out," "begin," "proclaim," "the word," "outside," and "places of wilderness" is strongly reminiscent of accounts of Paul's proclamation of the gospel among the Gentiles in Acts. And the result of this preaching is that Jesus finds it difficult to enter Capernaum—just as Paul experienced the hostility of Jerusalem once his gospel began to spread.

A Showdown with the Jewish Leaders

Both the circumstances of Jesus' confrontation with the scribes in Capernaum (2:1-12) and the language Mark uses to relate it leave us with several clues that, taken together, indicate this story was patterned after the story of Paul's confrontation with the Jerusalemite Christian leaders as told in Gal 2:1-14:

1) Jesus enters Capernaum "after [some] days" (2:1). This expression *di' hemeron* is composed of the noun *hemeron* (days) in the genitive case preceded by the preposition *dia*. The normal meaning of *dia* is "through"; with a genitive noun specifying a period of time the sense is usually "throughout," as can be seen in Acts 1:3. Rarely is the word *dia* used to mean "after," and in the four gospels we find it that way only here and in Mk 14:58//Mt 26:61. Since the Matthew text is dependent on Mark, that means only Mark uses *dia* in this unique way—and in the rest of the New Testament only Paul uses it this way. Moreover, the sole instance of *dia* meaning "after" in Paul's epistles is in Gal 2:1 (*dia dekatessaron eton*) in a context remarkably similar to this one: "after

---

13 The RSV translation here again is a misleading paraphrase rather than an accurate rendition of the original *exelthon erxato keryssein polla kai diaphemizein ton logon, hoste meketi auton dynasthai phneros eis polin eiselthein, all' exo ep' eremois topois en, kai erkhonto pros auton pantothen.*

14 years" Paul goes to Jerusalem where he will confront the Jerusalem Christian leaders; "after some days" Jesus goes into Capernaum where he will confront the scribes.[14]

2) The expression "and he was preaching the word to them" (2:2) corresponds to "and I laid before them the gospel which I preach among the Gentiles" in Gal 2:2.[15]

3) The house in Capernaum (2:1) corresponds to Simon's house (1:28), which as I indicate above represents the Jerusalem church. Consequently, the four carrying the paralytic would represent none other than the four apostles who are "called" in 1:16-20, 29: Simon, James, Andrew, and John. These (excepting Andrew) are the "pillars" of Gal 2:1-14.

4) The confrontation between Jesus and the scribes revolves around Jesus' authority, a theme which Mark has already mentioned twice in 1:22 and 27. Likewise, Paul's purpose in recounting the short history of his apostleship in Gal 2:1-14 is to defend his apostolic authority by showing how he acquired it—directly from God without human intervention, just as Jesus does—and how he used it to defend the gospel, as Jesus does in this conflict.

5) The result of the conflict is that "all" those gathered at Capernaum, signifying the church of Jerusalem and Judea, "glorified God," which brings to mind Gal 1:22-24 where we have Paul's description of how "the churches of Christ in Judea" reacted to him and his gospel.

One may conclude that the "crowd" of v.4 may well be a reference to the Gentiles, which will be corroborated later in v.13. The

---

14 The context is quite different in Mk 14:58: the hostile witnesses against Jesus are quoted as saying he claimed he would destroy the temple and raise it "after three days." See also *Gal* 6-7 for similar instances where a literary peculiarity of Paul's is reproduced elsewhere, particularly *eutheos* (immediately) and *he Syria kai he Kilikia* (Syria and Cilicia). The latter offers especially strong evidence that a Pauline text is being quoted verbatim.

15 Notice the use of the same verb *lalo* in Mk 2:2 and 7. Here again the RSV is misleading by using "was preaching" and "speaks," respectively. See also comments on 1:4-5.

reason then that the "four" were "not able" to draw near to him (v.4) may well be due to his mingling with the Gentiles, which was not allowed in the Judaism represented by James. Both these conclusions will be corroborated in the following pericope.

Table Fellowship

Thereafter, Jesus "goes out" "along the sea" (*para ten thalassan*). Since the latter expression is the same as in 1:16 where the "sea" is the "Roman sea," we may conclude that the setting where Jesus finds Levi—in other words, a Levite—and makes him a disciple (2:13-17) is Gentile territory. By the same token, the "crowd" Jesus was teaching is a reference to the Gentiles. The finding of a Levite in a Gentile land symbolizes the transfer of the unique holiness of Jerusalem and its temple service to the Gentiles. Not only that, but it is there that true discipleship starts, where "sinners" sit at table with the Holy One of God.[16] As Jesus explains, "I came not to call the righteous, but sinners." Jesus' determination to sit at table with "sinners" and the outraged responses of the "scribes" present a clear parallel in both content and terminology with the account in Gal 2:11-17 of Paul's determination to partake of table fellowship with Gentiles,[17] and the attempt by "men from James" to keep all Jews including him from doing so.

Closely connected to the issue of table-fellowship is that of Judaic rules prohibiting or allowing various foods,[18] which we find discussed in the subsequent pericope (2:18-22). Following Paul's teaching, if Jesus is the Messiah, then both Jews and Gentiles gather at his table as equal household members according to his household rules. The applicable rules will be those of the eschatological banquet that is usually spoken of in terms of a marriage

16 It is in 2:15 that we encounter for the first time the term "disciples of Jesus."
17 See my discussion of the equivalence between "Gentile" and "sinner" in Judaism, in *Gal* 83-84.
18 See 1 Cor 8; 10:23-33. See also Gal 2:12.

feast where the bridegroom is the Messiah himself.[19] At that feast
the rules are summed up in one law, *his* Law that requires love of
one's neighbor[20]—and every person dining at such a banquet is
the neighbor of every other person.[21] Immediately after the discussion of fast and feast, the statement is made about the utter incompatibility between the old and the new, the impossibility of
getting them to stay together, and thus the inevitability of a break
between them (vv.21-22), which is precisely what Gal 2:15-20 is
all about: the need to completely set aside the old (allegiance to
the Law) as a prerequisite for moving forward with the new (allegiance to Christ).[22]

The idea of a break is carried into the following passage
(2:23-28). Right at the outset it tells us that the disciples "began
to make (their) way by plucking the heads of grain" on the sabbath. There is no hint here that the disciples are picking the grain
in order to eat it; they are doing so just for the purpose of making
their way.[23] What they were doing that the Pharisees objected to,
then, is "making a way," and more specifically making a "new"
way: the word "way" connotes the "way" of the gospel,[24] and "began" emphasizes the newness of this "way."[25] In 2:15 the disciples
broke with the past by sharing table fellowship with sinners, and
here they are breaking the rules of Judaism once again. This time,
by doing something forbidden on the sabbath they are behaving

---

19 Mt 22:1-14// Lk 14:7-14; Mt 25:1-14; Jn 3:28-29; Rev 19:7, 9. See also 2 Cor
11:2; 21:2, 9; 22:17.
20 Rom 13:8-10; Gal 5:13-15; 6:1-2.
21 1 Cor 11:17-33.
22 A few examples are the remark warning against "building up what has been torn
down," the one about "dying to the Law in order to live for God," and the statement
that "it is no longer I who live but Christ lives in me." See *Gal* 81-89.
23 RSV mistranslates v.23. It has "as they made their way his disciples began to pluck
heads of grain" instead of "his disciples began to make (themselves) a way by/while
plucking the heads of grain."
24 See *Gal* 54-55 and Mk 6:8; 8:3, 27; 9:33-34; 10:17, 32; 11:18; 12:14.
25 This verb calls to mind its use with "the gospel" (1:1) which is the "new way" to be
followed by the disciples.

as only priests would, though they are not themselves priests.[26] Since the sabbath also represents the day of Israel's gathering around God's word, their actions symbolize the creation of a new gathering apart from, and not necessarily sanctioned by, the Jerusalem temple. Jesus then himself authorizes their actions by considering it equivalent to what the priests, authorized representatives of the temple, did in the past (v.26).[27] And the source of his authority is again ascribed to the lordship of "the son of man," which is now explicitly extended to the institution of the sabbath.

Empowering the Powerless

Mk 3:1-6 takes us back to the domain of Judaism through its mention of the synagogue of 1:21.[28] There Jesus empowers someone considered powerless or without voice by the authorities of Judaism (in the Old Testament "hand" signifies power or ability),[29] just as Paul gave equal voice and equal status to the Gentiles in the Messianic community. The combination of "wrath" (*orge*) and "hardening/hardness of heart" (*porosis tes kardias*) in 3:5 betrays its source, Romans. In that letter, written as his last endeavor to sway Jerusalem to fully accept the gospel, Paul speaks extensively of God's wrath upon the Jew who does not abide by God's will due to his "hardness" (*sklerotes*) and his impenitent "heart" (*kardia*) and refers to Israel's rejection of the gospel as "hardening/hardness" (*porosis*).[30] Mark's mention of "hardening of heart" in 3:5 coupled with the decision to "destroy" Jesus is an indication that the Jerusalem leaders actually did ultimately reject Paul's gospel even after his death.[31]

---

26 These actions and Jesus' words presume that there is no longer any differentiation between priest and layperson, i.e., between holy and unholy. Compare with the pericope on Levi in vv.13-17; see also my comments on Zech 14:20-21 in "Israel and the Nations," *St Vladimir's Theological Quarterly*, 38.2 (1994) 187-88.

27 See above on Mk 2:13-17.

28 Notice the "again" in 3:1.

29 See *OTI3* 58.

30 Rom 2:5, 8; 3:5; 4:15; 5:9; 11:7, 25.

31 On this issue see also the Introduction and my comments on 1:24 and on Philippians.

The Gospel Settles outside Jerusalem within the Confines of the Roman Empire

The result was that the gospel message was "shut out" from Jerusalem and consequently remained in the domain of Gentile Christianity into which everyone, including the Jerusalemites and Judahites, was invited. This is what the following pericope that concludes the first cycle (3:7-12) is all about. "And Jesus," the Messiah of Jerusalem, "with his disciples departed toward the *sea* and a great multitude from Galilee followed; *also from Judea and Jerusalem* and Idumea and from beyond the Jordan and from about Tyre and Sidon a great multitude, hearing all that he did, *came to him.*" The "sea" here is again the Roman sea, land of the Gentiles who are again referred to as "the crowd" (v.9). That is Jesus' destination, and those who would be his followers must go there also, including the Jews of Judea and Jerusalem. Just as they followed John the Baptist to the wilderness, they must follow Jesus to the Gentile land. It is there, in the domain of the Gentiles, that Jesus is confessed as "the Son of God," the Messiah.

Yet "he strictly ordered them not to make him 'known' (phaneron)." The term *phaneron* means "appearing in the open" and is also used to speak of Jesus' future coming in glory.[32] For the time being and until his coming, Jesus was to be confessed as he was preached in the gospel: God's crucified Messiah. God, and only God, would be able to make him "appear in the open," and God would do that in his own time.

---

32 1 Cor 3:13; 4:5; 2 Cor 5:10-11; Col 3:4.

13

The Second Cycle of Calling

The Call to the Apostles

The second cycle (Mk 3:13-6:6a) starts as the first did, with an apostolic call (3:13-19). The call in the first cycle took place "along the sea of Galilee," and the mountain from which Jesus calls here must be neither in nor near Jerusalem, but rather located in the same Galilee, representing the land of the Gentiles. The key word here is *apelthon* (they "went away" to him): one would "go up" to Jerusalem, not "go away" to it, and the same verb describes the disciples movement into the "wilderness"—another symbol for Gentile land—in 6:30-44.

The number of the apostles, twelve, is symbolic and refers to the totality of Israel. The first three are none other than the "pillars" of Gal 2:1-10. Indeed, Jesus expressly gives Simon, James, and John a special position by giving them, and only them, "surnames." "Peter" is the Greek counterpart of the Aramaic Cephas, but what about "sons of thunder"? I believe this appellation was intended to be taken as roughly equivalent to, or in the same class as, "Peter." The Greek name *Petros* derives from the noun *petra,* meaning "rock" or "mountain." Thunder is connected with the epiphanies of God on his mountain. In either case the reference would be to a position of authority in (the mountain) Jerusalem.

At the other end of the list of apostolic names we have another, complementary view of the same James and Simon, as the ones who ultimately betrayed Jesus and his message. This James is said to be the son of Alphaeus, i.e., the "brother" of Levi (2:14) and thus the "priest"[1] of the Jewish believers in Jesus as the Christ. Though Jesus relocated the new "priesthood" "along the sea" in

---

1 See my comments on Mk 1:44.

153

the land of the Gentiles,[2] James wants to chain it to Jerusalem. Simon is here the *Kananaios,* which means the zealot in Aramaic and alludes to the party of those who were stirring up Judea and Jerusalem to rise in armed revolt against Rome.

The last apostle's name, Judah (Judas in most English translations), as directly as possible refers to the Jews of Judea.[3] His surname *Iskarioth* is an Aramaic transliteration of the Latin *sicarius,* meaning one carrying a *sica* (sword), and thus corresponds to *Kananaios.* The connection between "Simon" and "Judah" is intentional and reflects what Cephas/Peter did at Antioch: according to Paul, Peter was trying to compel the Gentiles "to live like Jews" (*ioudaizein*; Gal 2:14). The verb *ioudaizein* was coined by Paul from the name *Iouda* (Judah).

Betrayal and Separation

Although Jesus "desired" (3:13) that James and Peter be his top apostles, they nevertheless betrayed him. That betrayal took place in Antioch (Gal 2:11-17), and the following pericope (3:20-30) is set against this background. Consider the following:

1) The "crowd" that gathers "again" around Jesus is none other than the crowd of the Gentiles.[4] This means that Jesus was inviting his apostles back to Gentile land which he considered to be as much his "home" (v.19) as Judaism was. But the apostles "could not even eat bread" there, i.e., were unable to engage in full table fellowship with the Gentiles due to, as will be seen in v.21, the pressure of their "kinfolk."[5] The relatives' role is central to the

2 On the phrase "along the sea," see comments on Mk 1:13-14.
3 *Iouda* is the Greek rendering of the Hebrew *yehudah.* It is the name of the patriarch Judah as well as of the kingdom, and later province, of Judah.
4 See comments on 2:4, 13 and 3:9.
5 See point 3 below where I point out that the kinfolk, "having heard," made an extreme accusation against Jesus, saying that he had lost his mind, and they were planning to seize him. What could they have heard about, except what is referred to in v.20, that he was meeting with the "crowd"? And if that were all, why the addition that he and his disciples could not eat? It is not the mere size of the crowd since later he multiplies the bread twice to a very large number.

next point I will bring up, but here in v.19 it is worth noticing the theme of not being able to share in a meal. That theme is central to Gal 2:11-14, where Peter and Barnabas were convinced by James' emissaries that sharing meals with Gentiles was not allowed for Jews.

2) The expression in 3:21 rendered "family" by RSV is *hoi par' autou*. Literally "those from him," it is an idiomatic expression meaning "those from his side/his party" or "those related to him in some way." These "relatives" of Jesus went out to seize him, for they[6] said that he "was beside himself." The verb translated by that phrase is *exeste*; it means literally "to stand outside" and can be used in that sense also. The general idea is that Jesus' kinfolk considered that he had put himself outside the family (of Israel) by having table fellowship with outsiders.[7] And since the kinsfolk are then identified as "scribes who came down from Jerusalem," we have a clear parallel to the scene described in Gal 2:11-14.

3) The text of Mark dwells at length on the theme of a schism within one household, while in Galatians the result of the arrival of "men from James" was a schism in the church of Antioch (Gal 2:11-14). There ensues in Mark a debate between Jesus and his opponents whom he castigates as being the real sinners (vv.28-30) after they make accusations against him; this corresponds to Galatians as a whole, in which Paul is defending himself against accusations and responds by proclaiming *anathema* against his accusers.[8]

4) The acuteness of the altercation is reflected in the incompatibility of the two stands: Jesus and the scribes each declare the other as being against God's spirit—the scribes consider Jesus to be an agent of Satan, possessed by an unclean spirit, while he considers them to be guilty of an "eternal sin" precisely because they made such accusations. The central theme throughout Galatians is likewise one of incompatible stands, as Paul proclaims there is

6 And not "people" as the RSV has it.
7 See Gal 2:15-17 and *Gal* 81-86.
8 See especially Gal 1:8-9; 5:4.

only one gospel, asserts that anyone who preaches any other version is accursed, and goes on to show that his and only his version is founded on scripture, while anyone who disagrees will be permanently cut off from Christ. [9]

The following story (3:31-35) returns to the theme of enmity between Jesus and his own relatives. Where earlier the relatives accuse him of "standing outside," here their own status of being effectively "outside" relative to Jesus is stressed:

> And *his mother and his brothers* came; and standing *outside* they sent to him and called him. And a crowd was sitting around him (*peri auton*); and they said to him, 'Your *mother and your brothers* who are *outside* are *asking for* you.'

The last italicized phrase, "asking for," renders the Greek verb *zetousin*, which as I showed in my comments on 1:36 has negative connotations in Mark, suggesting an intention to harm. Considering this passage along with the previous one, the impression one gets is that the original "relatives" of Jesus put themselves "outside" the real community of his followers by perverting or misrepresenting the gospel—which is what Paul's opponents stand accused of throughout Galatians.[10] But like Paul against his Jewish opponents, Jesus stood his ground, and the "crowd" (of the Gentiles) that sat "around him" (*peri auton*)—as opposed to those "from him/his relatives" (*par' autou*; 3:21)—stayed with him, thereby becoming his new family, a family taught by him to do the "will of God."[11]

Teaching in Parables

What follows these two pericopes is a new beginning: "Again he *began* to teach *along* (*para*) *the sea*. And a very large crowd gathered toward (*pros*) him, so that he got into a boat and sat in the sea; and the whole crowd was [oriented] toward (*pros*) the sea on

---

9   See Gal 1:6-9; 5:4; and *Gal* 80-81.
10 See especially Gal 1:6-9.
11 *thelema tou theou* is an expression Paul uses most often in reference to his apostleship (1 Cor 1:1; 2 Cor 1:1; Gal 1:4) or his apostolic work (Rom 1:10; 15:32; 2 Cor 8:5; 1 Thess 4:3; and very probably 1 Cor 16:12).

the land."[12] We have seen this terminology before (2:13; 3:23; 3:9),[13] but this time Jesus sits *in* the sea and the people *on the land* turn *toward* him. That is to say, Jesus' new center from which he teaches his entire Messianic community has moved out of Jerusalem and into the Roman empire at large; it is from there, and not Jerusalem, that *his* teaching (4:2), which carries divine authority,[14] originates. But this is just a new example of the New Testament following the pattern and example set by the Old: it was from the wilderness of Sinai that God's word in the *torah* was carried into Canaan, and it was from the foreign land of Babylonia that God's prophetic word was addressed to Jerusalem.[15]

After this comes the parable of the sower (4:3-20), and here again Mark leaves ample evidence that he intends to make a reference to Paul's teaching. A series of observations when considered together point firmly in this direction:

1) The choice of a parable dealing with sowing may have been triggered by Paul's use of the image of God's field to describe the nature of an apostle's work.[16]

2) The correlation between the seed in the parable (4:3-8) and those who hear the word in the parable's explanation (4:13-20), recalls the Pauline teaching that believers in the gospel are the product of the apostolic word, effectively the apostle's children or his "seed."[17]

---

12 RSV mistranslates several prepositions in this verse in the interest of making the English sound more natural; it also inserts an "it" in the phrase "sat in the sea."

13 Common words or phrases are "again," "teach," "along the sea," "unto him," "all the crowd/the whole crowd" (*pas ho okhlos*), "began," "boat."

14 Compare with 1:22 where we have the same expression "his teaching." Also notice the "Listen!" of 4:3 corresponding to the only other "listen" in Mark that occurs in the pericope of the transfiguration (9:2-8) where the divine voice orders Peter, James, and John: "This is my beloved Son; listen to him." (v.7)

15 See the Introduction.

16 1 Cor 3:9.

17 1 Cor 4:14; 2 Cor 6:13; Gal 4:19; Phil 2:22; 1 Thess 2:7, 11. Both the Hebrew *zera'* and the Greek *sperma*, meaning seed, are used in the Old Testament to refer to someone's progeny. This was taken up in the New Testament writings (Mt 22:24//Mk 12:29//Lk 20:28; Lk 1:55; Jn 7:42; 8:33, 37; Rom 9:7-8; 2 Cor 11:22 Gal 3:16, 19, 29; Rev 12:17).

3) Some of the seed fell on "rocky ground." The Greek *petrodes* (rocky) is closely related to the name *Petros* (Peter),[18] and this similarity can hardly be an accident, especially in light of the characterization of these people as being "scandalized when tribulation or persecution arises on account of the word" (v.17).[19] This is precisely what happened with Peter in Antioch (Gal 2:11-14). The explanation for this behavior, lack of "root" (*rhiza*), recalls the use of a "root" and "branches" metaphor in Rom 11:16-18.

4) Next come those in whom the seed "did not yield fruit," its explanation being that in these recipients the word "becomes fruitless" due to the love of riches. A reference to James would naturally follow one to Peter, and indeed it was James who considered that the riches God had granted Israel were only his to dispose of,[20] with the result that the Jewish church remained fruitless, failing to expand beyond Jerusalem and Judea. Paul, on the other hand, proclaimed that, "For there is no distinction between Jew and Greek; the same Lord is Lord of all and *bestows his riches* upon *all* who call upon him." (Rom 10:12)

5) The Roman empire at large, where Christ's teaching was firmly planted through Paul's preaching, became "the good earth/land" (*he ge he kale*) instead of Judea (the "good land" of the Old Testament).[21] This new "good land," the one that is "bearing fruit"[22] is none other than the land on which the "whole crowd" sat, listening to Jesus delivering his teaching while "in the sea" (4:1).

18 The Aramaic Cephas also means rock, and the Greek *Petros* is from *petra* (rock).
19 The RSV mistranslates *skandalizontai* as "fall away."
20 See further my comments on 10:17-31 and 12:41-44.
21 Ex 3:8; Num 14:7; Deut 1:25, 35; 4:22; 6:18; 8:7, 10; 9:6; 11:17; Josh 23:13, 15, 16.
22 Notice the imperfect tense here and in the corresponding *epheren* (was bearing) in v.8. The choice of the imperfect indicates the ongoing nature of the gospel's fruitfulness among the Gentiles. However, the verb "to sow," when used in regard to the good land, is in the aorist (the participle *sparentes*; v.20), meaning a one-time action. On the other hand, we have a present participle for "to sow" (*speiromenoi*) where it applies to those that did not bear fruit (vv.16 and 18). The connotation is that Paul's Gentiles have accepted the gospel and have been bearing fruit ever since, while it must continually be offered to Peter and James and their followers.

6) The participles *auxanomenon* (increasing/growing) and *karpophoroumenon* (bearing fruit) appear together here (vv.8 and 20) and in only two other places in the New Testament—Col 1:6 and 10—both times used in the same sense as they are here, once in reference to the gospel and the other time to those who believe in it.[23]

Yet, as Paul taught, the ultimate verdict regarding the bearing of fruits will be postponed until the Lord's coming as a judge,[24] and that is the theme of the following parable (4:21-23) and saying (vv.24-25). The lamp in the parable "comes" (*erkhetai*) in order to symbolize how all things will be "made manifest" (*phanerothe*) and will eventually "come into the open" (*elthe eis phaneron*). The verb "come" alludes to the Lord's "coming"; indeed, how could a lamp come, unless the lamp is in fact Christ himself?[25] Likewise, in Paul's epistles the adjective *phaneron* (along with verbal forms based on it, such as *phanerothe*) describes Jesus' future coming in glory.[26] The Pauline connection can also be detected in the use of the cognate words "hid" (*krypton*) and "secret" (*apokryphon*) in v.22, which occur several times in Paul's epistles in passages dealing with the same subject.[27] Moreover, the fact that the parable is intended to convey a message not necessarily made obvious by the literal meaning of its words is indicated by the remark attached to the end of it, "If anyone has ears to hear, let him hear." Finally, the fact that the message's

23 Which corroborates the point I make about the close relationship between this letter and Mark's gospel in the Introduction.

24 1 Cor 4:1-5. See *Gal* 271-277; 313-319.

25 The RSV, in its habitual attempt to make the English sound natural translates *erkhetai* into "is brought in" because a lamp cannot "come" all by itself. But this misses the point, besides rendering the Greek incorrectly.

26 1 Cor 3:13; 4:5; 2 Cor 5:10-11; Col 3:4. See also comment above on Mk 3:12.

27 Rom 2:16; 1 Cor 4:5. See also Col 3:3-4 where *kekryptai* (is hidden) occurs in conjunction with *hotan ho Khristos phanerothe* (when Christ will be made manifest). In 1 Cor 2:7 Paul speaks of the gospel as "God's wisdom hidden in mystery," which is picked up in Col 1:26//Eph 3:8 and Col 2:3. The only other instances in the New Testament are the Lukan parallel to our text (Lk 8:17) and "...thou hast hidden these things from the wise and understanding..." (Lk 10:21), which hearkens back to 1 Cor 1:19 (they both use the same Greek words *sophon* [wise] and *syneton* [understanding/clever]).

subject is God's final judgment is confirmed by the way Mark follows it first with a saying more clearly suggestive of a future judgment (vv.24-25) and then a set of parables explicitly about the "kingdom of God" (vv.26-32).

Jesus' practice of teaching in parables is rooted in the tradition of Ezekiel, whose message was also cast in "parables."[28] The connection is at its clearest in the following text, which effectively ties together the parable of the sower (4:3-20) with the following parables of the growing seed and mustard seed (4:26-32)—the entire sequence of parables in the cycle we are discussing:

> The word of the Lord came to me: Son of man, propound a riddle, and speak a parable to the house of Israel; say, Thus says the Lord God: A great eagle with great wings and long pinions, rich in plumage of many colors, came to Lebanon and took the top of the cedar; he broke off the topmost of its young twigs and carried it to a land of trade, and set it in a city of merchants. Then he took of the seed of the land and planted it in fertile soil; he placed it beside abundant waters. He set it like a willow twig, and it sprouted and became a low spreading vine, and its branches turned toward him, and its roots remained where it stood. So it became a vine, and brought forth branches and put forth foliage. And there was another great eagle with great wings and much plumage; and behold, this vine bent its roots toward him, and shot forth its branches toward him that he might water it. From the bed where it was planted he transplanted it to good soil by abundant waters, that it might bring forth branches, and bear fruit, and become a noble vine... Thus says the Lord God: "I myself will take a sprig from the lofty top of the cedar, and will set it out; I will break off from the topmost of its young twigs a tender one, and I myself will plant it upon a high and lofty mountain; on the mountain height of Israel will I plant it, that it may bring forth boughs and bear fruit, and become a noble cedar;

28 Jesus' use of parables is mentioned also in vv.10-11, 13, 30, 33-34. The Septuagint text of Ezekiel speaks of "parables" in the sense that the English word "parable" is a transliterated rendition of the Greek *parabolē*. See Ezek 12:21-23; 16:44; 18:2-3; 20:49 (21:5 in the Septuagint); 24:3. The book of Ezekiel in general makes profuse use of rich imagery to convey the word of the Lord.

and under it will dwell all kinds of beasts; in the shade of its branches birds of every sort will nest. And all the trees of the field shall know that I the Lord bring low the high tree, and make high the low tree, dry up the green tree, and make the dry tree flourish. I the Lord have spoken, and I will do it." (17:1-8; 22-24)

Ezekiel's paradigm also unlocks the meaning of the difficult passage where Jesus explains that the purpose of speaking in parables is to reveal the mystery of the kingdom of God but also *at the same time* to shut the door for repentance and forgiveness (4:10-12). Since a "parable" presents imagery intended to be comprehensible to anyone—sometimes extended into a story which is also fundamentally accessible—it is intended to communicate a teaching as clearly as possible.[29] If, then, someone does not understand and obey the message it must be a deliberate act, something done *willfully*. If the disciples are given the explanation of the parable (vv.14-20), the intention is to make them even more liable to judgment should they not heed its teaching (v.13). They represent the biblical Israel,[30] and it is precisely at the beginning of Ezekiel that we find the same train of thought, also addressed to Israel:

And he said to me, "Son of man, I send you to the people of Israel, to a nation of rebels, who have rebelled against me; they and their fathers have transgressed against me to this very day. The people also are impudent and stubborn: I send you to them; and you shall say to them, 'Thus says the Lord God.' And whether they hear or refuse to hear (for they are a rebellious house) they will know that there has been a prophet among them. And you, son of man, be not afraid of them, nor be afraid of their words, though briers and thorns are with you and you sit upon scorpions; be not

29 Besides the references in Ezekiel, two other examples are "My mouth shall speak wisdom; the meditation of my heart shall be understanding. I will incline my ear to a parable; I will solve my riddle to the music of the lyre" (Ps 48:3-4), and "Give ear, O my people, to my teaching; incline your ears to the words of my mouth! I will open my mouth in a parable; I will utter dark sayings from of old, things that we have heard and known, that our fathers have told us." (Ps 78:2-3).

30 See Rom 2:1-3:20; 9:19-28; 10:14-21, where biblical Israel is shown to be more liable to judgment.

afraid of their words, nor be dismayed at their looks, for they are a rebellious house. And you shall speak my words to them, whether they hear or refuse to hear; for they are a rebellious house. (2:3-7)

And he said to me, "Son of man, go, get you to the house of Israel, and speak with my words to them. For you are not sent to a people of foreign speech and a hard language, but to the house of Israel—not to many peoples of foreign speech and a hard language, whose words you cannot understand. Surely, if I sent you to such, they would listen to you. But the house of Israel will not listen to you; for they are not willing to listen to me; because all the house of Israel are of a hard forehead and of a stubborn heart. Behold, I have made your face hard against their faces, and your forehead hard against their foreheads. Like adamant harder than flint have I made your forehead; fear them not, nor be dismayed at their looks, for they are a rebellious house." Moreover he said to me, "Son of man, all my words that I shall speak to you receive in your heart, and hear with your ears. And go, get you to the exiles, to your people, and say to them, 'Thus says the Lord God'; whether they hear or refuse to hear." (3:4-11)

The same thought in more condensed form may be found in the book of Isaiah where the prophet was sent to deliver God's message to a similarly rebellious audience that would not accept it:

And he said, "Go, and say to this people: 'Hear and hear, but do not understand; see and see, but do not perceive.' Make the heart of this people fat, and their ears heavy, and shut their eyes; lest they see with their eyes, and hear with their ears, and understand with their hearts, and turn and be healed." (6:8-10)[31]

It is this version from Isaiah that Mark adopted, yet a dependence on Colossians also is apparent in the word "mystery" (*mysterion*) which occurs only here in Mark.[32] "The mystery of the kingdom of God" in Mark sounds remarkably similar to "this mystery which is Christ in you" in Colossians (1:26). The context of the latter verse is a discussion of the gospel proclaimed by Paul among the Gentiles, in which "mystery" is repeated several times (1:26-2:3; 4:2-4).

---

31 The prophetic message generally uses the metaphorical language of parables. Notice how God is referred to as a stone of offense, a rock of stumbling, a trap, and a snare in Is 8:14, which is part of the message in chs.7-12 introduced by ch.6 (see *OTI2* 117-129).

32 The RSV's "secret" is a mistranslation of *mysterion*.

It is thus the Gentiles who are "those around him" (*peri auton*) and form one community with "the twelve," which signifies God's Israel (4:10). These are the ones who are truly Jesus' disciples (v.34), in contradistinction to "those outside (*exo*)" (v.11), "his mother and brothers" who only *seem* to be close to him.

The concluding remarks (4:33-34) of the section on parables corroborate my reading of the entire section as an official presentation of Paul's gospel. Jesus "was speaking the word" (*elalei ton logon*) and "privately he was explaining everything" (*kat' idian epelyen panta*). The expression "speak the word" is a reference to the preaching of the gospel,[33] and the following remark offers a solution (the literal meaning of the Greek verb *epilyo*) for any difficulties this gospel may entail. Both instances of the verb "speak" (vv.33 and 34), as well as the verb "explain/solve" (v.34), are in the imperfect, suggesting that this was not a one-time event but something that continued over an extended period of time. Finally, and most importantly, the expression "privately" (*kat' idian*) is particularly interesting. It occurs only once in the entire Pauline corpus, in Gal 2:2: "I went up [to Jerusalem] by a revelation; and I laid before them—but privately (*kat' idian*) before those who were of repute—the gospel which I preach among the Gentiles..." This same expression recurs in Mark in most of the pericopes where Jesus is laying out his gospel (4:34; 6:30-31; 9:2; 13:3) and, more specifically, where he is correcting the misunderstandings of Peter, James and John (9:2) or Peter, James, John, and Andrew (13:3). As I shall show later, all of these passages are to be understood against the background of Gal 2:1-14. The remaining New Testament instance of *kat' idian* occurs in Mk 7:33 in conjunction with the healing of a deaf and mute man who I shall show to be patterned after Titus—the Gentile whom Paul took to the Jerusalem meeting as a test case (Gal 2:1)! Thus, all occurrences of the expression "privately" can be accounted for on the basis of its use in Gal 2:2.

33 See above my comments on 2:2.

Crossing Over

In 4:35 after teaching from a boat Jesus decides to "go across to the other side." Later he speaks to his disciples, "when evening had come" (*opsias genomenes*). This expression calls to mind the phrase "that evening" in 1:32, where it precedes the "very early morning" (1:35) when the gospel was proclaimed outside of Judea. He calls upon the disciples to take him to "the other side," and they obey by taking him "just as he was." What was it about him that was so remarkable as to require a comment like this? This otherwise inexplicable phrase can best be explained as an assertion that the preaching of the gospel by Paul and his followers to the Gentiles ("on the other side [of the sea]"[34]) did not entail any change in the reality of Jesus. In other words, Paul's gospel did not distort the real Messiah of Israel, a criticism leveled against him by James and his Jerusalemite party. The story of the calming of the storm (4:35-41) reflects the invitation by Paul to the Jerusalemite leadership to cross the Roman "sea" in spite of the dangers inherent in such an endeavor. The apparently sleeping (as though dead) Jesus arises (as though resurrected) and shows himself to be none other than the Lord who pacifies the raging waters[35] and brings them—here representing the Gentile Roman empire—to obedience.

The verb "obey" is typically Pauline terminology.[36] Understanding his apostleship as servitude to Christ,[37] he accordingly viewed the apostolic gospel's goal as the "obedience" of the Gentiles to the risen Christ as their Lord. This view is reflected in the prologue to Romans: "The gospel concerning his Son, who was de-

---

34 See 5:1.
35 Notice the mention of the waves and compare with Ps 93, where it is the Lord who is "mightier than the waves of the sea." (See *OTI3* 24-28).
36 Encountered in Mark only here (4:41) and in 1:27 where "the unclean spirits"—a reference to the Gentiles as outsiders—are said to obey him. See further comments on the following pericope, 5:1-20. Paul's use of "obey" and "obedience" to speak of the acceptance of the gospel are found in Rom 1:5; 6:16-17; 10:16; 15:18; 16:19, 26; 2 Cor 7;15; 10:5-6; 2 Thess 1:8.
37 Rom 1:1; 1 Cor 9:19; Gal 1:10; Phil 1:1.

scended from David according to the flesh and designated Son of God in power according to the Spirit of holiness *by his resurrection from the dead,* Jesus Christ our Lord, through whom we have received grace and apostleship to bring about *the obedience of faith* for the sake of his name *among all the nations/Gentiles...*" (Rom 1:4-5)[38]

The Gospel Is Effective in Gentile Territory

The following passage (5:1-20) takes us to the other side of the "sea" that was just conquered and tamed by Jesus, a symbol of the realm throughout which Paul's apostolic activity had brought the Gentiles under the obedience of Christ. That we are in Gentile territory is reflected in terminology referring to things considered unclean by, or foreign to, Judaism: tombs, unclean spirit(s), a demoniac, swine, Legion.[39] As he tamed the raging sea with his message, here too Jesus overpowers the Gentile world that James and his party were so afraid would engulf them. The language here indicates that Mark intended to warn his hearers not to fear that allowing Gentile converts to ignore the Law would water down Judaism.[40] At the same time he was warning against a fear of the Roman armies threatening Jerusalem during the Jewish war; such a fear could have been used by the zealots to convince people to join in their anti-Roman insurrection.

Mark's message is clear: Paul's gospel is no threat to Judaism. An "unclean" Gentile "goes away" and "begins to proclaim" (*erxato keryssein*) in the Decapolis, i.e., the Gentile Roman empire,[41] that he had been granted God's mercy.[42] In fact, Jesus or-

---

38 See also Rom 6:16-22; 1 Cor 7:21-23.
39 Tombs represent the lack of real life that is granted only through the living God's Torah. "Legion" is a reference to the Roman army.
40 See comments on 1:24.
41 The Greek Decapolis means "the (area of the) ten cities" and referred to a region east of the Jordan river where the Romans had a defensive line of ten city-fortresses.
42 A clear reference to Paul's teaching about God's mercy in Romans (9:23-24; 11:31; 15:9); see also Gal 6:16.

ders him to do so rather than come back with his benefactor into the domain of Judaism (v.21ff). In other words, Paul's gospel does not endanger Judaism because when it carries the good news to the Gentiles it requires them to spread it among themselves rather than try to convince Jews that the Law is passé.[43]

The Same Gospel Challenges the Jews

After this success among the Gentiles, making them obedient to God's gospel, Jesus returns to challenge both Judaism per se, symbolized by the older woman, and James' followers, symbolized by the young girl (5:21-43). Here again the terminology is revealing, this time pointing in the direction of Judaism: (ruler of the) synagogue, the name Jairus,[44] the number twelve, the company of Peter, James and John. Like the Jewish church led by James, the young girl is on the brink of death and requires "salvation" through the "hand," or power, of this Jesus who just offered God's mercy to the Gentiles.[45] Like Judaism per se, the older woman needs "faith" (in Paul's gospel)[46] in order to be "saved" and enjoy God's eschatological "peace."[47] The followers of Peter, James and John, on the other hand, are like the young girl here in that they need someone to open their eyes to the (Pauline) invitation, "*only* believe." Through faith (in Paul's gospel) *alone* will they be able to hearken to Jesus' command to arise and follow him, the resurrected Lord,[48] into (the) Galilee (of the nations) where they will be "given to eat" (at his Messianic table). And since this gospel of Jesus' resurrection *in close conjunction*

---

43 See Rom 1:1-5.

44 The Greek *Iairos* is a transliteration of the Hebrew verb *ya'ir* meaning "he enlightens/sheds light," which is a reference to the mission of the Jews toward the Gentiles who are considered to abide in darkness (Rom 2:19).

45 Vv.23, 30; also v.41 where Jesus "takes" (with his hand) the girl's hand.

46 See Rom 1:16-17; 3:22, 30; 4;11, 14-16, 24; 9:30-33; 10:4, 6, 14-21; 11;20; 13:11. See also Gal 2;15-16; 3:2, 5, 12, 22, 23-25.

47 See Rom 3:17; 5:1; 8:3-6; 14:18-19; 15:13. See also Gal 6:16.

48 Notice the wordplay between "the girl *aneste* (got up)" in v.42 and "And...*anastas* (he rose)..." in 1:35 (see comments above).

with his suffering and death will not be revealed until 8:31-9:1, "he strictly charged them that no one should know this."

Jerusalem's Refusal of the Gospel

From the following pericope (6:1-6), one learns that Paul's attempts to persuade Jerusalem to acknowledge the fruits of his apostolic endeavors among the Gentiles, by accepting their token financial offering, fell on deaf ears.[49] The passage describes precisely Paul's predicament vis-à-vis his own Jewish "relatives" which he laments so often in his letters: the Jews—"his own country" (*patris*), "his own kin,"[50] "his own house" (*oikia*)[51]—rejected him, "were scandalized"[52] at him, and took a stand of "disbelief" (*apistia*) with regard to him.[53] If this situation remained true after Paul's death, as the gospel of Mark was being written, then Paul's personal efforts to win over the Jerusalemite church must have failed.

The passage's intent to allude to Paul's situation may also be indicated by the word *tekton* which means "builder," but is usually translated as "carpenter." It occurs nowhere else in the New Testament except in the parallel text Mt 13:55—but it closely resembles *arkhitekton* (architect/master builder) of 1 Cor 3:10, a text that was certainly well known by Mark. In 1 Corinthians Paul uses this word to refer to his own role as an apostle.

If Mark's intention in this passage is to convey a message about the nature of Paul and his gospel, it stands to reason that the per-

---

49 See the Introduction.

50 V.4. The Greek *syngeneus* occurs only here in Mark and is akin to *syngenes* that is found only in Romans (9:3, and also 16:7, 11, 21) in the entire Pauline corpus.

51 The same word as in 1:28 and 3:25-27.

52 V.3. Notice the same verb *skandalizomai* that occurred in 4:17 to speak of Peter's stand also there; see comments above.

53 This word occurs only in Romans among Paul's epistles, all four times in reference to the Jews' refusal of the gospel (3,3; 4:20; 11:20, 23). Elsewhere in the New Testament, it is found in the Matthean parallel to Mark (Mt 13:58) and in 1 Tim 1:13; Heb 3:12, 19.

sonal names of Jesus' "brothers" related in it were carefully chosen to serve the same purpose. The significance of James, Judah, and Simon has already been discussed. What about Joses (*Ioses*), who is mentioned only three times in the New Testament, all of them in Mark?[54] The evidence for determining the intended symbolism of this name is shakier here than it is with the other names I have so far analyzed, but it is possible to formulate a hypothesis that makes sense here and in the other places where this name appears. While the name is not attested to even in the LXX, it is cast in a way that brings to mind the Greek noun *ios* meaning "poison/venom."[55] Mark's intention may then be to allude to someone named *Ioseph* (Joseph) whom he wishes to suggest is poisonous. The fact that Matthew changes the name to "Joseph" lends credence to this supposition.[56] Against whom, then, would Mark be warning his readers?

Considering that Judah refers to the tribe of Judah, and thus Judea or Palestinian Judaism,[57] Joseph "the venomous one" could be the tribe of Joseph, the main representative of the Northern kingdom that was dispersed without any indication that it ever returned. It could then represent the Judaism of the diaspora, the eleven lost tribes. This would not explain Mark's negative attitude toward "Joseph" unless we take the hypothesis one step further and focus on the element of splitting apart, of "brothers" effectively abandoning the one true community. Paul and Barnabas were granted responsibility together for the Gentile mission (Gal 2:9), but they had a very sharp divergence of views when Barnabas

---

54 Here and at 15:40 and 47.

55 *Ioseph* is a very well known name; the hearer will immediately think of *Joseph* without the connotation of anything else. But when he hears an unusual name (actually, this name doesn't exist as a name) his attention is drawn to something else. *Ioseph* is undeclinable, whereas *Ioses* is declined into *iosetos*, which draws the attention in the direction of a Greek word.

56 He does this in Mt 13:55 which is parallel to Mk 6:3 and in 27:56 which is parallel to Mk 15:40. Lk 4:22 and Jn 6:42 which are parallel to Mk 6:3 have "son of Joseph."

57 See comments on the list of the twelve in 3:13-19.

joined the judaizing camp. In Paul's view, then, at that point Barnabas effectively became "venomous" (Gal 2:11-14).

Jesus' brothers' names can all be accounted for, then, as names of Jewish Christian leaders (James and Peter) or representatives of Judaism as a whole (Judean and diaspora Judaism), and possibly one Jewish leader of the Gentile mission. This leads to the conclusion that Mary herself, the mother of them all, represents not all followers of Christ in general but specifically Jewish believers in Jesus as the Messiah.[58] Here in Mark the latter group is first rebuked for its lack of faith (in Paul's gospel; 4:35-41), then is asked to "believe" (5:36) as the Gentiles already have (5:1-20). But in fact they have persisted to the end in rejecting this entreaty. This series of stories is thus about Gentile acceptance and Jewish rejection of the gospel and so presents in narrative form the theme of Paul's epistle to the Romans.

---

58 In tribal traditions, the name of a forebear is also the name of the totality of his progeny. Thus, the name of Jesus' mother, Mary, became Mark's symbol for Judeo-Christianity. The choice of Mary over her husband Joseph is rooted in the Old Testament tradition where Israel, God's community, is spoken of in terms of a wife (Hos 1-3) or a woman (Ezek 16 and 23). In the case of Hosea, Israel is both the mother and the children, which corresponds closely to what we find in Mark here and in 3:13-35. Another example is the case of Abraham's wife, Sarah. Second Isaiah refers to her as a symbol of the new Jerusalem and its inhabitants, which he views as a tribe, the progeny of Sarah (see Is 51:1-3 and 54:1-3, and my comments thereon in *Gal* 244-46 and 249).

14

The Third Cycle of Calling

Another Call to the Apostles

This cycle (6:6b-8:21) deals more specifically with Jerusalem's "hardening of heart" with regard to Paul's gospel. It starts with Jesus calling upon the apostles to preach the gospel freely (6:6b-13). They are not to be concerned about a lack of bread to eat or money to buy it with, even though they will eventually be called upon to "feed" the crowd (6:30-44; 8:1-10). Their sole and sufficient source of "authority" is to be the staff (*rhabdos*) of genuine fatherhood.[1] And wherever they genuinely carry the gospel, their witness is to become a "testimony against" (*eis martyrion autois*) those who reject it. That instruction is identical to the one Jesus gave to the leper who symbolized Paul in 1:40-45, which implies that he is calling upon the apostles to be like Paul by taking a stand (giving testimony) for the true gospel in the face of any opposition, even from the Jerusalem priesthood or leadership.

The Death of John the Baptist

At this point the pericope about John the Baptist's death (6:14-29) abruptly interrupts the one about Jesus sending out the apostles. Its character as a story complete in itself inserted into the middle of another one, with little or no attempt at integrating the two, can be seen in the way the text flows so well from v.13 to v.30— one could remove vv.14-29 entirely without it being apparent that anything was missing. Why was it inserted here, especially

1   1 Cor 4:21, in a passage on fatherhood.

considering the fact that John's imprisonment was already mentioned way back in 1:14?

A key theme or purpose of the story may be found in the statement that some were calling Jesus the "resurrected" John (vv.14, 16). This shows the intimate relation between the messenger and the one who sends him; John witnessed so faithfully and truthfully to the message that Jesus himself also proclaimed that he became an image of Jesus, or in the eyes of some, Jesus was an image of him. And John's faithfulness to that message is what led to, and ended with, his death, as would later happen to Jesus. But there the similarity ends, because Jesus' "preaching" did not end with his death—in fact, it effectively began *after* his own death and resurrection, for it was then that Paul, and now Mark as well, spread throughout the known world the gospel of Jesus as the resurrected and coming Lord.[2] John's death here, then, prefigures Jesus' death in a way that focuses the attention on Jesus rather than John, for the difference between them is that John's death is final while Jesus' death blossoms into a glorious new beginning. In this sense John proclaims the image of Jesus as effectively in his death as in his life; or in other words, the martyred John is the visible face of the invisible resurrected Jesus. This idea—that the weakness or death of Christ's apostle is itself a faithful image of Christ himself—is what Paul taught all along:

> ...you know it was because of a bodily ailment that I preached the gospel to you at first; and though my condition was a trial to you, you did not scorn or despise me, but received me as an angel of God, as Christ Jesus... My little children, with whom I am again in travail until Christ be formed in you! (Gal 4:13-14, 19)

> But we have this treasure in earthen vessels, to show that the transcendent power belongs to God and not to us. We are afflicted in every way, but not crushed; perplexed, but not driven to despair; persecuted, but not forsaken; struck down, but not destroyed; always carrying in the body the death of Jesus, so that the life of Jesus may also be manifested (*phanerothe*) in our bodies. For while

---

2   See comments on 1:2-15, especially vv.14-15.

we live we are always being given up to death for Jesus' sake, so that the life of Jesus may be manifested (*phanerothe*) in our mortal flesh. So death is at work in us, but life in you. Since we have the same spirit of faith as he had who wrote, "I believed, and so I spoke," we too believe, and so we speak, knowing that he who raised the Lord Jesus will raise us also with Jesus and bring us with you into his presence. (2 Cor 4:7-14)[3]

In my comments on 1:2-11 I pointed out that, in Mark, John the Baptist is a symbol for Paul, and the depiction of his life resembles Paul's. In addition, this section contains Pauline terminology and themes. Two of these may be found in the introductory phrase, "for Jesus' name had become known (*phaneron*)." The Lord's "name" is connected with the preaching of the gospel in Paul's epistles,[4] and *phaneron* in Mark suggests the Lord's coming, which is a central feature of Paul's gospel.[5] All of this explains why Mark inserted the story of John's beheading in the middle of the story of the apostle's call and travels: he wanted to make sure the former would *immediately* follow the last apostolic call itself in order to suggest to the reader that John—and through him Paul—represented the paradigm of the true apostle who gives his life for the gospel.

And in death as in life, we can find parallels between John and Paul. By adopting "the faith he once tried to destroy" (Gal 1:23) Paul put himself outside the realm of his contemporary Judaism which was a legal religion in the Roman empire. In so doing, he opened himself to the risk of being accused by Roman officialdom of promoting a "new," and thus illicit, religion, an action punishable by death. Similarly, by taking a stand against Herod, the Jewish king and thus representative of the Jews, John the Baptist placed his life in jeopardy and ultimately did become Herod's victim. But in Mark the blame for his death lies less with Herod himself than with his

---

3 Notice the closeness of this text to 6:14 whose last words are: "that is why these powers (*dynameis*) are at work (*energousin*) in him."

4 See Rom 10:13-17; 15:20; 1 Cor 1:2, 13-17; 6:11.

5 See comments on 1:1-15; 3:12; 4:22.

"courtiers and officers and the leading men of Galilee" (6:21). The explicit mention of Galilee in this context, considered along with the other parallels between Paul and John, is another indication that "Galilee," in Mark, acts as a symbol for Rome.

The "Roman connection" in this passage is further reflected in the manner of execution and in the term *spekoulator* applied to the "soldier of the guard" who carries it out. Beheading was strictly reserved for Roman citizens (Paul was a Roman citizen, John most likely was not), while *spekoulator* is the Greek transliteration of the Latin *speculator,* a Roman title.[6]

There is one more indication that John, in this story of his death, is meant to resemble Paul. Consider the similarities between the "young girl" *(korasion;* vv.22, 28) here and the one in 5:41-42 who symbolized James' followers:

1) The word occurs only in these two places in Mark.

2) Both times the girl is first introduced as "daughter" *(thygatrion/thygater,* 5:23, 34, 35; 6:22) and later as "young girl" *(korasion;* 5:41, 42; 6:22, 28).

3) Both texts place a special focus on the term "young girl" by means of a quick transition to it from "daughter." In the earlier one, the translation into Greek of an Aramaic expression is expressly marked by the convoluted phrase "that is, in translation" *(ho estin methermeneuomenon;* v.41) instead of simply "that is" *(ho estin).* In the later one, the shift from *thygatrion* to *korasion* happens almost as quickly, within the same verse (v.22).

If this is indeed the same "young girl," Mark's message is clear: her complicity in John's death represents the complicity of James and his followers with Paul's judaizing opponents, which ultimately helped lead Paul to his death.

---

6 *Speculator* is the guard or spy from *specula* (elevation, observatory).

Table Fellowship

The remainder of the story of the sending out of the apostles (6:30-44) returns to the familiar theme of table fellowship. What Mark intends to say through the symbolic language of this story and the way he inserts the story of John's death before it is that although Paul is gone, it is now Jesus himself—the resurrected and coming Lord—who calls upon the apostles to follow the Pauline "way" and accept full table fellowship between Jews and Gentiles. In these verses Jesus instructs the apostles, who thought they were teaching correctly (v.30), to stop teaching for a while, after which he will attempt to reorient their thinking by means of the miracle of the bread and the fish. They must go to "a lonely place" (*kat' idian*)[7] which is none other than the "place of wilderness" of 1:35, that is, the land of the Gentiles.[8] They could only get there by "going away" (*apelthon*; also reminiscent of 1:35) "in the boat"; the implication being that they are again moving to the other side of "the sea of Galilee."[9] As we saw earlier in 4:1, it is there that the true teaching, by Jesus, "begins."

When the disciples suggest that he dismiss the "crowd" and not eat with them, Jesus requires them to share *their* food with them.[10] This food they are to share with the "outsiders" is the *Torah*, the "five" loaves symbolizing its five books. Yet the disciples try again to differentiate between themselves and the crowd of outsiders by mentioning two fish, that is, two separate communities, one of Jews and one of Gentiles, as separate components of an overarching Messianic community—which is precisely what Paul fought against.[11] The fact that Jesus "divided the two fish among them *all*" shows that Mark introduces this idea of two communities precisely to reject it by stressing the oneness of the new community. The same emphasis is

---

7 The phrase *kat' idian* is drawn from Gal 2:11-14; see comments above on 4:34.
8 The primary importance given this matter is reflected in the repetition of both expressions *kat' idian* and *eremon topon* (vv.31, 32).
9 See 4:36 and 5:1.
10 Notice Jesus' question: "How many loaves have you?" (v.38).
11 See comments on 1:16-17 and *Gal* 38-39.

evident in the number twelve of the baskets, since the twelve tribes represent the fullness of Israel. And in the number five thousand the "five" again represents the Torah, of which all partake equally, and "thousands" emphasizes that "all" are included. This confirms a principle Paul repeats frequently: "For there is no distinction between Jew and Greek; *the same Lord is Lord of all and bestows his riches upon all* who call upon him."[12]

Crossing Over into Gentile Territory

As the story continues in 6:45, Jesus "compels" (*enankasen*) his reluctant disciples to go into the boat and go before him to "the other side," here identified as Bethsaida. The Aramaic *bethsaida* means "house of hunting/fishing" or "house of the provision that comes from hunting/fishing," which indicates that Jesus was prodding the disciples into going to the "Galilee of the nations" *before* him so that they would be there when he would, at a later time, come in glory from "the mountain, the house of prayer," i.e., the divine sanctuary (v.46). Here again, the crossing takes place "when evening came" (*opsias genomenes*), a phrase that Mark uses to introduce texts about Jesus' epiphany in "Galilee."[13] The disciples departed but "were making headway painfully"—they were reluctant to leave Jerusalem for Galilee. Jesus set an example for them to the extent that he even "meant to pass by them" (v.48) and lead the way toward "the other side"; when that alone didn't work, he tried to augment the example he was giving by "speaking"[14] to them. Still, they did not "understand"[15] the lesson of "the loaves" because "their hearts were

12 Rom 10:12; see also Gal 3:28; 1 Cor 12:13; Col 3:11.
13 See comments on 1:32 and 4:35.
14 The verb *lalo* in Mark typically refers to speaking or preaching the gospel; see comments on 1:34; 2:2, 7; 4:33. The implication is that Jesus' disciples, who themselves are supposed to be spreading the gospel, in fact need it preached to them. This is precisely what we find Paul doing to Peter in Gal 2:11-14.
15 See comments on 4:12. There it is the outsiders who don't "understand"; thus, by not understanding Jesus' message, the disciples were effectively making themselves outsiders; see also following note.

hardened."[16] The gospel message was nevertheless carried to the Gentiles (vv.53-56), and they were "saved" (*esozonto*) by touching Jesus' garment, in exactly the same way as did the woman with the flow of blood, representing Judaism (5:27-28).

A Debate with the Leaders

Immediately thereafter the scribes and Pharisees move to impede these Gentiles' salvation (7:1-22), just as the Jerusalem Christian leaders tried to impede the salvation of Paul's Gentile converts in Antioch (Gal 2:11-14). The similarities between the two situations are striking:

1) In Mark, "Pharisees and scribes" come "from Jerusalem"; in Galatians "certain men" come "from James" (who is headquartered in Jerusalem).

2) In Mark, these men from Jerusalem question the acceptability of table fellowship with "unclean" disciples;[17] in Galatians they convince all the Jews to stop having table fellowship with Gentiles, who are unclean by definition in Judaism.

3) Jesus calls these men "hypocrites" (*hypokritai*)—the only occurrence of that word in Mark. Paul laments the way all the Jews "followed [Peter] in hypocrisy" (*synypokrinomai*) and Barnabas in turn was carried away by their "hypocrisy" (*hypokrisis*)—the only words based on that root in Paul.[18]

16 See comments on 3:5. There I explained *porosis* against its use in Romans where Paul criticizes James for not accepting the Gentiles; here the *porosis* lies in Jesus' disciples' not wanting to understand the necessity of table fellowship with Gentiles.

17 The use of the expression "eating the loaves" in vv.2 and 5 connects this pericope with that of the feeding of the five thousand in 6:30-44 (RSV dismisses the term "loaves" without cause in both instances). The second "feeding" gives the ultimate meaning of table fellowship where everyone is included in the same community.

18 The RSV shows its double standard by translating the verb as "with him...acted insincerely" and the noun as "insincerity" when directed toward Peter and Barnabas, but more straightforwardly as "hypocrites" when directed toward the scribes and Pharisees.

4) The references to Jewish dietary customs as "the tradition of the elders" or "the tradition of men" or "your tradition," unique instances in Mark, recall "traditions of my fathers" of Gal 1:14, a unique occurrence in Paul.

5) One of these phrases in Mark, "the tradition of men" reflects the "Colossians connection"[19] since it is found only here and in Col 2:8. But the latter verse in turn points back to Galatians, for it reads: "...according to the tradition of men, according to the elemental spirits of the universe (*ta stoikheia tou kosmou*)..."—and the latter expression is unique to Galatians (4:3, 9) and Colossians (2:8, 20) in Paul.

6) Beginning with 7:8, Mark uses the word "men" instead of "elders" in speaking of the Jewish tradition, in order to help show the incompatibility between human traditions and "the commandment of God" or "the word of God." This opposition is reminiscent of the one between men and God in Gal 1:1 and 1:11-12.

7) The Galatians connection is also suggested by the verbs "nullify/reject" (*atheto*; v.9) and "annul/make void" (*akyro*; v.13), key verbs in Paul's argument there concerning the unchangeable character of God's promise to Abraham (Gal 3:15, 17).[20]

8) According to Jesus, what matters is behavior according to God's will (vv.10-12, 20-23), which is precisely the point of Gal 5:13-26.[21]

The Gospel Is Preached to and Received by the Gentiles

Having "declared all foods clean," thereby putting Jews and Gentiles on a par, Jesus, "having risen" (*anastas*), "went away" (*apelthen*)[22] to the region of Tyre (7:24).[23] Tyre had been an ally

19 See p. 163.

20 In Paul, *atheto* occurs again in Gal 2:21 in conjunction with God's grace, and in 1 Thess 4:8 in relation to God's giving his Holy Spirit. As for *akyro*, it is found only in Galatians and Mark (and its Matthean parallel Mt 15:6).

21 See also Rom 2:17-29.

22 See on these two verbs my comments on 1:35; there as here, they describe movement out to Gentile territory.

23 "...and Sidon" is an addition in some manuscripts, whose intent is to make Mark conform to Matthew (15:21).

of Jerusalem but deserted it when Jerusalem fell to the Babylonians in 587 B.C., resulting in a lengthy oracle against it in Ezekiel (chs.26-27).[24] In Tyre Jesus meets a woman who had "heard of him" (an allusion to apostolic preaching) and who is introduced as "a Greek, a Syrophoenician by birth (*to genei*)," or in other words, a Gentile in every respect (v.26).[25] She asks to be fed from the table of the "children (of Israel)" and is granted her wish due to her "faith"; in fact, she is the first person in Mark who confesses Jesus as "Lord" (v.28). Unlike the Jew Jairus' daughter who was healed but then became the "young girl" who delivered Jesus' forerunner to death, this Gentile woman's daughter was healed of her "uncleanness" (vv.25-30).[26]

The next verse (7:31) is particularly interesting in the way it confirms that "sea of Galilee" in Mark symbolizes the Mediterranean sea and thus the Roman empire as a whole. It reads: "Then he returned from the region of Tyre, and went through (*dia*) Sidon to the Sea of Galilee, through (or "in the middle of"; *ana meson*) the region of the Decapolis." Now, Sidon is north of Tyre, while the sea of Galilee and the Decapolis are southeast of it—so how could one go *through* an area to the north in order to reach an area to the southeast? And the Decapolis is further from Tyre than the sea of Galilee, so how could one go *through* the farther-away area to get to the closer area? Or if one interprets *ana meson* as "in the middle of," making the end of this sentence merely an observation that the sea of Galilee is located within the Decapolis, why would Mark only here, after so many references to that sea, mention its location in the Decapolis? The best way to explain an otherwise incomprehensible statement is to conclude that Mark was using "Decapolis" as a symbol for

24 See also Is 23.
25 The combination of Greek and Syrophoenician, i.e., Canaanite, is striking: it combines the two classic biblical terms for "Gentile."
26 The intended parallelism between the two stories (for the purpose of showing a contrast) is unmistakable: in either case the daughter is first referred to as *thygatrion* (5:23; 7:25), then as *thygater* (5:34, 35; 7:26, 29).

the Roman empire,[27] and the sea of Galilee as a symbol for the Mediterranean sea which lies "in the middle" of the Roman empire. This statement would then mean that Jesus was carrying the gospel away from Jerusalem northward (through Tyre and *then* Sidon) toward the center of the Roman empire.

In the region of the Decapolis he encounters a deaf-mute whom he heals (7:37). Earlier Jesus said to those around him together with the twelve, "Understand (literally, "see") what you hear" (*blepete ti akouete*; 4:24).[28] In other words, the Jew who *hears* the divine word (being read at a synagogue service) needs to "see" it in the sense of understand it.[29] In comparison, the Gentile who is not privy to hearing scripture is "deaf" and consequently "dumb" in the sense that he cannot "speak" of the scriptural God. Thus, the pericope here in 7:31-37 reflects Paul's struggle to have the "deaf and dumb" Gentiles acquire a "voice" in the church just like the Jews, to be able to "speak" the gospel message.[30]

But even if the deaf-mute represents Gentiles as a class, the details of his story indicate Mark may have modelled him after a specific individual he knew or knew about. This is not just any deaf-mute but one whom Jesus specifically singled out "from the crowd" (*apo tou okhlou*), met with him privately (*kat' idian*), and healed him by means of particularly dramatic actions. Who, then, could be his prototype? The terminology in the verse relating his healing is particularly enlightening: "And his hearing/ears (*akoai*) were opened, and the bonds (*desmos*) of his tongue were released, and he was speaking (*elalei*) straight/correctly (*orthos*)."[31] These key words once again point us in the direction of Galatians:

27 This is how it is used in 5:20, the only other occurrence of Decapolis in Mark.
28 And not "take heed unto" as the RSV has it. The same RSV translates the same Greek verb *blepo*, in v.13, as "understand."
29 Of course, the equivalence between seeing and understanding is just as true in English.
30 The verb *lalo* (v.35, 37) is virtually a technical term in Mark for preaching the gospel; see comments on 1:34; 2:2, 7; 4:33; 6:50.
31 The RSV translation of v.35 is extremely poor: "And his ears were opened, his tongue was released, and he spoke plainly."

1) While this is the sole occurrence of *akoai* in Mark in the sense of ear or hearing, the same word appears in Gal 3:2 and 5 (*akoe*, singular of *akoai*) with the dual meaning of "hearing" and "proclamation."[32]

2) The adverb *orthos* (straight/correctly) also occurs only here in Mark, and it too resembles a word used in Galatians: the verb *orthopodo* (walk straight) in Gal 2:14 comes from the same root, means "walk (live) according to the gospel" in its Galatians context, and is found nowhere else in the entire New Testament. The resemblance between Mark and Paul becomes even more striking when one notices that the adverb here qualifies the verb *lalo*, which, as I point out above, is in Mark typically an allusion to "speaking" the word of the gospel.[33]

3) "Bonds" (*desmos*), unique in Mark, brings to mind Paul's struggle for the *freedom* of the Gentiles, which is the theme of Galatians.[34]

4) Finally, as I show above in the comments on 4:34, the phrase *kat' idian* in Mark is identical to what we find in Gal 2:2 and appears in Mark in similar contexts.

If, then, Galatians influenced the writing of the deaf-mute pericope, the prototype for the deaf-mute himself may also be found there, and one individual mentioned there does fit this description: Titus. As I show above, the deaf-mute is a Gentile, and Titus was a Gentile. He became Paul's helper in the proclamation of the gospel and was brought along deliberately to the Jerusalem summit as a test case, in order to verify that he would not have to be circumcised.[35]

---

32 See *Gal* 99-100.
33 Considering this to be an allusion to preaching the gospel, which is not a one-time act but an on-going activity, would also explain why, unlike the verbs *enoigesan* (were opened) and *elythe* (was resolved/released) that are in the aorist (preterite), the verb *elalei* (was speaking) is in the imperfect, thus referring to a continual action.
34 Gal 3:23, 24, 28; 4:3, 8, 8, 22, 23, 26, 30, 31; 5:1, 18.
35 2 Cor 7:6-14; 8:6-23; Gal 2:1-5; see *Gal* 62-63. The theme of a man's mouth being opened to speak the gospel also resembles Paul's story, but the deaf-mute is intended

Because that summit did result in an agreement emancipating the Gentiles from the need to observe Jewish Law, Titus did play a significant, if passive, role in helping the Gentiles to acquire a "voice" in the church.

Full Equality at the Lord's Table

As more and more Gentiles do not merely accept Jesus' beneficence but go around proclaiming the gospel as the apostles themselves do, it becomes even clearer that they cannot be excluded from full equality in table fellowship. Jews must accept them as full equals in order to manifest the full unity in Christ's community between Jews and Gentiles. Throughout the entire world there must be one and only one, united community, for that is the will of the one and only God himself. This is the theme of the next miracle of the loaves (8:1-10), which acts as a symbolic description of the Gentiles gathered around the resurrected Jesus at the divine Messianic table. Again the "crowd" has "nothing to eat." It has been "abiding with" Jesus for "three days," and "some of them have come from afar." The loaves are now seven, which is the divine number. And because the *one* God can have only *one* community,[36] we have this time not two fish representing the disciples' attempt to preserve two separate communities,[37] but "some small fish" (*ikhthydia*) representing undifferentiated individuals, since there is no longer a difference between Jew and Gentile. Indeed, "there is no longer Jew nor Greek" in the Messianic community of the risen Christ, for all are "Abraham's seed."[38] The remains filled seven baskets, which is again the divine number. The number four thousand represents the totality

to represent the Gentile who follows Jesus. Besides, throughout Mark it is Jesus who "is" Paul, while John the Baptist "is" Paul in his Jewish aspect, as representative of the Old Testament; otherwise, the only exception is the leper at the beginning.

36 See *Gal* 138-143.

37 See comments on 6:30-44.

38 Gal 3:26-29; see *Gal* 185-188.

of the people at the four corners of the universe (one thousand each), meaning that the new community encompasses the entire world.

This interpretation makes sense of the story's closing statement: "And immediately he got into the boat with his disciples, and went to the regions of Dalmanoutha." The "boat," now filled with "his disciples" is heading to a place we can no longer even identify with certainty. The cryptic word Dalmanoutha, unique in the entire New Testament, is probably a reference to Dalmatia (the coastal area of present-day Yugoslavia), east of Illyricum (inland Yugoslavia). This conjecture would then link Jesus' travels to Paul's travels as recounted in Romans:

> For I will not venture to speak of anything except what Christ has wrought through me to win obedience from the Gentiles, by word and deed, by the power of signs and wonders, by the power of the Holy Spirit, so that *from Jerusalem and as far round as Illyricum* I have fully preached the gospel of Christ, thus making it my ambition to preach the gospel, not where Christ has already been named, lest I build on another man's foundation... (15:18-20)

Final Break

At this point the gospel message has crossed fully into the heart of Gentile territory, and this means a final break with James' Jerusalem, which is confirmed by the story of the Pharisees' desire for a "sign from heaven," a divine endorsement of Jesus (8:11-13). Jesus simply ends the discussion immediately by telling them they will be given no sign besides the one sign of the "end."[39] And that "end" has not yet come, for, as he explained earlier, "the gospel must first be preached to all nations" (13:10), but time is short. That is why his own journey must continue: "And he left them, and getting into the boat again he departed to the other side." This is precisely

---

39 See 13:4. The term *semeion* (sign, in the singular) is found only in this passage (three times) and in 13:4 in the entire gospel of Mark.

what Paul did: he continued his journey, making a special effort to preach in uncharted areas, the pressing task of a true apostle. The other "apostles"—those content to sit in Jerusalem—are called upon here to do the same. The chance for talking about the matter will soon end, and the same Lord, who called each of them, will, at his coming, give his verdict.

The next pericope (8:14-21) concludes the gospel's first part. The remainder of Mark will relate Jesus' journey to his death, during which journey he will explain openly the "gospel of the cross." Here, in preparation, his followers are strongly urged to "see, see" (*horate, blepete*; v.15), to "comprehend, understand" (*noeite, syniete*; v.17), to have eyes to see and ears to hear (v.18), and to understand (v.21).[40] To do so means to avoid the influence of the Pharisees (meaning James' party)[41] and Herod (meaning the Jews),[42] who are trying to "trouble" and "agitate" the Pauline following into an "uprising"[43] against his teaching. The disciples of Paul and Christ are not to side with Jerusalem in its stand against the Romans,[44] but rather to go out of Jerusalem in order to bring to those Romans the gospel message of peace, the message about the one who has already conquered and is seated at the right hand of God. Any reluctance on their part is due to "hardness of heart" and must be overcome so that they can proceed to Bethsaida, the "house of fishing," as Jesus has been all along trying to "compel" them to do (6:45).

---

40 Contrast with 4:12 where the "outsiders" are said to see and not perceive, to hear and not understand.

41 See comments on 8:11.

42 See comments on 6:14-29.

43 See my comments in *Gal* 280 on Gal 5:8, the source of the image of leaven in Mk 8:15 (the only instance in this gospel). In texts written before Mark, "leaven" occurs only in Gal 5:8 and 1 Cor 5:6-8.

44 See the Introduction.

15

The First Cycle of Teaching the Gospel

Timothy, Type for the Pillars to Follow

In Bethsaida a blind man is brought to Jesus, who opens his eyes in a dramatic way (8:22-26), similar to what he did with the deaf-dumb person earlier. As a counterpart to the latter, who represented the Gentile Titus,[1] this person must be intended to represent Timothy, Paul's main Jewish disciple. A closer look at the terminology reveals that the blind man, like Timothy, is a Jew who carries the gospel to the Gentiles:

1) In my comments on 7:31-37 I pointed out that in Mark there is a contrast between the Jew's need to "see" scripture in the sense of understand it, while the Gentile, who does not even have the opportunity to hear scripture at all, is "deaf" and consequently "dumb" in the sense that he cannot "speak" of the scriptural God. A blind man would then be a symbol of the Jew who does not (yet) understand scripture.

2) The blind man's Jewish background is also suggested by the presence here of the adverb "clearly" (*telaugos*). While the word itself is unique in the New Testament, the cognate verb "see clearly" (*augazo*) occurs in one other place, 2 Cor 4:3-4:

> And even if our gospel is veiled, it is veiled only to those who are perishing. In their case the god of this world has blinded the minds of the unbelievers, to keep them from *seeing* (*augasai*) the light of the gospel of the glory of Christ, who is the likeness of God.

The context of this passage (2 Cor 3) is a discussion of the Jews'

---

1 See comments above.

inability to see due to the veil over their hearts[2] and the "harden-ing" (*porosis*) of their minds.[3]

3) Jesus takes the blind man out of "the village" (*he kome*) and does not allow him to return to it. Considering that *he kome* does not recur in the singular anywhere else but in 11:2 where it either means Jerusalem or a village very near Jerusalem, the implication here could be that the man is not to "enter Jerusalem" in the sense of joining the Judeo-Christian Jerusalemite party.[4] Instead, Jesus "sent him (*apesteilen*) to his home," that is, outside of "the village." The verb *apostello* (send) is a reference to the apostolic message the healed blind man was to carry to his "home," outside Judea.[5] According to Acts 16:1-2, Timothy's home was Lystra, in Asia Minor (i.e., outside Judea); and his mission was not to Judea but to the Jewish diaspora and the Roman empire.

4) Why is there an intermediate healing stage in which the blind man speaks of "the human beings"?[6] A broadly inclusive phrase like "the human beings" suggests "all human beings," which implicitly includes Gentiles along with Jews. And "trees" may represent symbolically the Jewish view that Gentiles will be cut down and thrown in the apocalyptic fire of God's wrath.[7] In contrast, the re-jection of that view implies acknowledgement of Paul's view that all—Gentile as well as Jew—are objects of God's mercy and grace.

Of course, other individuals might fit the pattern here that I am suggesting was designed to fit Timothy. But part and parcel of that suggestion is the idea that regardless of the actual identity of the pro-totype for the blind man, Mark is offering him here as a paradigm,

---

2 The RSV has "minds."
3 Later Paul again takes up the theme of "hardening" of hearts or minds, in Romans, in reference to Jews who reject the gospel. See comments on Romans in Part I.
4 See comments below on 11:1 where I show that Timothy was "sent"—from the Greek *apostello*—to Jerusalem to deliver the Pauline gospel to James' party.
5 Compare with Acts 16:1-5.
6 Incorrectly rendered "men" in the RSV.
7 See Mt 3:10//Lk 3:9; Mt 7:19; 12:33-37.

an example to be followed. As long as he is understood that way the reader will understand Mark's intended message whether or not he recognizes that this character was modelled after a specific individual. However, my goal is a fuller understanding of the thought behind the creation of this complex work of literature, so I am presenting a thesis based on the known fact that Paul's followers were very few at the end of his life.[8] Given that fact and considering the ones we do know, who would be the natural paradigm of the good disciple for the writer? The most likely one is Timothy. To summarize, then, the function of the blind man in the text is to provide an example of the Jew who follows Jesus (the most likely prototype for this example being Timothy), as compared to the deaf-mute, who is a Gentile (the most likely prototype being Titus).

The Confession of Faith at Caesarea Philippi

Just as Paul along with Timothy crossed to Philippi in Macedonia[9] where the "beginning of the gospel" took place,[10] here also "Jesus went out (*exelthen*) with his disciples to the villages (*komais*) of Caesarea Philippi." (8:27) Notice that Jesus goes not to Caesarea Philippi itself, but to its villages; he goes out of the "village" Jerusalem into the "villages" of a city whose name recalls the Roman city Philippi.[11] Put otherwise, after having tried to drill into his apostles the necessity of "going out" (of Jerusalem and Judea) to the Gentiles of the Roman empire, Jesus takes the final step and along the way (*en te hodo*)[12] he explains to them and the hearers of Mark's book the

---

8   In other words, I am doing here what other scholars have done in the case of the starets Zosima in Dostoevsky's "The Karamazov Brothers": trying to identify the prototype of a literary character. This can be enlightening, but ultimately it is not necessary because ultimately it is the function of the literary character in the text that counts. Whether or not the blind man was modelled after Timothy, he is paradigmatic, an example the reader is advised to follow.

9   Compare with Acts 16:6-15.

10   See comments on 1:1 as well as the Introduction.

11   See the Introduction.

12   The "way" is the "way of the gospel"; see comments on 2:23-28.

gospel of suffering and shame, which is none other than Paul's "gospel of the cross" (1 Cor 1:18) and the suffering Christ.

Indeed, at the occasion of Peter's confession of Jesus' Messiahship (8:29), Jesus "ordered" his disciples not to say anything to any one "about him" until he delivered unto them the correct teaching. Thus, it is here that he "began teaching"[13] his disciples concerning the Messiah (8:31-9:1), presenting himself as the "son of man," who has authority and is Lord, and who will accede to the seat of divine authority and Lordship through suffering, rejection, and death at the hands of his kinfolk.[14] This was the essence of the true gospel, as the comment of 8:32a clearly indicates: *kai parrhesia ton logon elalei* translates "and with boldness he was speaking[15] the word."[16] Besides the expression "speaking the word,"[17] the noun *parrhesia* (boldness), unique in Mark,[18] is very telling. It occurs in Paul only four times, all four in conjunction not only with the gospel, but with suffering for its sake.[19] The "dispute" over this "gospel" between Jesus and Peter recalls the one between Paul and Peter in Antioch:

1) The sharpness of the disagreement between Jesus and Peter is reflected in the same strong verb *epitimo* (rebuke, scold, order harshly)[20] used to describe the way each rebukes the other. Like-

13 See comments on 4:1; there he was beginning to teach in parables, now he is explaining the true meaning and correcting any misunderstandings.
14 2:7, 10, 28; 8:31; see comments on 1:37; 3:6, 32; 6:14-28.
15 Notice the imperfect which means that Jesus spent some time expanding on the statement of v.31, as opposed to the aorist (preterite) which would have emphasized the mere fact that he completed the explanation.
16 The RSV's rendering of this phrase is particularly inaccurate: it paraphrases by replacing the key expression "the word" with just "this" ("and he said this plainly") and it mistranslates *parrhesia* by making it sound as though the emphasis was merely on ensuring there were no misunderstandings, rather than saying something "openly" or "boldly" that heretofore had been hidden.
17 See comments on 1:34; 2:2, 7; 4:33, 34; 6:50; 7:35, 37.
18 It occurs only here in the entire synoptic tradition (Mark, Luke, and Matthew).
19 2 Cor 3:12 in the context of 3:1-4:12; 2 Cor 7:4 in the context of 7:2-7; Phil 1:20 in the context of 1:3-26; Philem 8 in the context of vv.8-13.
20 Also used in 1:25; 3:12; 4:38; 8:30.

wise, in Antioch Paul rebuked Peter, even calling him "condemned" (2:11). Notice also that in Galatians Paul delivered his rebuke "before them all," while Jesus similarly made sure his disciples were present before rebuking Peter—in contrast to the several other instances where the disciples are spoken to "privately" (*kat' idian*; 2:14). While we do not hear of an attack on Paul by Peter personally in Galatians, the sharpness of his opponents' attacks are in evidence throughout that epistle.

2) Jesus' calling Peter "Satan" is similar to Paul's branding as "accursed" (*anathema*) anyone who preaches a different gospel than his.[21] Moreover, Peter's "satanism" is linked to his "thinking" (*phrono*) about the matters "of men" and not those "of God," an opposition occurring frequently in Galatians in the same context where Paul uses the word *anathema*.[22]

3) The centrality of the gospel *message* in the Markan pericope is parallel to the same theme in Galatians. In Mark this is reflected in two expressions found nowhere but in this gospel: "for my sake and the gospel's" and "of me and of my words."[23] The presentation of (the crucified) Jesus Christ and the gospel as the two sides of the same coin is characteristic of Galatians.[24]

4) After the dispute with Peter, Jesus "called to him the crowd with his disciples" to teach them. This is identical to Paul's actions after the episode in Antioch: he proceeded with his disciples to evangelize the Gentiles. Peter's lack of faith and attempted interference was unable to stop either Jesus or Paul.

5) Jesus teaches that true discipleship revolves around the cross, which is central to Paul's gospel throughout his epistles but is especially prominent in Galatians.[25]

21 Gal 1:8-9.
22 Gal 1:1, 10, 11-12.
23 See also 10:29.
24 1:6, 11-12, 16; 3:1; 4:13-14, 18; 5:4.
25 2:20; 3:1, 13; 6:14. On suffering, see also 3:4; 4:29; *Gal* 103-105; 251-253.

6) The notion of "shame" associated with the cross recalls Paul's refusal to "boast" in anything "except in the cross of our Lord Jesus Christ" (Gal 6:14). In Galatians it is the one who does not accept the "rule" of Christ (6:16) who deserves to be "accursed" (*anathema*); in Mark the member of the "adulterous and sinful generation"[26] who does not accept Christ's "cross" due to being ashamed of it is likewise "cursed"[27] insofar as Christ will be ashamed of (and thus will reject) him.

One may add here two other Pauline connections. The first is that a close link between boasting/glory and the day of judgment (as in v.38) is typical of Paul.[28] The other is the pair of verbs "to gain" (*kerdo*) and "to forfeit/lose" (*zemio*) in v.36, both unique in Mark. A parallel use of these verbs occurs just one other time, in Philippians: "But whatever gains (*kerde*) I had, I counted as loss (*zemian*) for the sake of Christ. Indeed I count everything as loss (*zemian*) because of the surpassing worth of knowing Christ Jesus my Lord. For his sake I have suffered the loss (*zemio*) of all things, and count them as refuse, in order that I may gain (*kerdo*) Christ." (3:7-8)[29]

The Transfiguration

Only now, when the gospel of the cross has been taught, does Jesus speak of the kingdom of God "coming with power" (9:1). The ultimate epiphany of God as king and ruler of all is linked in the Old Testament to the feast of booths or tabernacles. This is the back-

---

26 *hamartolos* (sinner/sinful) applies technically to Gentiles, while adultery is the biblical expression of sin *par excellence* (see e.g. Hos 2).

27 Implied already by the terms "adulterous" and "sinful."

28 Rom 2:5-10; 5:1-11; 11:13-15; 1 Cor 9: 15-27; 15:29-34; 2 Cor 1:12-14; 5:11-15; Gal 6:4-5; Phil 2:16; 1 Thess 2:19-20.

29 The nouns *kerde* (gains) and *zemian* (loss) are cognates of *kerdo* and *zemio*. Notice in the same part of Philippians the reference to boast/glory (v.3) and sharing in the suffering and death of Christ (v.10). The noun *kerdos* also appears by itself in Phil 1:21 in conjunction with dying for Christ's sake (and the gospel's, taking into account the entire context of Phil 1:3-26).

ground for the pericope of the transfiguration (9:2-13).[30] "After six days," i.e., on the seventh day of the feast, which is the last before the solemnity of the eighth and final day, "Jesus took with him Peter and James and John, and led them up a high mountain apart by themselves (*kat' idian monous*)." This last expression recalls *kata monas* (alone) and *kat' idian* (privately) of 4:10 and 34, when Jesus was explaining the "parables of the kingdom of God."[31] Here again Jesus is "*the* teacher" (*rabbi*)[32] even in the presence of Elijah and Moses, the representatives of the Prophets and the Law and thus the Old Testament scriptures as a whole;[33] hence the divine command to "listen to him," referring to the teaching he is about to convey in vv.9-13. As he earlier stood "alone" when he was "forcing" his teaching upon his disciples (6:45, 47), here also he is "alone" in conveying to the Jerusalem "pillars" the "meaning" of the resurrection, which is at the heart of the gospel message.[34] This is precisely what Paul tried to do at the Jerusalem meeting. And here again, as Paul consistently and insistently taught, the "suffering" of the son of man came about "as it is written" (9:12), and if so then according to God's will. The suffering itself is then the key to understanding the resurrection and glorification.

At this key juncture the person of Paul himself is introduced through that of Elijah, the forerunner.[35] As I showed earlier, Mark presents Paul, in the person of John the Baptist, as the precursor of "Jesus coming into Galilee to preach the gospel of God."[36] My reading is corroborated by the fact that Elijah is also said to have "endured much," "as it is written," just as John the Baptist had— also an image of Paul.[37] Mark is thus presenting Paul, through the

---

30 Notice the reference to booths in v.5.
31 See earlier my comments on *kat' idian* in 4:34.
32 V.5. RSV has "master."
33 See *OTI2* 204.
34 1 Cor 15:1-11.
35 V.11. See Mal 4:5-6.
36 1:14. See comments on 1:1-15
37 6:14-29.

mention of the gospel of the suffering Christ, as the messenger of
the end times, accurately reflecting the way Paul himself viewed
his own role.[38] Paul acted as a forerunner by coming and challenging the Jerusalem "pillars" with the gospel, which they rejected; now the resurrected Lord comes to give them one last
chance. If they reject him too, they will have refused the intervention of God himself "with power" (v.1), thereby committing the
sin of "blaspheming against the Holy Spirit."[39]

Jesus and the Unclean Spirit

The phrase "blasphemy against the Holy Spirit" alludes to what took
place at Antioch (Gal 2:11-14), and once again that episode, a recurring theme in Mark as has already been seen, is taken up in the following passage (9:14-29). In the presence of a "great crowd," a
debate takes place between the disciples and the "scribes." As I show
above in my comments on 3:20-30, the "scribes" who in that text
"came down from Jerusalem" represent the "men from James" in the
Antioch episode. Here again Jesus shows his "faithless" disciples that
a deaf and dumb Gentile can be rendered able to speak,[40] and that it
is made possible by faith.[41] Thus it is faith that allows a Gentile to
reap the benefits of the resurrection promised to God's people. As for
the disciples, they will have to understand that they cannot do what
Jesus did *unless* (*ei me*) they "pray"[42] over the deaf and dumb Gentile, i.e., *unless* they move the (place of) "prayer" into the domain of
the Gentiles, as Paul did.[43]

38 Rom 1:1-5; 11:1-10; 15:15-21; 2 Cor 3:1-4:15; Gal 1:15-16; Phil 2:16-17.
39 3:29. Concerning the connection between "(divine) power" and "Holy Spirit," see *I
    Thess* 48-50.
40 Compare with 7:31-37.
41 V.23; RSV translates *pisteuonti* as "him who believes."
42 Some manuscripts add here "and fasting" after "prayer" as they do in 1 Cor 7:5. The
    shorter reading should be considered the original one since it is the *lectio difficilior*,
    i.e., the reading more difficult to account for. The later addition of "and fasting" is
    attributable to the development of a tradition (common among other religions as
    well) of viewing prayer as a spiritual exercise usually coupled with fasting.
43 See comments on Mk 1:35.

16

The Second Cycle of Teaching

The next cycle of teaching (9:30-10:31) begins with the second foretelling of the passion. As always in Mark, it is via Galilee that Jesus is "on his way" toward Jerusalem.[1] His presence in Galilee is kept secret as he explains to his disciples that his resurrection can only take place *following* his deliverance unto death at the hands of not only his kinfolk (8:31), but also of "men," i.e., the Gentiles.[2]

Why the secrecy? The first part of Mark deals mainly with the fact that in order to fulfill the prophecies, the gospel must be preached among, and accepted by, "all the nations" of the Gentiles. This may be considered one essential aspect of the gospel, but the other essential aspect is the story of Jesus' sacrificial death. This part—the idea that the *power* of God is revealed in *weakness*, the weakness of the cross, or put more generally, that victory is wrought through defeat—is a scandal even for the Gentiles (see 1 Cor 1:23-24). For this reason, any reference to Jesus' power must be held in check until his death on the cross so that only the true gospel may be known, the gospel of the cross which proclaims that true power comes only through weakness.

Instructions to the Pillars

With this message Jesus goes into Capernaum (9:33-37), the domain of Judaism,[3] where he will try to get the Jews there to accept

---

1 His destination is mentioned in 10:32.
2 See comments on 6:14-28.
3 See 1:21-28 for an explanation of how the name "Capernaum" acts as a symbol for Judaism in Mark.

the gospel. He teaches the twelve, who were debating "on the way" as to who was "greater," that in order to be first, one must be "last of all" and "servant of all." Both expressions are used by Paul to describe his role as an apostle: the former comes from 1 Cor 15:8, while the term "servant" (*diakonos*) by itself appears several times (1 Cor 3:5; 2 Cor 3:6; 6:4; 11:23). As for the assertion that a true servant willingly receives even a child, a Jew would look upon a Gentile as a kind of "child"—someone with no rights or power—so this would then be another exhortation to the Jewish believers of James' camp to accept Gentiles in the name of Jesus Christ, since this is the will of God.

The following pericope (9:38-41) calls upon the Jerusalem "pillars" to recognize that they are not automatically lords over all of Jesus' Gentile followers. It ends by exhorting these leaders to accept the Gentiles who accepted Paul's gospel so that they themselves might share in the "reward"[4] that God will grant through his Christ, which is the thesis of Romans chs.9-11.

The subsequent passage details the consequences of the "pillars'" refusal to accept Paul's understanding of the gospel (9:42-50). If they scandalize the "little" (i.e., Gentile) believers by not accepting them, they will be liable "to be thrown into hell." It is safer to be rid of anyone who commits such an action, and that was precisely what Paul did after the dispute at Antioch: he separated himself from his closest associate, Barnabas. The references to fire, especially v.49, recall Paul's teaching that "everyone's work" will be tested through fire (1 Cor 3:13). And following Paul's lead in speaking of apostolic activity in terms of the priestly office,[5] this "work" is referred to as a cultic offering. The link between salt and fire comes from Lev 2:1-13:

> When any one brings a cereal offering as an offering to the Lord, his offering shall be of fine flour; he shall pour oil upon it, and put

---

4   Taken from 1 Cor 3:14; see also 9:17-18.
5   Rom 15:16; Phil 2:16-17; 1 Thess 2:10. See *I Thess* 95-96.

frankincense on it, and bring it to Aaron's sons the priests. And he shall take from it a handful of the fine flour and oil, with all of its frankincense; and the priest shall burn this as its memorial portion upon the altar, an offering by fire, a pleasing odor to the Lord... And you shall bring the cereal offering that is made of these things to the Lord; and when it is presented to the priest, he shall bring it to the altar. And the priest shall take from the cereal offering its memorial portion and burn this on the altar, an offering by fire, a pleasing odor to the Lord... You shall season all your cereal offerings with salt; you shall not let the salt of the covenant with your God be lacking from your cereal offering; with all your offerings you shall offer salt. (vv.1-2; 8-9; 13)

Those who consider themselves apostles must consider themselves to be "salt" necessary for the acceptability of the sacrifice/offering of the Gentiles. But that responsibility means they will be liable to a harsher judgment if they fail—total destruction with no hope of salvation.[6] Indeed, what else would be done with salt that "has lost its saltness," that is, with an apostle who destroys God's temple instead of building it? Finally comes another exhortation to Jews and Gentiles to share table fellowship: "Have salt among[7] yourselves, and be at peace with one another." Sharing salt and bread is tantamount to sharing the same table, which in turn is an image of the eschatological peace at the table of the kingdom.

The Issue of Divorce

With this call to accept the Gentiles without reservation, Jesus, "having risen" (*anastas*),[8] proceeds into Judea proper where, "as was his custom, he was teaching them" (10:1). Notice here again

6 Compare v.15 with 1 Cor 3:16-17.
7 And not "in" as the RSV has it. Usually in Hellenistic Greek, *en* followed by a plural means "among," and in this case the expression stands in parallel with the following one, "be at peace."
8 See comments on 1:35 and 7:24. In each case, Jesus goes out to the Gentiles after "having risen" (*anastas*). The *anastasis* (resurrection) thus takes place ultimately only in Gentile territory and from there comes as the gospel to Jerusalem.

the cyclical nature of Mark's gospel: Jesus keeps repeating his teaching in order to drill it into the hearers.

His teaching this time begins with a pericope about divorce (10:2-12) that reflects another way in which Paul's teaching freed Gentiles from requirements or teachings of Judaism. The book of Ezra illustrates how a strict approach to Judaism would require Jews to divorce their Gentile spouses:

> While Ezra prayed and made confession, weeping and casting himself down before the house of God, a very great assembly of men, women, and children, gathered to him out of Israel; for the people wept bitterly. And Shecaniah the son of Jehiel, of the sons of Elam, addressed Ezra: "We have broken faith with our God and have married foreign women from the peoples of the land, but even now there is hope for Israel in spite of this. Therefore let us make a covenant with our God to put away all these wives and their children, according to the counsel of my lord and of those who tremble at the commandment of our God; and let it be done according to the law. Arise, for it is your task, and we are with you; be strong and do it." Then Ezra arose and made the leading priests and Levites and all Israel take oath that they would do as had been said. So they took the oath... All these had married foreign women, and they put them away with their children. (10:1-5, 44)

Paul realized that such an attitude would invite Gentiles unhappy with spouses to accept the gospel with the intention of "lawfully" getting rid of them after they converted, since according to Ezra's example a believer would be called upon to divorce an unbelieving spouse. To forestall any such behavior he issued the following commands to his own converts:

> To the married I give charge, not I but the Lord, that the wife should not separate from her husband (but if she does, let her remain single or else be reconciled to her husband)—and that the husband should not divorce his wife. To the rest I say, not the Lord, that if any brother has a wife who is an unbeliever, and she consents to live with him, he should not divorce her. If any woman has a husband who is an unbeliever, and he consents to live with her, she should not divorce him. For the unbelieving

husband is consecrated through his wife, and the unbelieving wife is consecrated through her husband. Otherwise, your children would be unclean, but as it is they are holy. But if the unbelieving partner desires to separate, let it be so; in such a case the brother or sister is not bound. For God has called us to peace. Wife, how do you know whether you will save your husband? Husband, how do you know whether you will save your wife? (1 Cor 7:10-17)

Jesus' discussion of this topic in Mark is clearly based on Paul's ruling. Answering his disciples' inquiry, Jesus says: "Whoever divorces his wife and marries another, commits adultery against her; and if she divorces her husband and marries another, she commits adultery." Both the Deuteronomic ruling quoted in v.4 (Deut 24:1-3) and the Ezra passage speak only of a man divorcing his wife, but Jesus' reply concerns the woman as well as the man. This two-sided approach—addressing man and woman separately and on an equal footing—occurs nowhere else either in the Old Testament or the New Testament except in 1 Cor ch.7.

The Little Children

Now that the resurrected Christ is approaching Jerusalem (10:32) and time is running out, he becomes "indignant" (10:14) at its leaders for hindering the Gentiles from sharing fully in God's kingdom announced in the gospel (10:13-16). The Jewish tradition allowed only male adults—at least 30 years of age—to speak out and teach; thus, the children in this story are symbolic of the Gentiles whom the Jewish-Christian authorities in Jerusalem did not allow to have equal voice. Mark's wording recalls 1 Thess 2:10-12, 14-16:

You are witnesses, and God also, how holy and righteous and blameless was our behavior to you believers; for you know how, like a father with his children, we exhorted each one of you and encouraged you and charged you to lead a life worthy of *God, who calls you into his own kingdom* and glory... For you, brethren, became imitators of the churches of God in Christ Jesus which are in

Judea; for you suffered the same things from your own country-
men as they did from the Jews, who killed both the Lord Jesus and
the prophets, and drove us out, and displease God and oppose all
men by *hindering us from speaking to the Gentiles that they may be
saved*—so as always to fill up the measure of their sins. But *God's
wrath has come upon them* at last!

The Rich Man

The following pericope (10:17-31) closes the cycle containing the
second announcement of Jesus' suffering, death, and resurrection. It repeats both the theme and language of Gal 2:15-3:29 by
calling upon the Jew, "rich" in the Law compared to the Gentile,
to endorse the (Pauline) gospel.[9] Both texts speak of inheritance,[10] (eternal) life,[11] the Law's not being sufficient for entering
God's kingdom,[12] the virtual identity between the person of Jesus
and the gospel,[13] and suffering and persecution.[14] And in both
the main individual being addressed is Peter.[15] The pericope ends
one cycle with a look ahead to the next through the final statement: "But many that are first will be last, and the last first." This
theme will be taken up in the first story of the following cycle
(10:35-45) dealing with James and John, who are the "first" in
the sense that they are heads of the Jerusalemite church.

---

9   A link between the previous pericope and this one is made through the introduction
    of the notion of blessing (of the children/Gentiles) at the end of the previous one
    (v.16), a notion that is central to Paul's argument in the Galatians passage (3:8-9, 14).

10 10:17 and Gal 3:18, 29.

11 10:17, 30 and Gal 2:19; 3:11.

12 10:21 and Gal 2:16.

13 10:29 and Gal 3:1, 13-14, 19, 24. See also Gal 1:6-16 and comments above on Mk 8:35.

14 10:30 and Gal 3:4 (see my comments in *Gal* 104, 251-53).

15 10:28-31 and Gal 2:14. Notice how Peter says to Jesus, who asked the rich man to
    "follow" him (10:21): "Lo, we have left everything and followed you." (v.28)

17

The Third Cycle of Teaching

Third Announcement of Jesus' Death

The third and last prediction of Jesus' death and resurrection (10:32-34) opens up the last part of Mark that deals with the coming of the resurrected Christ into God's city, Jerusalem. The gospel message he proclaims calls upon the city's residents to move into the "Galilee of the nations" where the gospel originated and where it is now preserved and proclaimed by the Pauline community under Timothy's leadership.[1]

Presentation of the Gospel to the Pillars

Jesus' "followers on the way (*en te hodo*) were afraid" because of the mention of persecutions earlier (v.30). But Jesus "begins" to tell "the twelve" that in fact persecution—by the Gentile authorities as well as the Jerusalemite Jews and Jewish-Christians[2]—is the lot of Jesus and his followers.[3] The march toward Jerusalem starts with a castigation of its Jewish-Christian authorities in the persons of James and John, sons of Zebedee,[4] and conversely an open endorsement of Paul's gospel with its ideal of sacrificial service (10:35-45). The two Jewish-Christian leaders effectively wanted to accept the gospel while rejecting its essential character as the gospel "of the cross." They still wanted to have a share in the rule over the Gentiles, which is God's prerogative, and God's

1 See the Introduction.
2 See the Introduction and comments on 6:21.
3 The inevitability of persecution is discussed in my comments above on 6:14-29. Remember also the parable of the sower—besides the fact that it too mentions persecution as the lot of Jesus' followers, it shares some of the same terminology, i.e., Jesus "begins" to teach (4:1), and he explains the parable to "the twelve."
4 The name Zebedee has negative connotations; see comments on 1:19-20.

alone; even Jesus *in his glory* is ultimately "subject" to his Father, as Paul taught (1 Cor 15:20-28).

Notice here again a clear link to Galatians: throughout the New Testament, *hoi dokountes*[5] (those who consider/have in mind) is found only in Mark 10:42 and Gal 2:2, 6, in each place meaning those who "consider themselves to be of special value." We are told that they intend to "rule over the Gentiles" and, by doing so, to actually *"lord* it over" and "exercise *authority* over" them; a stand Paul fought against bitterly at the Jerusalem meeting.

James and John are told that they would still be, as believers in Jesus the Christ, part of the Messianic community, "but to sit at my right hand or at my left is not mine to grant, but it is for those for whom it has been prepared."[6] This, replies Jesus, is not his to give. He can only offer them the way toward that end, and it is the way he himself is following: that of "baptism," in this case meaning a leader's self-sacrifice for the sake of his community.[7] That self-sacrifice is the same as Paul's path of servanthood as it is outlined in vv.43-44. These verses repeat the terminology of 9:35, with the addition of a word Paul frequently applies to himself: *doulos* (slave/servant). Beyond that, the sacrificial nature of the true leadership of Christ's church is presented against the image of the Isaianic "servant of the Lord" (Is 53:12). Here again we are fully on Paul's territory, as evidenced by numerous references or allusions in his epistles to Isaiah's "servant."[8]

---

5   The RSV translation "those who are supposed to" obscures the link between Mark and Galatians, which is striking in the Greek original.

6   The mention of "right hand" in this context recalls the "right hand of fellowship" these apostles exchanged with Paul in Gal 2:9.

7   Notice how the mention of baptism is linked to that of the cup to be drunk (v.38), a reference to Jesus' sacrificial death (see 14:23-24).

8   Compare (in the original Greek for the New Testament and the Septuagint for the Old) Gal 1:15 with Is 49:1; Phil 2:16 with Is 49:4; 2 Cor 6:2 with Is 49:8; Rom 8:33 with Is 50:8; Rom 10:16 with Is 53:1; Rom 4:25 with Is 53:4-5; 1 Cor 5:7 with Is 53:7; Rom 5:19 with Is 53:11.

18

Timothy Offers Jerusalem Paul's Last Message

Timothy Is Paul's Successor

With this notion in mind, of a sacrifice that would redeem others, Jesus proceeds to Jerusalem via Jericho (10:46-52). As his namesake Joshua before him led God's people, he leads "his disciples and a great multitude" from Galilee (of the Gentiles) where his gospel originated—just as God's *Torah* did in the wilderness of Sinai and his word borne by Ezekiel, from "the wilderness of the nations."[1] Unlike his predecessor, however, Jesus does not need to linger in or around Jericho ("And they came to Jericho; and as he was leaving Jericho...") because he is not coming to claim the "land." Instead, he is the savior announced by Second Isaiah (Is chs.40-55), coming into his city Jerusalem to establish his righteous justice proclaimed in the gospel and thus to draw to it all the nations from afar.[2] And herein lies the main question for the Jews: Is "Jesus of Nazareth" truly the "son of David," the Messiah, the "holy one of God" here to save the Jews—or has he instead "come to destroy them" (1:24)?

Facing the many who did not want him to confess Jesus as "the son of David," the blind man Bartimaeus insistently does so.[3] Who might this blind man be, who was sitting "by the way" (*para*

---

1 See the Introduction. "The multitude" or "the crowd" is also a symbol for the Gentiles in Mark.
2 See *OTI2* 166-184.
3 The RSV translates *typhlos...prosaiton* as "a blind beggar" instead of "a blind (person)...asking insistently/begging."

ten hodon) and finally was "saved" through "faith," "having his eyes opened" and "following"—as a disciple would—Jesus "in the way" (*en te hodo*)? Based on a limited range of evidence I suggested above that the blind man of 8:22-26 represented Timothy, and the evidence leads to the same conclusion in regard to the blind man of 10:46-52.

Mark devotes an unusual amount of attention to this blind man's name: "the son of Timaeus, Bartimaeus, blind, was sitting..." It is also telling that the translation of the Aramaic "Bartimaeus" *precedes* rather than follows the name. All these circumvolutions most likely reflect a cryptic attempt at referring to Timothy, Paul's "son" par excellence,[4] who was the only non-apostle to have his name included as co-sender in Paul's letters.[5] *Timaios* is the closest possible Greek name to *Timotheos*. Besides, it is close as well as akin in meaning to the adjective *timios* that means "honored, revered," which is what Paul was among his disciples. Hence, Timothy was the "son of Timaeus," understand "of the revered one." In 8:22-26 he was led by Paul to the true understanding of Jesus' Messiahship and joined him in the "beginning of the gospel" at Philippi (8:27-38); now that Paul is dead, he is called to lead the way of the resurrected Jesus into (James' and the Jews') Jerusalem.

The Entry into Jerusalem

The pericope of the entry into Jerusalem (11:1-11) opens with an awkward phrase: "And when they drew near to Jerusalem, to Bethphage and Bethany, toward the Mount of Olives..." The most likely meaning of this confusing combination of names is that the road to the Mount of Olives, where the Lord's final epiphany would take place (at the feast of booths),[6] can be taken through either Bethphage or Bethany. The former translates as

4   Rom 16:21; 1 Cor 4:14-17; Phil 2:19-20; 1 Thess 3:2.
5   2 Cor 1:1; Phil 1:1; 1 Thess 1:1; Philem 1.
6   See Zech 14:4-5, 16.

"the house of (unripe) figs" or "the house of food,"[7] and the latter as "the house of the poor/afflicted/humble." The first would be the road of the Jews who decided to take up arms against the Roman armies and would take refuge in the orchards of the blossoming fig trees where they could hide behind the leaves and consume the figs as food; the second would be the way recommended by Timothy, that of the "poor" who would wait for the epiphany of their crucified Lord. As for the colt, it represents the young Jewish-Christian community of Jerusalem: it is "tied" in the sense that it has not yet been freed by following Paul's gospel, and thus "no one has ever sat" on it because it has not yet fulfilled its duty and destiny (a donkey's duty and destiny is to serve as a beast of burden). It can now accept the offer of freedom ("untie") which Jesus "sends"[8] it through two of his disciples who proclaim Paul's gospel to them,[9] or it can join the Jewish insurrection against the Romans. That it must choose between two divergent paths is indicated by the remark that it was still "before the (city) gate outside *at the bifurcation*" (*epi tou amphodou*). James' community will be untied, i.e., freed from its slavery, only if it lets itself be guided by the Jesus whom Paul preaches, and joins the disciples in confessing him as the sole Messiah.

This Jesus enters Jerusalem and the temple "made with (human) hands" (14:58), only for a visitation, not to settle in it. When it was evening, he went out "with the twelve" (i.e., his entire discipleship) to Bethany, "the house of the poor." The next morning (11:12) he would return from there to enter Jerusalem in order to establish the "heavenly Jerusalem" Paul proclaimed (Gal 4:25-27) around a different temple, one "not made with (human) hands."

Coming out from Bethany (11:12-14) Jesus sees that the leaves of the fig trees of Bethphage were alluringly misleading; the

---

7   If the latter half *phage* is taken to refer to the Greek verb that means "eat."
8   The Greek verb *apostello* in v.1 is from the same root as the noun *apostolos* (apostle).
9   Most probably a reference to Timothy and Mark.

figs were unripe because it was not "their time." This episode represents another attempt to convince the disciples[10] not to follow the way of the Jewish armed insurrection, which he declares anathema because it is contrary to Paul's gospel and its call to accept the way of the cross.[11]

Jesus' Authority

Then Jesus cleanses the temple (11:15-19) to take it from under the monopoly of the Jewish Jerusalemite leadership and in order to make out of it "a house of prayer for all the *nations*." The full quotation from Isaiah makes clear this emphasis on including the Gentiles:

> Thus says the Lord: "Keep justice, and do righteousness, for soon my salvation will come, and my deliverance be revealed. Blessed is the man who does this, and the son of man who holds it fast, who keeps the sabbath, not profaning it, and keeps his hand from doing any evil." Let not the foreigner who has joined himself to the Lord say, "The Lord will surely separate me from his people"; and let not the eunuch say, "Behold, I am a dry tree." For thus says the Lord: "To the eunuchs who keep my sabbaths, who choose the things that please me and hold fast my covenant, I will give in my house and within my walls a monument and a name better than sons and daughters; I will give them an everlasting name which shall not be cut off. And the foreigners who join themselves to the Lord, to minister to him, to love the name of the Lord, and to be his servants, every one who keeps the sabbath, and does not profane it, and holds fast my covenant—these I will bring to my holy mountain, and make them joyful in my house of prayer; their burnt offerings and their sacrifices will be accepted on my altar; for my house shall be called a house of prayer for all peoples. Thus says the Lord God, who gathers the outcasts of Israel, I will gather yet others to him besides those already gathered." (Is 56:1-8)

It is clear then that no Gentile would be shut out of the new "heavenly Jerusalem," which is God's city. The Jewish leadership's reaction to

---

10 V.14 has "heard him," not "heard it" as in the RSV.
11 Gal 1:8-9; 6:11-16.

Jesus' words and actions was to seek Jesus' destruction,[12] whereas "all the crowd (i.e., the Gentiles) was astonished at his teaching." And again, when evening had come, Jesus went out of the city in preparation for the "early morning."[13]

The following pericope (11:20-27) begins with the following "early morning" when the "cursed" fig tree of Bethphage (representing the Jewish armed insurrection) is "withered away *to its roots*," as Jeremiah had predicted concerning the temple of Jerusalem.[14] In reply to Peter's surprise the disciples are told: "Have faith in God. Truly, I say to you, whoever says to this mountain, 'Be taken up and cast into the sea,' and does not doubt in his heart, but believes that what he says will come to pass, it will be done for him." "This mountain" can only be the temple mount of Jerusalem, God's throne, which must finally be thrown into the "sea" (of the nations) according to the prophecies of both Isaiah and Jeremiah. And it can be accomplished through faith in the God preached in Paul's gospel. Indeed, his gospel teaches that *all*, Jews as well as Gentiles, are sinners;[15] it also teaches that God is "father" to "all those who trespass," Gentiles as well as Jews.[16]

The debate about Jesus' authority in Jerusalem in the subsequent passage (11:27-33) is another reference to the Jerusalem meeting described in Gal 2:1-10,[17] with "the chief priests and the scribes and the elders" representing the "pillars" of the Jerusalemite church. The link between Jesus and John the Baptist is remarkable at this junction. As I established earlier, John the Baptist

---

12 See comments on 1:37; 3:6, 32; 8:11-12.

13 11:20; see comments on 1:35 and 16:2.

14 7:1-15. This was prepared for by the reference in the preceding pericope to Jeremiah's accusation that the Jerusalemite leadership made the temple into "a den of robbers."

15 Gal 2:15, 17. The mention of Peter in 11:21 betrays a link between this pericope and Gal 2:11-17.

16 11:25; compare with Gal 3:21-4:7.

17 This reference to the Jerusalem meeting comes directly after a mention of forgiveness of trespasses, just as in 2:1-12 a discussion about Jesus' authority to forgive sins represents that same Jerusalem meeting.

represents Paul in Mark's gospel, and given that understanding, Mark is saying here that the resurrected Jesus explicitly links his own authority to that of Paul.[18] He leaves it up to the Jewish-Christians of Jerusalem to decide whether they will accept leadership "from God" or from men;[19] no one can make the decision on their behalf.

Last Words of Teaching before the Announcement of the Last Test

To clarify that their decision is ultimately concerning the resurrected Messiah, the Son of God, Mark offers the following pericope (12:1-12). This is the last time the gospel[20] will be offered to the "farmers" (*georgoi*) of God's vineyard, i.e., those in charge of the Jerusalem church,[21] in parables. This parable is the same one used by Isaiah to address the leaders of his Jerusalem (Is 5:1-2), with the "beloved son" being the one on account of whom the Jewish-Christian Jerusalemite leaders are finally held accountable. As a result of their rejection of him as *the* representative and sole heir[22] of God who planted the vineyard, God gives the vineyard over to the care of "others." Put more plainly, Paul's disciples are now the ones to whom the "inheritance" falls, as "fellow heirs with Christ" (Rom 8:17). That the test for retaining title of the church's leadership hangs on the recognition of Jesus' Messiahship, in spite of his apparent rejection on the cross, is further underscored by the reference to Ps 118:22-23 in vv.10-11, since that

18 Compare to Gal 1:11-12, 15-16.
19 Compare to Gal 1:1, 10-12.
20 Notice the verb "began." See my comments above on 1:1, 45; 5.20, 62. Note especially that with 4:1 and 2 (the beginning of the verses) Jesus is teaching in parables just as he is here. Notice also here in 12:1 the verb "speak" (*lalo*), which as I show above in my comments on 2:2; 5:36; 8:32; and 4:33-34 is an allusion to speaking *the gospel* (note especially that 4:33-34 is in the same context as the parable of the sower).
21 The use of "[farming] field" (*georgion*) as a metaphor for the church occurs in 1 Cor 3:9.
22 See Rom 4:13-14; 8:17; Gal 3:18-19, 29; 4:1-7, on the matter of inheritance.

psalm portrays God's king as his chosen one in spite of his rejection by those around him.[23]

The four following pericopes all emphasize the same point. They are included in order to give James' party one last chance to accept the crucified Jesus as the Messiah, the true liberator of Jerusalem from its slavery,[24] to convince it not to fall into the trap of joining their fellow Jews in insurrection against Rome as though there were another Messiah yet to come, and consequently to prepare them to take the right stand at the time of the final test (ch.13). They all thus look forward to, and prepare for, chapter 13.

The first of the four (12:13-17) teaches the Pharisees (representing Jewish-Christians) and the Herodians (the Jews), that the eventual fall of Jerusalem to Caesar is not to be equated with the defeat of God and his cause, as Jeremiah himself had taught long ago in similar circumstances.

The same message is reiterated in the following passage (12:18-27)[25] along the lines of Rom 4:13-24, in which Paul writes that God granted Abraham a "progeny" (*sperma*)[26] although his body was "already given unto death" (*ede nenekromenon*) and in spite of the "mortification/state of death" (*nekrosis*) of Sarah's womb,[27] on the basis of Abraham's faith in God "who gives life to the dead."[28]

---

23 See *OTI3* 76 for the kingly nature of this psalm. As for its allusion to the king's rejection, notice especially vv.17-18: "I shall not die, but I shall live, and recount the deeds of the Lord. The Lord has chastened me sorely, but he has not given me over to death."

24 See comments on 11:1-11.

25 The link between this passage and Mk ch.13 is secured through the use of the verb *plano/planomai* that occurs only in 12:24, 27 and 13:5, 6 in Mark. The RSV is misleading since it translates it as "be wrong" in the first case and "lead astray" in the latter.

26 Which is precisely the issue in the story presented by the Sadducees. Indeed, not only does the story deal with the Mosaic ruling of Deut 25:5 regarding the securing of a *sperma* (progeny) to a deceased who did not have any (Mk 12:19). The term *sperma* itself is repeated in vv.20 and 21.

27 V.19.

28 V.17. The Greek *zoopoiountos tous nekrous* (who gives life to the dead) is behind

This passage acts as a reminder that God is not defeated if Rome defeats the Jews and Jerusalem, for death itself is not final and therefore not in itself to be considered a defeat.

There follows in 12:28-34 the teaching that "to love one's neighbor as oneself is much more than all whole burnt offerings and sacrifices," which recalls Rom 13:8-10 as well as 12:1-21 where we are told of "a living sacrifice, holy and acceptable to God" attainable through "renewal of your mind."[29] Rom ch.12 and 13:8-10 are related in that the former is woven around the notion of brotherly love, on which the latter focuses directly.[30]

Finally, in 12:35-37, those who are expecting the Messiah as a kingly, i.e., victorious,[31] "son of David" who would lead their revolt against the Roman enemy, are reminded, through David's own words, that the true Messiah is *kyrios* (Lord), as the crucified Jesus already is.[32]

The connection with Romans can be detected in the way the first, third, and fourth Markan pericopes follow the sequence in Rom 13, which is comprised of the following sections: obedience to rulers (vv.1-7),[33] brotherly love (vv.8-10),[34] and Christ's coming as Lord (vv.11-14).[35] The connection can also be seen in the final pericopes of Mk ch.12—vv.38-40 and vv.41-44. In the former the scribes are condemned for their refusal to engage in table fellowship, and thus in full communal fellowship as one com-

---

Mark's concluding remark *ouk estin theos nekron alla zonton* (He is not God of the dead, but of the living; 12:27).

29 Vv.1-2. Notice how the scribe is told by Jesus, in Mk 12:34, that he answered *nounekhos* (mindfully/wisely), an adverb based on the same word translated "mind" in Romans (*nous*), and which is unique in the New Testament.

30 See particularly the reference to love in 12:9.

31 See *OTT3* 17-32 and 62-63.

32 Compare with Rom 1:3-4.

33 Compare with Mk 12:13-17.

34 Compare with Mk 12:28-34.

35 Compare with Mk 12:35-37. Notice Jesus' answer to the scribe: "You are not far from the kingdom of God" (v.34), which recalls "For salvation is nearer to us now than when we first believed" of Rom 13:11.

munity, with the Gentiles,[36] which is reminiscent of Rom 14:1-12.[37] The reference to the "widows" in Mk 12:39 looks ahead to the following passage about a poor widow's offering to the temple. Here again we are at the heart of the purpose of Paul's letter to the Romans, namely, to invite James' party to accept the offerings of the believing Gentiles.[38] Through this offering the latter are putting at risk their "entire life" (*holon ton bion*); indeed they, many of them slaves, have apostatized from the Roman civil religion, which leaves them open to the death sentence at any moment. James' followers should then not be afraid to lose their lives for Christ's sake by abandoning their fellow armed Jerusalemite Jews and choosing instead to accept fellowship with Paul's Christian Gentiles.

---

36 The scribes are said to "walk" (i.e., according to the Law) in a way that gives them "priority" (*protokathedria, protoklisia*) over others in the synagogues and at tables, while they "devour/eat up" the houses (i.e., houses of prayers) of the widows (i.e., the Gentiles) and make up an "excuse/pretense" to pray *makra* (far away/at a distance) from them. The RSV translates *makra* as "long prayers," reading it as an adjective neuter plural; but the same form functions in Greek adverbially also.

37 Notice that in Mk 12:40 the scribes "will receive the greater condemnation" (*lempsontai perissoteron krima*), which clearly refers to "will incur judgment" (*krima lempsontai*) of Rom 13:2. The intention of "greater" (*perissoteron*) in Mark is to say that they will have to answer to the true "Lord" (*kyrios*) whose judgment is much harsher than that of the Roman emperor.

38 See pp. 9-10. The terminology of Mk 12:44, "abundance" (*perisseuon*) and "poverty" (*hysteresis*), is reminiscent of that of 2 Cor 8:14, "abundance" (*perisseumai*) and "want" (*hysterema*). 2 Cor 8-9 consists of Paul's appeal to his Christian Gentiles to raise a collection of money he intended to take up with him to the church in Jerusalem.

19

Last Call before the Lord's Coming

Beginning with the questioning of Jesus' authority (11:27-33) and up to the pericope of the poor widow's offering (12:41-44), Jesus is in the temple giving the authorities there one last chance to understand that he is the Messiah coming to Jerusalem to fulfill God's plan of salvation right there among them. They reject that opportunity, and he leaves the temple for the last time to its own destiny, informing his disciples that it is only man-made (14:58) and thus is bound for destruction just as its predecessor in Jeremiah's and Ezekiel's time was (13:1-2).

Then, while on the Mount of Olives from where the Lord will come to make Jerusalem the city of his righteousness and salvation for Jews and Gentiles alike,[1] four disciples—Peter, James, John, and Andrew—ask him when the destruction of the temple will take place and what the "sign," which he had refused to give earlier (8:11-12), will be. As I point out above,[2] these four together represent the new temple of Jewish-Christianity, and the unique relevance to them of the old temple's destruction explains why they and only they are the ones who pose the question (they do so "privately" / *kat' idian*)[3] and receive its answer (13:3-36).

Now Jesus "begins" for the last time to declare the gospel message.[4] This time he introduces it with stern warning: "Take heed that no one leads you astray. Many will come in my name, saying, 'I am he!' and they will lead many astray." His disciples must wait

---

1 See Zech 14.
2 See comments on 2:1-12.
3 On the importance and meaning of this expression see my comments above on 4:34.
4 See comments on "beginning" and "began" earlier.

until he comes in glory, as was traditionally expected of the Messiah. Meanwhile they must remember that he is still the crucified Jesus who was "delivered up" unto the hands of both Jews and Gentiles, and they will have to share in his fate as a testimony to their faith in him, exactly as Paul did.[5] "For they will deliver you up to councils; and you will be beaten in synagogues; and you will stand before governors and kings for my sake, in testimony against them (*eis martyrion autois*)."[6]

It is immediately before these words that the caveat "Take heed (that you not be led astray)" is repeated. The point here is that a good beginning does not guarantee a good end, for only "he who endures to the end will be saved." The "end" is then defined as some time after *the gospel*[7] is preached to "all the nations/Gentiles" (*eis panta ta ethne*). Put otherwise, it is not the eventual appearance of false messiahs, wars, or rumors of wars (vv.6-7) that will herald God's final coming, but rather the acceptance of Paul's gospel by the Gentiles and the acknowledgment of the truth of that acceptance (through reception of the Gentiles' offering) by the Jerusalemite church leaders. Only then will the Holy Spirit have spoken (v.11)!

In the following passage (vv.14-22) the phrase "abomination of desolation" or "desolating sacrilege" comes from the book of Daniel, where it refers to Antiochus Epiphanes' desecration of the temple in 167 B.C. by setting up the statue of Zeus on its altar of sacrifice and abolishing the Jewish sacrifices to God.[8] Here in Mark it applies to what a Roman general would do upon con-

---

5   See comments on the three predictions of suffering, death, and resurrection (8:31; 9:31; 10:33).
6   Note the phrases "for my sake" and "testimony against them." My comments on 1:44; 6:11; 8:35; 10:29 show that they are connected with witnessing to the gospel in Mark. Throughout Mark ch.13 the central theme is the gospel, and not only in v.10, which is considered by many as the center of a chiasm.
7   Notice the use of the absolute "the gospel" without any qualification, which is none other than what is presented in Mark's work.
8   Dan 9:27; 11:31; 12:11. See also 1 Macc 1:54.

quering Jerusalem. That event would be an opportunity for the "false christs and false prophets" (representing Jews leading the rebellion against Rome) to pressure the "chosen ones" (the Jewish-Christians), in order to "lead them astray" from the gospel. But the four disciples, and through them all the disciples, will be prepared by having been forewarned: "take heed; I have told you all things beforehand." Finally, the true Messiah, the suffering "son of man," will appear in glory and will gather his "chosen ones" who have shared in the only meaningful suffering, that which is endured for the sake of the crucified Jesus and his gospel (vv.24-27).[9] All that matters when this end comes is Jesus' "words" which "will not pass away" even when everything else does (vv.28-31). And his words are:

> But of that day or that hour no one knows, not even the angels in heaven, nor the Son, but only the Father. *Take heed, stay awake; for you do not know when the time will come.* It is like a man going on a journey, when he leaves home and puts his servants in charge, each with his work, and commands the doorkeeper to be on the watch. Watch therefore—for you do not know when the master of the house will come, in the evening, or at midnight, or at cock-crow, or in the morning—*lest he come suddenly and find you asleep.* And what I say to you *I say to all: Watch.* (vv.32-37)

These words are unmistakably intended to prepare the hearer for the real test that lies ahead: "to lose one's life for the sake of the gospel" (8:35); in other words, to die for the true God who reveals himself through the gospel of the crucified Jesus Christ. And everyone must realize that this will be a difficult undertaking, for even the apostles Peter, James, and John fall asleep during the time of test, in spite of Jesus' warnings (14:32-42).

---

9 See Dan 7.

20

Jerusalem's First Refusal of the Gospel

At the start of chapter 14 the priests and scribes "seek" to arrest and "kill" Jesus "in stealth/by guile" (*en doloi*; vv.1-2), a combination of expressions found nowhere else in the New Testament except 1 Thess 2:3. Mark's presentation of Jesus again appears to be based on Paul's life, but it is also based on Paul's teaching: in spite of all Jesus' enemies' careful planning to avoid killing him during the feast of Passover, he will end up dying at precisely that time after all, thus becoming the paschal lamb as Paul taught (1 Cor 5:7-8).[1]

Anointing at Bethany

In Bethany, the "village of the poor,"[2] Jesus confronts his hearers with an either/or choice: to side with the Christ of the Pauline gospel or with the Judean insurgents (14:3-11). Peter is called "Simon the leper," thus putting him in the same class Paul was in when he was persecuting the church of Christ (Paul is represented as a leper in 1:40-45). Again we find a passage that recalls the controversy at Antioch (Gal 2:11-14). In the "house" of Simon, i.e., at his "table," the recognition of Jesus' Messiahship/kingship by a

---

1   Notice the close correspondence in terminology between Mk 14:2 ("It was now two days before the Passover (*paskha*) and the feast of Unleavened Bread (*azyma*). And the chief priests and the scribes were seeking how to arrest him by stealth, and kill him; for they said, 'Not during the feast (*heorte*), lest there be a tumult of the people.'") and 1 Cor 5:7-8 ("Cleanse out the old leaven that you may be a new lump, as you really are unleavened (*azymoi*). For Christ, our paschal lamb (*to paskha hemon*), has been sacrificed. Let us, therefore, celebrate the festival (*heortazomen*), not with the old leaven, the leaven of malice and evil, but with the unleavened bread (*en azymois*) of sincerity and truth.")

2   See comments on 11:1.

woman (representing the Gentiles)[3] through the pouring of oint-
ment (*myron*) over his head, was criticized. Simon allowed his
company to give its own interpretation of the Messiah's role,
namely that he would lead the Judean "poor"[4] to victory in an
armed combat against their enemies. However, Jesus teaches that
the issue at stake is not the "poor" and their fate, but recognition
of the true Messiah—which literally means "the one who is
anointed"—and acknowledging him as king for his "burial." This
teaching is part and parcel of "the" gospel that is to be "preached
unto the whole world": the apparently vanquished Jesus is the
sole true Messiah even for the besieged Jerusalemite Jews. But under the leadership of James, the Christian as well as non-Christian
Jews of Jerusalem do not want to accept this view of the Messiah,
and their refusal represents nothing less than a betrayal of Christ.[5]
That betrayal is represented here by the betrayal of Judas, whose
name, as pointed out above, stands as a symbol for the Judean
Jews of Mark's day.

Passover

In 14:12-21 Jesus sends two of his disciples[6] to prepare the Passover for Jesus and the twelve. That Mark intends to offer here a
new teaching regarding the true meaning of this feast is suggested
by his use of "the teacher/master" (*ho didaskalos*) as the title for Jesus. And here again the stress is on the notion of the betrayal of
this new teaching by one of the twelve, notably the one closest to
him.[7] The assertion that someone sharing Christ's paschal meal is

---

3 Most likely representing the Pauline community; see further my comments on
   Mary Magdalene in 15:40.
4 See 2 Cor 6:10 and Gal 2:10 for the use of "poor" in reference to the Jerusalemite
   and Judean Christians.
5 See comments on 3:19.
6 Most probably Timothy and Mark, as in Mk 11:1 where we encounter the same
   phrase *apostellei dyo ton matheton autou* (sends/sent two of his disciples).
7 Compare 14:18 with 1 Cor 11:23 (and 10:14-23).

still under judgment—i.e., that merely partaking in it does not guarantee anyone his favor—is none other than Paul's teaching as presented in 1 Cor 11:27-34.

Mark's account of the last supper itself (vv.22-26) also reproduces themes from 1 Corinthians. Jesus offers the food as only a host does; the eucharistic table is thus *his table*, just as in 1 Cor 11:20 where the meal that the believers partake of is the Lord's. Yet he himself is also the food consumed at that table, according to the *words* he utters while dispensing that food, both here and in 1 Cor 11:24-25.[8] He becomes food by being *sacrificed* as the Messiah, as is clear from the explanation he gives when he offers the chalice—and the validity of this teaching for all the disciples is underscored through the phrase "and they *all* drank of it." Finally, all of this points to the future kingdom of God that will be established at the Lord's coming, as is implied here and explicit in 1 Cor 11:26. Evidence that Mark also had this theme in mind is found in v.26: "And when they had sung a hymn, they went out to the Mount of Olives." The Mount of Olives is the place of God's final appearance according to Zechariah (14:16-17), and now it becomes the seat of the coming Lord, whose Messianic community gathers around him there. Whenever the disciples are gathered at the eucharistic meal, they are preparing to join in the hymnology of praise for the coming one, not at Mount Zion, but at the Mount of Olives, God's eschatological site where the "survivors" from among the Gentiles as well as the Jews will "worship the King, the Lord of hosts."[9] The pattern here—mention of Christ's sacrifice on the cross immediately followed by waiting for his coming in glory—is typical of Mark.[10] The emphasis on this pattern results in a de-emphasis on the resurrection itself, which explains the absence in Mark of any pericopes about Jesus' post-resurrection appearances.

---

8 Notice also that Paul received "from the Lord [himself]" (v.23)—i.e., "by the *word* of the Lord" (1 Thess 4:15)—the teaching as to the meaning of the eucharistic meal.

9 Zech 14:16-17. See also my comments on 11:1 and 23.

10 See also my comments on ch.13.

Since the only true Messiah is the one preached in the (Pauline) gospel,[11] he is to be found in Galilee (of the nations) where Paul preached, rather than in Jerusalem. And once again, Mark calls upon the followers of Peter, the apostle to the circumcision,[12] to set their eyes on Galilee and join Paul's followers in proclaiming the one gospel throughout the entire Roman world (vv.27-31). The fact that the Messiah must be proclaimed as the *crucified* Jesus will prove to be a stumbling block (*skandalon*) that not only Peter but all the disciples will have to face.[13]

The Test of Gethsemane

Immediately after the disciples swear to their loyalty, the "pillars" among them immediately fail the most basic test of their discipleship (vv.32-42).[14] This passage is another version of the parable of the vineyard and the tenants (12:1-12). The name Gethsemane is a Hebrew/Aramaic combination of *gat* (winepress) and *šamen* (fat, plenteous, fertile). The original version of this parable in Is 5 uses the word *šamen* to describe the vineyard, in the phrase "on a very fertile hill" (*beqeren ben-šamen*). On the other hand, the noun *gat* occurs in the prophetic writings only in Isaiah 63:2 and Joel 3:13, both times in reference to God's judgment of sinners before establishing his final kingdom. In Isaiah it is part of a long text (63:1-66:17) following a passage about the eschatological Jerusalem (ch.62) and preceding one about God's final kingdom (66:18-24). The middle section containing the word *gat* is similar to Mk 14:32-42 in two other ways: the speaker in it recounts his

---

11 See my comments on 13:3-13 and 21-23.

12 Gal 2:8. As such he has responsibility for Jews throughout the Roman empire and is not bound to Jerusalem.

13 The original of "You will all fall away" (v.27) is *pantes skandalisthesesthe* and the original of "they all fall away" (v.29) is *pantes skandalisthesontai*. The scriptural quotation in v.27b is taken from Zech 13:7, the chapter that speaks of God's judgment and is followed by ch.14 where we are told about his eschatological epiphany on the Mount of Olives.

14 In v.38 we find the only instance of *peirasmos* (test, temptation) in Mark.

abandonment by those who should have been his friends, and the prayer in it addresses God as "Father":

> Who is this that comes from Edom, in crimsoned garments from Bozrah, he that is glorious in his apparel, marching in the greatness of his strength? "It is I, announcing vindication, mighty to save." Why is thy apparel red, and thy garments like his that treads in the wine press (*gat*)? "I have trodden the wine press (*purah*) *alone,* and from the peoples *no one was with me;* I trod them in my anger and trampled them in my wrath; their lifeblood is sprinkled upon my garments, and I have stained all my raiment. For the day of vengeance was in my heart, and my year of redemption has come. I looked, but there was *no one to help;* I was appalled, but there was *no one to uphold;* so my own arm brought me victory, and my wrath upheld me..." I will recount the steadfast love of the Lord, the praises of the Lord, according to all that the Lord has granted us, and the great goodness to the house of Israel which he has granted them according to his mercy, according to the abundance of his steadfast love. For he said, Surely they are my people, sons who will not deal falsely; and he became their Savior...But they rebelled and grieved his holy Spirit; therefore he turned to be their enemy, and himself fought against them...Look down from heaven and see, from thy holy and glorious habitation. Where are thy zeal and thy might? The yearning of thy heart and thy compassion are withheld from me. For thou art *our Father,* though Abraham does not know us and Israel does not acknowledge us; thou, O Lord, art *our Father,* our Redeemer from of old is thy name...Yet, O Lord, thou art *our Father;* we are the clay, and thou art our potter; we are all the work of thy hand. (63:1-64:7)

The "pillars" failed to pray the Isaianic prayer insofar as they refused to acknowledge God as the Father of *all* those who repent.[15]

15 The *'abba, ho pater* (Mk 14:36) is patterned after what we find in Gal 4:6 and Rom 8:15, where it emphasizes that God is the Father of all believers, Jews and Gentiles alike (see for more details *Gal* 201-217). The passage in Isaiah following the one quoted above also emphasizes the universality of God's salvation: "For I know their works and their thoughts, and I am coming to gather all nations and tongues; and they shall come and shall see my glory, and I will set a sign among them. And from them I will send survivors to the nations, to Tarshish, Put, and Lud, who draw the

While they cannot accept God's will that through the Messiah's sacrifice God deigns to become the Father of all those who accept his salvation (Is 63:1), Jesus does accept it and remains faithful to it. This is precisely the story related in Gal 2:1-14. And in both places Peter is singled out from the rest as one of whom much is expected but who falters in the end (vv.29-31 in the immediately preceding passage, v.37 in this one).

The end of this pericope (vv.41-42) introduces the story of Jesus' betrayal. As will be seen, that story is also about Paul's gospel: it represents the rejection by the Jerusalemite Jews of the last chance for a change of mind, which Paul had offered them through his letter to the Romans.

Jesus Betrayed

That the betrayer Judas ("Judah") represents the Jerusalemite Jews in the story of the betrayal (vv.43-51) is clear from the company he keeps: "And immediately, while he was still speaking, Judas came, one of the twelve, and with him a crowd with swords and clubs, from *the chief priests and the scribes and the elders.*" All these people rejected the Isaianic gospel preached by Paul, according to which God's salvation is offered equally to all those who seek him through repentance, Jews and Gentiles alike.

As for those who would take up the sword, ostensibly to defend their Messiah, they are sadly misguided. If the gospel is the good news of God's peace, then one does not defend it militarily. Yet this is precisely what the Jerusalemite Jews, under pressure from the zealots, decided to do. In what sense was their action a "kiss of betrayal" to the Jesus Paul knew and preached? Due to the Jewish insurrection in Judah the Romans would look with suspicion upon all Jews in the empire; and since Timothy and Mark

bow, to Tubal and Javan, to the coastlands afar off, that have not heard my fame or seen my glory; and they shall declare my glory among the nations." (66:17-18)

and many of the disciples were Jews, a Jewish insurgency would jeopardize their ability to preach the gospel freely.

At the end of this section is a seemingly superfluous mention of a "young man" who was with Jesus but flees.[16] The "young man" is Mark himself, and in this text he is beginning to set himself up as an example for Peter and his followers, whom Mark's gospel calls upon to return to the true Messiah after having fallen away from him. Just as Acts pictures Mark as someone who at first failed the test of following in Paul's footsteps (15:37-38), so Mark flees from Jesus—but only temporarily. The "young man" will return to proclaim the risen Lord in 16:5,[17] as an example to Peter, who can also return to the fold and proclaim the crucified and risen Lord, after having temporarily fallen away.

Jesus and Peter under Trial

The pericope of Jesus' trial (vv.53-65) probably represents the last encounter in Jerusalem between James, represented by the high priest,[18] and Paul who was bringing to him the Gentiles' money collection. The entire discussion revolves around the temple, the seat of Jerusalem's God, and its purpose is to show that the temple is *not* the seat of the Messiah's God. This argument was already made in Old Testament days. The prophets, especially Jeremiah and Ezekiel, preached that God was no longer to be found in the *torah* (teaching) of the Jerusalemite priesthood, but rather in the *dabar* (word) of the prophets.[19] What that means in Mark's time is that God is no longer communicated through the teaching of the Jerusalemite "pillar" James, but rather through the word of Paul's gospel. Indeed, wherever the crucified Jesus is

---

16 The phrase *synekolouthei auto* can mean "was following him together with others" or "was following him for some time"; in any case it is in the imperfect, which stresses the ongoing nature of the action indicated by the verb.

17 The Greek *neaniskos* occurs in Mark only in these two places.

18 See comments on 1:44.

19 See *OTI3*, 175-177. Notice the "Prophesy!" in v.65.

preached as the Messiah, there is God's community (*qahal, ekklesia*), Christ's body, God's temple "not made with (human) hands."[20] The Messiah does not keep a kind of headquarters in the earthly Jerusalem but will be revealed when he returns as the Son of Man, from the book of Daniel, whose abode is on God's heavenly throne and to whom "was given dominion and glory and kingdom, that *all peoples, nations, and languages should serve him...*"[21] The resemblance between Mark's Son of Man and Daniel's can also be seen in the way both endure persecution.[22]

The mention of Peter waiting for the outcome of Jesus' trial sets the stage for an independent pericope whose purpose is to show him failing another test of true discipleship (vv.66-72). He does not correctly use his authority (*exousia*) as would one "in charge"[23] of God's household, who should watch for his lord's return as a doorkeeper (13:34). That we have here a reference to the parable of 13:34-36 is indicated by the theme of the cock's crowing that appears in both.[24] That a reference to Peter's rejection of Paul's gospel is meant here may be seen in the way Peter vigorously denies being a "Galilean." That name, as we have seen, is a key word in Mark's gospel connected with the acceptance of Gentiles on an equal footing with Jews in the church. The word

20 See *I Thess* 22-26; Rom 7:4; 12:4-5; 1 Cor 6:12-20; 12;12-27; 1 Cor 3:9-17; 6:19; 2 Cor 6:16; also Eph 2:21 (notice the use of the same word *naos* [the temple building, i.e. the holy and holy of holies] in these passages and in Mk 14:58). On "not made by human hands" see 2 Cor 5:1 and Col 2:11.

21 Dan 7:13-14.

22 Dan 7:21-22, 25. There may also be another link to Paul here. It is striking that the spitting (*emptyo*) in 14:65 (see also 10:34 and 15:19) is reminiscent of its mention (*ekptyo*) in Gal 4:14, the sole New Testament instance of the latter word, where Paul compares himself with "an angel (messenger) of God" and with "the Christ Jesus" himself. The other instances of *emptyo* in the New Testament, occurring at Mt 26:67; 27:30; Lk 18:32 follow Mk 14:65; 15:19; 10:34, respectively.

23 The RSV's "puts his servants in charge" (13:34) is a paraphrase; a literal translation would be "gives his servants the power."

24 The noun *alektrophonia* in 13:35 is unique to the entire New Testament and is the only other word in it made from the word *alektor* (cock).

anathematizein which Peter uses to express that denial means "to invoke a curse on oneself" and also calls to mind Galatians, where Paul proclaims *anathema* against all who preach a gospel other than the only true gospel (Gal 1:8-9).

21

Jerusalem's Second Refusal of the Gospel

Jesus before the Roman Authorities

The theme of accusation in the pericope about Pilate's questioning of Jesus (15:1-5) recalls the same theme in the story of the healing of the withered hand in 3:1-6. The earlier passage conveys a message about the empowerment of Gentiles as equal members with Jews in the Messianic community, relying heavily on the terminology of Romans, Paul's last attempt to invite the Jerusalemite leadership to accept his gospel. Here we find that the invitation was ultimately rejected. By its accusations against Jesus, the Jerusalem leadership (the "chief priests") shows its refusal to accept a "King of the Jews" who silently accepts defeat at the hand of the Romans instead of leading an armed uprising against them.[1] Paul proclaimed a suffering Messiah, and it is precisely this Messiah that they rejected.

Who was Barabbas, or rather what function does he fulfill in this story (vv.6-15)? He shows once again that when the Jerusalemite leadership had to choose between rebellion and suffering they chose the former. The name *bar 'abba* means "son of the father," and consequently alludes to the appellation "Son of God," the title of the Messiah. Hence the term "so-called" (*ho legomenos*) prefixed to his name, which connotes "false."[2] Because this "Messiah" is the very opposite of Jesus, rebellious and insurrectional,[3]

---

1 Notice how Jesus does not answer Pilate beyond acknowledging that he is the King of the Jews (vv.2, 5).
2 See Mk ch.13 where reference is made to the false "christs" (vv.21-22) who consider war as a prerequisite to, or condition to, the establishment of God's kingdom (vv.6-7).
3 Barabbas is a Greek form of Aramaic *bar 'abba*. It may also very well be a play on *bar 'abba* and *bar 'abbas*; the last word is the inverse of the Hebrew *saba'* meaning service in war or fighting men, army. (See further comments below on Joseph of Arimathea). Notice also how Pilate asks the question about Jesus as the King of the Jews

he is especially appropriate for graphically depicting the nature of the Jerusalemite leadership's rejection of Paul's suffering Messiah.[4]

As is true throughout Mark, Paul in his person is seen to represent the Jesus he preaches, and here that may be seen in the fact that the chief priests deliver up Jesus due to "envy" (*phthonos*). This noun occurs in Phil 1:15 as a description of those who took advantage of Paul's imprisonment to promote their own agenda.[5]

Finally, as in the case of Peter's denials, Jesus' accusers are given three opportunities to change their minds (vv.9, 12, 14). Instead, they continue to view the cross as a sign of God's repudiation of Jesus' Messiahship, a viewpoint that represents Paul's opponents' refusal to accept the "gospel of the cross" as the only true "word (of God)."[6] Their stubborn refusal to accept the "gospel of the cross" suggests that those who follow the true Messiah must abandon such leaders rather than try to follow or convert them.

The mocking of Jesus (15:16-20) serves to confirm Paul's contention that the cross is a stumbling block not only to the Jews, but also to the Gentiles (1 Cor 1:20-25). The Roman soldiers, representatives of the "rulers of this age," joined the Jews in spitting on Jesus and leading him to be crucified. Both groups consider the very idea of Jesus' kingship to be ridiculous, an attitude befitting the "rulers of this age" as they are described in 1 Cor 2:8: "None of the rulers of this age understood this; for if they had, they would not have crucified the Lord of glory."

Crucifixion and Death

Within the crucifixion narrative we find yet another invitation to Peter and his followers to abandon the Jewish supporters of

not once but twice (vv.9, 12): the emphasis here serves to point out that the Jews *insisted* on sticking to their wish to follow an insurrectional messiah.

4 "But the chief priests *stirred up the crowd* to have him release for them Barabbas instead." (v.11)

5 This is the one instance in the Pauline corpus where it is not part of a list of evil deeds (as in Rom 1:29; Gal 5:21; 1 Tim 6:4; Tit 3:3).

6 See Gal 3:1; 6:11-16; 1 Cor 1:17-18; 20-25; 2:1-5, 8; Phil 2:8; 3:16; Col 1:20; 2:14.

armed insurrection and follow instead the Pauline gospel of the cross (vv.21-32). That gospel is presented here and in the following pericope along the lines of Psalm 22, which depicts a suffering king.[7] The reference to Peter may be found in the person of "Simon of Cyrene." The Greek *Kyrenaios* resembles the Hebrew *qeren* (horn),[8] a word that can connote "power" (in leadership), especially the power of the king as God's messiah.[9] Now, as I have shown to be the case throughout this gospel, Mark frequently chooses names for their symbolic value in helping him convey a message. If so, then what would the most likely purpose behind his combining the first name "Peter" with the surname "*Kyrenaios*"? The answer that best fits the rest of what we know about his purpose in writing the gospel is that Mark is calling upon Peter to become the *qeren*, or leader, of the Pauline Gentile[10] church which is the true Messianic community. To do so, however, he has no choice[11] but to accept unconditionally the Pauline gospel of the cross.[12] The play on the consonants k-r-n is repeated in v.22 where Golgotha is explicitly translated as "the place of the skull" *(kraniou topos)* where the crucifixion takes place. In accepting the burden of Jesus' cross Peter would prove himself a fol-

---

7   Ps 22:18, 7, and 1 are quoted or referred to in Mk 14:24, 29, and 34, respectively. See *OTI3* 75-76.

8   Since Hebrew has no vowels, it is the correspondence of the consonants (krn—qrn) that matters, and since the Greek does not have the letter "q" it uses "k" instead.

9   See 1 Sam 2:1, 10; 2 Sam 22:3; Job 16:15; Ps 18:2; 75:4, 5, 10; 89:17, 24; 92:10; 112:9; 132:17; 148:14; Jer 48.25; Lam 2.3, 17; Ezek 29. 21; Dan 8.

10 The names of Simon's sons, Alexander and Rufus (*Rouphos*), may also have symbolic significance. The first is the name of the founder of Hellenism and the second a rendering of the common Latin—and thus Roman—name *Rufus*. The choice of Rufus may have had to do with the fact that its Greek counterpart begins with *Ro*, the first two letters of Rome. These are the Gentile lands over which Peter is called to exercise leadership as a father would.

11 Notice the verb *angareuousin* (they compelled) at the beginning of v.21.

12 Notice how the expression *are ton stauron autou* (to carry his cross) here uses the same terminology found in Jesus' injunction to the multitude together with his disciples, i.e., to *all*: "If any man would come after me, let him deny himself and take up his cross (*arato ton stauron autou*) and follow me." (9:34)

lower of Jesus, who not only accepts crucifixion but rejects any Messianic anointing (the significance of myrrh in v.23) that is not linked to the Pauline gospel of the cross.[13]

The function of the two robbers in vv.27 and 32 is also to stress the incompatibility between the Pauline gospel and the teaching of the Jerusalemite Christian leadership. Indeed, earlier those Jewish-Christian leaders are themselves branded as robbers (11:17).[14] The idea here is that even if one accepts crucifixion, it means nothing if it is for the wrong reason; many of the Jewish armed rebels were crucified, but they were "false messiahs" (13:22). The true Messiah is the one who, fulfilling Isaiah's prophecy, would open the door of God's house to *all the nations* (11:17). As indicated in Jesus' discourse in ch.13, false messiahs can be very convincing in their appearance; it is only the "content" of the teaching that can differentiate true from false. And the inclusion of *all the nations* (13:10) is essential to the content of the true gospel.[15] Notice how the two robbers are said to have "also reviled him" (15:32) although they were "crucified with him" (*syn auto staurousin* in v.27 and *synestauromenoi* in v.32). The source of the latter phrase is clear: it is the exact same terminology Paul uses to speak of being "crucified with Christ" through acceptance of his gospel.[16] But false prophets and false messiahs will not accept crucifixion; they understand salvation as *renunciation* of the cross insofar as they advocate armed rebellion. Hence, even the two who are literally crucified with him nevertheless "revile him," as do those on the ground:

> And those who passed by derided (literally, "blasphemed"—*eblasphemoun*) him, wagging their heads, and saying, "Aha! You who would destroy the temple and build it in three days, *save* yourself,

---

13 See 14:3-9 and comments above.
14 The plausibility of my thesis that there is a connection between 11:17 and 15:27 is based on the fact that the term "robbers" is found only in these two instances in Mark.
15 This concern is also reflected in the use of Ps 22 that reads: "All the ends of the earth shall remember and turn to the Lord; and all the families of the nations shall worship before him. For dominion belongs to the Lord, and he rules over the nations." (vv.27-28)
16 Rom 6:6; Gal 2:19; 5:24; 6:14.

and *come down from the cross!*" So also the chief priests mocked him to one another with the scribes, saying, "He saved others; he cannot *save* himself." (vv.29-31)

It is the equating of salvation with rejection of the cross that is the blasphemy in this text.[17]

The pericope about the death of Jesus (15:33-41) also uses Ps 22 but adds a reference to Ps 69, another kingly psalm.[18] Whereas the former deals with the nations' favorable response to the Lord's anointed, the latter speaks of the king's enemies among his own people: "I have become a stranger to my brethren, an alien to my mother's sons. For zeal for thy house has consumed me, and the insults of those who insult thee have fallen on me. When I humbled my soul with fasting, it became my reproach. When I made sackcloth my clothing, I became a byword to them. I am the talk of those who sit in the gate, and the drunkards make songs about me." (vv.8-12) While the Gentile centurion confesses that the crucified Jesus is the Son of God, which is precisely what the gospel is all about, the Jews are still waiting for Elijah to "bring him down" from the cross, not understanding that Elijah has already come in the person of Paul,[19] who preached Jesus as the Messiah *revealed as such in his crucifixion.*

But who are the women who "look on *from afar*" (15:40), that is, keeping themselves at a distance from the crucified Jesus? In my comments on 6:3 I indicated that Mary (and her children) represented the Jewish kin of Jesus and Paul.[20] Here we have two Mary's, each of them also representative of a whole group. The second of the two represents the party of James and Joses; as noted above, "Joses" is close to the Greek for "poison" and is meant as a

---

17 See 3:28-29 and compare with 2:7 and 14:64.
18 Ps 69:21 is referenced in v.36. See *OTI3* 76.
19 See my comments on 4:8 and 9:9-13.
20 See also my comments on 3:31-34. Notice that James as well as Joses/Barnabas is criticized; the appellation "the lesser" (*tou mikrou*) literally belittles him, particularly considered in contrast to his reputed status as "pillar" or elder.

reference to the party of Barnabas.[21] The first is called Magdalene, which recalls the Hebrew *migdal*[22] ([watch]tower) of the vineyard in Is 5:2 and Mk 12:1.[23] This could allude to Timothy's group that remained faithful to the Pauline gospel and in that sense was the sole true vineyard of the Lord.

The name Salome most likely represents an allusion to Jerusalem and, more specifically, the temple: notice the similarity in consonants between this woman's name on the one hand, and those of Salem, Jerusalem's original appellation, and Solomon, the temple's builder, on the other. The community Salome represents would then be the Jerusalemite Jews in particular, and all Jews throughout Judea in general. All three groups, including Mary Magdalene, were at a loss after Paul's (and possibly Timothy's) death, left alone to deal with the end of Jerusalem at the Romans' hands; hence their "looking on from afar."

Burial into Oblivion

Who was Joseph of Arimathea (15:42-47)? The surname, *Harimathaia* in Greek, offers few clues. It may have been derived from the Hebrew *har-rimmat(h)aim* (mount of decay), in which case it would prepare for the subsequent play on the words "corpse" (*ptoma*) and "body" (*soma*).[24] The remainder of what we know about this person, however, is sufficient to postulate a specific individual as Arimathea's prototype: the name "Joseph" itself; the description, "a respected member of the council (Sanhedrin), who was also himself looking for the kingdom of God"; and his

---

21 See comments on 6:3.
22 My reader is reminded that Hebrew has no vowels, so only the consonants *mgdl* are to be taken into consideration to see the correspondence.
23 See comments above on 12:1.
24 The RSV has "body" in v.49 but the word there is *ptoma* (corpse), not *soma* (body). *Harimathaia* could also be interpreted as a combination of the Hebrew *har*, meaning mountain, and the Greek *mathaia*, from a root meaning teaching. The combination of two languages in one word makes this alternative less plausible.

action of taking Jesus down from the cross. All this suggests that Joseph represents Paul's coworker-turned-opponent Barnabas:

1) I interpreted Joses in 6:3 as an allusion to "Joseph" in the sense of the tribe of Joseph, or the Northern Kingdom which split away from Judah. The image of a brother abandoning his brother resembled what Barnabas did when he abandoned Paul.

2) Barnabas was a respected member of the church of Jerusalem, which is what gave him authority in the eyes of the church community in Antioch and made him an acceptable link between it and Jerusalem.[25]

3) Until Paul and Barnabas separated, they worked hand in hand in the service of the gospel of the kingdom of God, and were in that sense looking for its coming.[26]

4) Keeping in mind how closely interrelated the synoptic gospels are, and how the later ones are dependent on the same traditions Mark draws upon, it is worth pointing out additional evidence in the later Lukan tradition. Joseph of Arimathea in Luke is linked to Barnabas in Acts by the fact that the introduction to each individual begins by calling him a "good man" (*aner agathos*),[27] an expression not found elsewhere in the entire New Testament.

5) The positive things said about Joseph make him appear to be a good character, but that goodness is superficial and/or short-lived. In fact, his action of "taking Jesus down from the cross" runs counter to Paul's gospel as it is presented throughout Mark and is tantamount to a betrayal of Paul's gospel of the cross. I will explain this in more detail momentarily: for now let me point out that if my analysis of the negative character of Arimathea's actions is true, the way he is presented again fits Barnabas remarkably well. Barnabas is the one who started out well as Paul's closest coworker, then later abandoned him, following instead Paul's juda-

---

25 Acts 11:22-24, 30.
26 Gal 2:1-10; Acts 11:25-30; 13; 14. See Mk 1:14-15.
27 Lk 23:50 and Acts 11:24.

izing opponents, whose attitude Paul considered tantamount to being ashamed of, or denying, the cross ...or in other words, taking Jesus down from the cross.

There are additional hints concerning this last point about the negative character of Joseph's actions. Consider the remark about his "seeking the kingdom of God" and compare it with the remarks about the "kingdom of God" in 12:28-34. There a scribe (which in Mark represents a Pharisee) is told that the entire Law lies in the love of God and neighbor,[28] he enthusiastically endorses that summary, and Jesus tells him that he is "not far from the kingdom of God." After that pronouncement "no one *dared* to ask him [Jesus] any question." Now, they were asking Jesus questions to test him, to try to trip him up,[29] so if they did not "dare" to ask him again it was because they no longer "dared" to do something directed against Jesus, something expressing a lack of faith in him. The only other place in Mark that the verb "dare" (*tolmo*) appears is in 15:43: Joseph of Arimathea "*dared*"[30] to approach Pilate and ask for the body of Jesus in order to bury it in a tomb that would be sealed with a "very large" stone that could not possibly be rolled away (16:3-4). Like the intention of Jesus' interrogators, Joseph's is not to be considered benign but rather an attempt to consign Jesus' body to the oblivion of death. But Mark has already made clear that any such attempt would be bound to fail, since Jesus' body would be raised again as God's temple not made with human hands, and he would be preached, understood, and lived as such within the Messianic community founded by and gathered around Paul's gospel.[31]

By requesting from Pilate the body of Jesus (v.43) Joseph of Arimathea is taking an anti-Pauline stand in yet another way. He

---

28 A summary of the content of Paul's gospel; see Rom 13:8 and Gal 5:14.
29 See the Sadducee's question in the immediately previous passage, 12:18-27.
30 The RSV, assuming Arimathea is an entirely positive character, translates the verb *tolmo* as "took courage" here, although for the same verb it has "dared" in 12:34.
31 See earlier my comments on 13:52-65.

is acknowledging that Rome has the ultimate power over the crucified Jesus and can do with him as it pleases. Not so, Paul repeatedly taught—Jesus' body is under the authority and power of God alone, and, as Mark insisted earlier, God will raise him on the third day as a new temple built by God alone (14:58; 15:29). Mark's reluctance to grant the Roman authorities such power over the crucified Jesus is reflected in his careful choice of words: Pilate was able to hand over to Joseph not the "body" (*soma*) of Christ but only a "corpse" (*ptoma*; v.45).[32]

Unconditional *de facto* submission to the power of Rome was contrary to the Pauline gospel. Far from submitting to Rome and its emperors, Paul proclaimed allegiance to a different and higher power. He brought to Rome, the heart of the Roman empire, a gospel that would replace the emperor as source of God's power and salvation. He called upon *all* the inhabitants of the Roman empire and *all* of the emperor's subjects—not just Jews but also Gentiles, including both Greek and barbarian—to submit in full obedience not to the emperor but to the gospel.[33]

Joseph of Arimathea took Jesus down from the cross. He did what the bystanders at the cross called upon Elijah to do, but which Elijah never came to do. Joseph's action and Elijah's refusal to act correspond to the behavior of the people they represent in Mark: in Paul's view Barnabas denied the cross, and thus effectively took Jesus down from the cross, when he joined Paul's judaizing opponents;[34] Paul, on the other hand, remained faithful to his own gospel by consistently refusing to deny the cross, and thus refusing to take Christ down from the cross, like Elijah in Mark's narrative.[35] At the very heart of Paul's gospel is the conviction that the last memory

---

32 Another misleading translation in RSV, which has "body" here; the basic idea of the verse is rendered adequately for the English reader, but the very important difference between the words *soma* and *ptoma* is obscured.
33 See Rom 1:6, 14-16 and my comments on them above.
34 See my comments on Gal 2:12-21 in *Gal* 75-90.
35 See comments on 9:4-5 and 15:36.

one may have of Jesus before his resurrection is of him hanging crucified on the cross.[36] Until his coming, Jesus must remain "the Lord of glory, *crucified*" (1 Cor 2:8), in the sight of all authorities in this world, Roman or otherwise.

Jesus is laid in a tomb hewn out of a "rock." This "rock" represents the mountain of the temple,[37] as indicated by the striking absence of Salome in v.47 (compare to v.40): since she represented the temple, she did not need to be mentioned along with the "rock" of Jesus' tomb which carries the same symbolic meaning. Joseph of Arimathea, then, is symbolically putting his faith in Jerusalem by not just putting Jesus in the temple but sealing him in there for good with an immovable stone (15:46; 16:4). It is not difficult to see in Joseph's action a reference to the zealots who fought Rome in the Jewish war of 66-70 A.D. because of their (misplaced) faith in the earthly Jerusalem. Mark refutes that belief by showing that Jesus could not be held down even by the "rock," and thus was not subject to the Jerusalem temple. This in turn is merely a faithful rendering of the conception of God's relationship to the temple in the prophetic tradition. As Jeremiah and Ezekiel taught, God's abode moved out of the Jerusalem temple and into the person of his representative, the prophet himself. The person of the prophet then became the locus around which the new Israel was to congregate.[38] Consequently, the defeat and destruction of "God's city" could not mean God's own defeat, for God was no longer fully identified with "his" city. Nor could the destruction of the Jerusalem temple mean Jesus' defeat, for his body was "the temple not made with hands" that was about to be built in three days (14:58).

---

36 Gal 3:1; 5:11, 24; 6:12, 14; 1 Cor 1:13, 17-18, 21; 2:2; 2 Cor 13:4; Phil 2:8; 3:18; also Col 1:20; 2:14; and Eph 2:16.
37 See my comments on the Hebrew *sur* (rock, mountain) in *OTI3* 42-44
38 See *OTI3*, 136-139; 155-160. See also comments on 13:52-65.

22

A Final Offer Extended to Jerusalem

The three communities represented by three women had at face value no choice but to accept Joseph of Arimathea's lead in considering that the fate of Jesus' body was sealed within the tomb (of the doomed Jerusalem). But the hearer of Mark's gospel had been informed by the pericope of the anointing at Bethany that the only valid anointing of Jesus' body is that of the woman who acknowledged him as the Messiah.[1] Thus, at the tomb, all three are faced with the alternative offered them by the young man, representing Mark himself, the new leader of the Pauline disciples, now baptized in Paul's gospel (16:1-8).[2] He instructs them to acknowledge that the crucified Jesus is now risen and waiting for them. They, and especially the Petrine group, are to seek him in Galilee (of the nations), where he has been since "the beginning of the gospel."[3] At any rate, they must all leave the tomb, i.e., Jerusalem, due to the raging war and try to settle somewhere else (v.8).

It only becomes possible to hear Mark (the young man) and follow his instructions "when the sabbath is past," because it is only possible when one leaves behind the "sabbath" in the sense of James' Judaism.[4] Otherwise, even with the tangible Jerusalem gone, one could keep the mental attitude of forcing the Gentile

1 See 14:3-9 and my comments thereon.
2 He is dressed in the baptismal garment, the "white robe."
3 1:1, 9, 14, 16; see my comments on those verses.
4 Notice how in this verse the second Mary is said to be the mother of James alone. Barnabas is not considered as a partner in the dialogue any more; the sole partner at this time is the Jerusalemite community gathered around James. While Paul was considered the true apostle in the domain of the Gentiles (outside Jerusalem and Judah), at the beginning Barnabas was his co-apostle. But later Barnabas betrayed the gospel and consequently ceased to be an apostle.

disciples to "judaize," which is what Paul's opponents constantly were attempting to do.[5] The importance of this point can be seen in the repeated reference to the sabbath at the outset of the last two pericopes:

> And when evening had come, since it was the day of Preparation, that is, the day before the sabbath; (15:42)

> And when the sabbath was past, Mary Magdalene, and Mary the mother of James, and Salome, bought spices, so that they might go and anoint him. And very early on the first day of the week (*ton sabbaton*, literally, "of the sabbaths") they went to the tomb when the sun had risen. (16:1-2)

Only then could there be a new beginning, a sunrise, a new day, a new set of sabbaths (weeks) where "neither circumcision counts for anything, nor uncircumcision, but a new creation" (Gal 6:15) and where God's peace and mercy will prevail upon his Israel and upon all those who abide by Paul's rule, his gospel (v.16). It is neither Joseph of Arimathea, nor Mary the Magdalene, nor Mary the mother of James and Joses, nor Salome, who can bring this eschatological rule of God throughout the Roman empire and thus the entire inhabited world, but solely the *call* uttered by the young man dressed in a white robe. The content of that call is Paul's gospel, which Mark has presented here in written form; if its reader and hearers fail to heed the call, trembling and fear, the opposite of God's peace, will prevail.

Two Later Endings for Mark

With v.8 ends the original gospel of Mark according to two major manuscripts, *Aleph* (Sinaiticus) and *B* (Vaticanus). These are among the most important and most reliable of the extant witnesses to the original text of Mark. Other manuscripts add the section appearing in English bibles as verses 9 through 20, which is referred to among scholars as "the longer ending." Still other manuscripts have instead what is called "the shorter ending,"

---

5 Such was attempted in Antioch (Gal 2:14).

which English versions sometimes give in a footnote. Both the "shorter" and the "longer" endings are later additions and I shall deal with them in the last volume of this series.

This means the original text of Mark contained no accounts of Jesus' post-resurrection appearances, a fact some have found confusing or hard to accept. However, as I explained in my comments above on 14:22-26, this becomes understandable when one realizes that in Mark Christ's sacrifice on the cross is the immediate preamble to his coming in glory. In this too Mark merely follows Paul. Consider, for example, the striking omission of any mention of the resurrection in 1 Cor 11:26, which summarizes the purpose of the Lord's supper after the account of its institution in vv.23-25. Just as we find here at the end of Mark, Paul jumps from the crucifixion to the second coming: "For as often as you eat this bread and drink the cup, you proclaim the Lord's death until he comes."

Selected Bibliography

B. Byrne, *Romans*, (Sacra Pagina), Collegeville, 1996.

C. E. B. Cranfield, *Romans: A Shorter Commentary*, Grand Rapids, 1985.

J. D. G. Dunn, *Romans, vols 1 and 2* (WBC), Dallas, 1988.

J. Fitzmyer, *Romans* (Anchor Bible), Garden City, 1993.

H. Conzelman, *1 Corinthians* (Hermeneia), Philadelphia, 1975.

R. B. Hays, *1 Corinthians* (Interpretation), Louisville, 1997.

E. Best, *2 Corinthians* (Interpretation), Atlanta, 1987.

R. Bultmann, *The Second Letter to the Corinthians* ET, Minneapolis, 1976.

R. Martin, *2 Corinthians* (WBC), Word Books, Waco, 1986.

J. L. Martin, *Galatians* (Anchor Bible), Garden City, 1997.

F. Matera, *Galatians* (Interpretation), Louisville, 1992.

G. Hawthorne, *Philippians* (WBC), Waco, 1983.

P. T. O'Brien, *Philippians* (NIGTC), Grand Rapids, 1991.

J. D. G. Dunn, *Colossians and Philemon* (NIGTC), Grand Rapids, 1996.

E. Lohse, *Colossians and Philemon* (Hermeneia), Philadelphia, 1971.

B. R. Gaventa, *1 & 2 Thessalonians* (Interpretation), Louisville, 1998.

C. A. Wanamaker, *1 & 2 Thessalonians* (NIGTC), Grand Rapids, 1990.

R. Guelich, *Mark 1-8:26* (WBC), Waco, 1989.

M. Hooker, *The Gospel According to Saint Mark*, Hendrickson, 1991.

J. D. Kingsbury, *The Christology of Mark, Philadelphia*, 1984.

W. Marxsen, *Mark the Evangelist: Studies on the Redaction History of the Gospel* ET, Nashville, 1969.

W. Telford (ed.), *The Interpretation of Mark* (Issues in Religion and Theology 7), Philadelphia, 1985.

L. Williamson Jr., *Mark* (Interpretation), Louisville, 1983.

Index of Scriptural References

Index of Subjects

247